WEST INDIAN LITERATURE

Macmillan International College Editions (MICE) will bring to university, college, professional and school students in developing countries low cost but authoritative books covering the history and cultures of the Third World, and the special aspects of its scientific, technical, social and economic development. In other parts of the world MICE will satisfy the growing demand for information about the developing countries. The MICE programme contains many distinguished series in a wide range of disciplines, some titles being regionally biased, others being more international. Library editions will usually be published simultaneously with the low cost paperback editions. For full details of the MICE list, please contact the publishers.

Macmillan New Literature Handbooks
General Editor: Professor A N Jeffares

These are literary and historical guides to the major 'new' literatures in English. They survey the major authors and their works in a historical context, by *genre* and against the background of the worthwhile works of minor prose writers, poets and playwrights.

The books in this series are lively and enjoyable to read; they will be useful to students at universities, and at extra-mural classes, polytechnics, liberal arts colleges, teachers' colleges and later secondary school classes.

General readers approaching non-British English literature for the first time will find here ideal guides to the 'regional' literatures which interest them.

First titles
Bruce King (editor): *West Indian Literature*
Alastair Niven: *West African Literature*
Alastair Niven: *East African Literature*
Bruce King: *The New English Literatures*

West Indian Literature

Edited by
BRUCE KING

First published 1979 by
THE MACMILLAN PRESS LTD
London and Basingstoke
Associated companies in Delhi   Dublin
Hong Kong   Johannesburg   Lagos   Melbourne

Filmsetting by Vantage Photosetting Co. Ltd., Southampton
and London
Printed in Hong Kong

British Library Cataloguing in Publication Data

West Indian Literature. – (Macmillan new literature handbooks).
   1. West Indian literature (English) – History and criticism.
   I. King, Bruce, b.1933
   810'.9'9729   PR9210

   ISBN 0–333–23590–8
   ISBN 0–333–23591–6   Pbk

To Adele and Nicole

Other books by Bruce King

Dryden's Major Plays
Marvell's Allegorical Poetry
A Celebration of Black and African Writing
Literatures of the World in English
Introduction to Nigerian Literature
Dryden's Mind and Art
Twentieth Century Interpretations of All for Love

Contents

1   Introduction *by Bruce King*   1

2   The Background *by Rhonda Cobham*   9

3   The Beginnings to 1929 *by Anthony Boxill*   30

4   The Thirties and Forties *by Reinhard W. Sander*   45

5   The Fifties *by Sandra Pouchet Paquet*   63

6   Since 1960: Some Highlights *by Edward Baugh*   78

7   Edgar Mittelholzer *by Michael Gilkes*   95

8   Samuel Selvon *by Michel Fabre*   111

9   George Lamming *by Ian Munro*   126

10   Derek Walcott *by Mervyn Morris*   144

11   V. S. Naipaul *by Bruce King*   161

12   Wilson Harris *by Hena Maes-Jelinek*   179

13   Jean Rhys *by Cheryl M. L. Dash*   196

14   Edward Brathwaite *by J. Michael Dash*   210

Notes   229

1 Introduction *by Bruce King*

Despite the long history of West Indian creative writing, it is still a comparatively new field of literary study in which reputations, achievements and influences remain subjects of heated debate. It was not until 1968 that the first books surveying the literature of the region were published, followed a year later by the establishment of a course at the University of the West Indies, Mona.[1] As there is still an insufficient body of useful commentary and historical information readily available for the general reader and student, it seems worthwhile to bring together an up-to-date introduction to Caribbean literature in English. In commissioning this collection of new essays I have tried—as far as possible within a book of this length—to provide a survey of the literary history of the West Indies, to offer comprehensive introductions to the major authors, to present an assessment of recent work by both established and younger writers, and to relate the creative writing to the social and historical background. The attention given the period before 1950, the evaluation of recent writing, the reassessment of the work of Edgar Mittelholzer, and a new approach to the poetry of Edward Brathwaite are, I think, among the significant directions in criticism noticeable in the following pages. But as any division into historical periods, or selection of major authors, is open to discussion, some introductory comments may be useful.

Although West Indian creative writing has existed from the eighteenth century onwards, it was not until the first quarter of the present century that authors of real ability began to appear.

The novels written for Thomas MacDermot's 'All Jamaica Library' may be described as the beginning of a consciously Jamaican literature, but the venture failed to take hold.[2] H. G. de Lisser, after giving an unnaturally happy ending to the realistic portrait of a poor servant girl in *Jane's Career* (1914), increasingly turned to exotic historical novels about pirates, witchcraft and romantic love. Despite the many literary and debating clubs of the period, local society offered few opportunities for artists and emigration usually followed. Claude McKay, after publishing two slim volumes of dialect poems (1912), left for the United States; it was not until *Banana Bottom* (1933) that he returned to Jamaican subject-matter, giving an exile's romanticised view of peasant country life.

The 1930s saw the emergence in Trinidad of the journal *The Beacon* (1931–3) and a group of writers—Alfred Mendes (*Pitch Lake*, 1934, and *Black Fauns*, 1935), C. L. R. James (*Minty Alley*, 1936)—influenced by the Russian Revolution and the Indian nationalist movement, who attempted to align creative writing to local radical politics. Their fiction realistically portrays the lives and speech of the lower-middle classes and the poor. Vivian Virtue's *Wings of the Morning* (1938) should be mentioned as having set a new standard of technical competence which was necessary before a more experimental and consciously West Indian poetry could develop during the next decade. Of the journals which began publication in the 1940s, *Kyk-over-al* (1945–61) was associated with nationalism in Guyana, and *Focus* (1943, '48, '56, '60) with the nationalist movement in Jamaica. *Bim* (1942–), from Barbados, a more purely literary journal for the region, co-operated with the influential B.B.C. *Caribbean Voices* radio programme.

The usefulness of such places of publication to the development of West Indian literature can be seen from V. S. Naipaul's comments on problems facing writers before 1950. His father, Seepersad Naipaul, wrote a collection of short stories, *Gurudeva and other Indian Tales* (1943), published at his expense, which he sold locally in Trinidad:

A reading to a small group, publication in a magazine soon lost to view: writing in Trinidad was an amateur activity, and this was all the encouragement a writer could expect. There were no magazines that paid; there were no established magazines; there was only the *Guardian*. . . . My father was a purely local writer, and writers like that ran the risk of ridicule. . . .

But attitudes were soon to change. It was local publication that brought Derek Walcott and his *Twenty-Five Poems* to our attention in 1949. In that year, too, the Hogarth Press published Edgar Mittelholzer's novel, *A Morning at the Office*; Mittelholzer had for some time been regarded as another local writer. And then there at last appeared a market. Henry Swanzy was editing *Caribbean Voices* for the BBC Caribbean Service. He had standards and enthusiasm. He took local writing seriously and lifted it above the local: he got Roy Fuller to review Derek Walcott's *Twenty-Five Poems*. And the BBC paid; not quite at their celebrated guinea-a-minute rate, but sufficiently well—fifty dollars a story, sixty dollars, eighty dollars—to spread a new idea of the value of writing.[3]

During the immediate post-war years, West Indian literature was a reflection of growing nationalism, hopes of a regional federation, feelings of anti-colonialism, and interest in local culture. Significant publications included V. S. Reid's *New Day* (1949), Roger Mais's *The Hills Were Joyful Together* (1953), and Martin Carter's excellent *Poems of Resistance* (1954), which were conscious expressions of the new movements. John Hearne's *Voices Under the Window* (1955) reflects the social and cultural presence that had developed among the middle class of the period and the increasing awareness that their values were not necessarily those of the populace. While the 1950s are perhaps the most important decade of West Indian writing in the sense of their having established an identity, an awareness of common themes and a canon of significant writers and texts, it should be noticed that many of the best known literary works were published during the 1960s. By the early 1970s many writers had become involved in the debates concerning ideology, neo-colonialism, black consciousness, folk traditions and an African heritage which resulted from the failure of independence to bring into being social justice and authentic national culture.

Edgar Mittelholzer was the first author of the generation which established the reputation of West Indian writing abroad during the 1950s to dedicate himself to a literary career. His early success in London set an example soon followed by Samuel Selvon and George Lamming. *Corentyne Thunder* (1941) has been called 'the first novel published that explored Guyanese peasant life'.[4] *A Morning at the Office* (1950), set in Trinidad, and the *Kaywana* trilogy, which gives epic continuity to the confused history of Guyana, were impressive in their era for exploring the problems of mixed blood and the presence of different races and cultures in the region. Mittelholzer had tremendous energy and wrote compelling, if flawed, novels in which he anticipated themes and subject-matter which have continued to be treated by later authors. *My Bones and My Flute* (1955) deserves more attention than it has received.

It would be difficult to imagine a book on West Indian literature in which the Trinidadian Samuel Selvon was not given a prominent place. *A Brighter Sun* (1952) and *Turn Again Tiger* (1958) contributed to the tradition of the West Indian novel through their use of local speech, delineation of social problems, and sense of comedy. Even when writing of the loners, hustlers and other exiles on the fringe of West Indian society in England, in *The Lonely Londoners* (1956), Selvon created characters who seem typical and representative. Indeed he was among the first to capture the picaresque quality sometimes characteristic of West Indian lives.

George Lamming's *In the Castle of My Skin* (1953) was the first West Indian novel to achieve classic status. A semi-autobiographical record of a child growing up in 'Little England' during the 1930s and '40s, its poetical style, close observation of village life, understanding of social change and sensitive use of Barbadian speech showed how local material could be given dignity and significance in literature without resorting to protest, exoticism or idealisation. Originally a poet, Lamming has since written allegorical novels which imaginatively and symbolically examine the larger problems raised by the early history, colonisation and subsequent independence of the islands.

While other writers of the 1950s became expatriates, Derek Walcott stayed within the Caribbean working at his poetry and plays. Ever since the publication of *In a Green Night* (1962), he has been recognised as a poet of international stature. His early mastery of the techniques of English verse has been supplemented by the selective use of dialect and patois, and the development of a vision of the Americas as a new beginning. He has written lovingly of his home island, St Lucia; by using a full range of poetical techniques and allusions he has given the particularities of West Indian experience a timeless, universal, classical dignity. His play, *Dream on Monkey Mountain* (1970), and autobiographical poem, *Another Life* (1972), are among the best works of West Indian literature.

V. S. Naipaul has looked at the region with the clear eyes of a reporter; sceptical of and disenchanted with cultural myths, he has become the critic of slogans and false hopes. His early satiric novels, *The Mystic Masseur* (1957) and *The Suffrage of Elvira* (1958), brought a sophisticated sense of economy and stylistic precision to the West Indian novel. Where others had attempted through realism and protest to describe local problems, Naipaul's method was the humorous novel of social manners. If his irony upset many, it might be argued that such scepticism reflected the political and cultural confusion of the previous decades. He is perhaps one of the best writers in English at present; *A House for Mr Biswas* (1961), based on his father's life, has been described as 'the finest study ever produced in the West Indies . . . of a minority, and the herculean obstacles in the way of its achieving a room in the national building'.[5] His subsequent novels examine the social and cultural problems of newly independent nations in the postcolonial world.

Wilson Harris's *Palace of the Peacock* (1960) and the other novels of his *Guiana Quartet* are difficult to read casually, but the difficulty is similar to that of other innovating, experimental writers such as James Joyce and T. S. Eliot. One reads Harris as if the novels were poetry, following the flow of images, symbols and events without worrying about causa-

tion. Such fluidity, fragmentation and improbability of narrative are used by the author to show that the West Indies are a
new society, a new beginning. The past, rather than being a
burden, offers varied materials with which the imagination can
build a new culture from the many races and peoples in the
Caribbean. While it is possible to suffer impatience with
Harris's densely textured fiction, it is also possible that he is
one of the great writers of our time.

Jean Rhys, from Dominica, established a literary reputation
in Paris during the 1920s and '30s and then dropped from sight.
In 1966 she unexpectedly published *Wide Sargasso Sea*, a major
novel portraying the collapse of white creole society after
Emancipation; the creoles are rejected by and ill adapted to
Europe, yet cut off by race and the history of slavery from the
black West Indians. Although Jean Rhys's reputation is now
based on *Wide Sargasso Sea*, the theme of alienation in Europe is
apparent in her earlier novels where the heroine feels an
outsider in a cold world and remembers affectionately the
warmth and more relaxed culture of the islands. Indeed her
early novels should be seen, along with the work of H. G. de
Lisser, Claude McKay and Eric Walrond, as among the first
significant fiction published by a West Indian. The narrator of
Good Morning, Midnight (1939) says, 'I have no pride—no
pride, no name, no face, no country. I don't belong anywhere.'
Jean Rhys's feelings of alienation, of drift, of victimisation, of
being uprooted have become common themes of other West
Indian writers.

In recent years, since the publication of *Rights of Passage*
(1967), the first volume of *The Arrivants: A New World Trilogy*,
Edward Brathwaite has earned a reputation as a major West
Indian poet, someone who has utilised the resources of popular
speech, folk culture and African and Caribbean history. He is
perhaps the first poet in English to express the 'black consciousness' of the sixties and seventies through sophisticated
literary techniques.

West Indian is one of many new English literatures that
began under colonialism and 'emerged' after the Second World
War, mostly as a result of the social, political and cultural
changes which had started in the late 1930s and which picked

up speed during the war and with the ending of the Empire. As with other new literatures its development has paralleled the rise of national movements and its themes and subject-matter have often been the problems resulting from colonialism and independence. Characteristics shared with other developing new literatures include the creation of myths of the past; the use of local scenery; the study of local, especially peasant lives; an emphasis on the community, nation, or race; the treatment of individuals as representative or typical; and the modification of standard English as a literary language by the use of local forms and rhythms of speech.[6]

Along with other new literatures, the early imitation of English models was followed by an emphasis on local colour and landscape, social realism which was felt to be more nationalistic, a protest tradition, the exploration of a divided cultural heritage, the discovery of how to treat regional sub-ject-matter more poetically and artistically, and a contempor-ary literature which is both local in its particularities and in tune with modern writing elsewhere. But is is also true that the various period styles of West Indian literature have been modifications of a prevailing metropolitan or international fashion; the Parnassian poetry of W. A. Roberts, the social realism of the 1930s, the myth-making of Wilson Harris, Derek Walcott's confessional verse, each is a local variation of an influential style or mode of its time.

Particular to the region are its varied multiracial composi-tion and the lack of visible, evolving continuity between the inhabitants and the culture of their origin. Consequently West Indian literature has been concerned with such contrasts as the poor and middle class; history and the present; the desire for and suspicion of education; dispossession and freedom; racial difference and creolisation; metropolitan and regional culture; local pride and embarrassment. Common themes include the search for 'roots' and for identity, social and historical injus-tices, feelings of imprisonment, the desire for order, the dis-covery of traditions or a folk culture, and the creation of a new society.[7]

The notion of a West Indian literature is largely a product of the period after the Second World War when a sense of community between writers of the various parts of the region was established through publication in the new journals, the *Caribbean Voices* broadcasts, travel between the islands, the shared experience of those who emigrated to London, the rise of independence movements and self-government, and plans for a federation. Significantly, earlier literary critics speak rather of local, Jamaican or Guyanese literature than the West Indies.[8] Despite the collapse of the federation, the concept of a West Indian literature is useful. Besides the shared history, problems and language of the English-speaking communities of the region, and the fact that writers continue to see themselves as part of a West Indian society, there is the practical consideration that no one country has yet had a sufficient number of major authors to be able to speak of a developed literature of its own. This may change in future as more writers contribute to their national tradition and as significant earlier works are rediscovered and reassessed; but it is noticeable that there has been a renewed interest in federation expressed through literary anthologies, festivals and other cultural manifestations.

2 The Background *by Rhonda Cobham*

From the time of their discovery by Christopher Columbus at the end of the fifteenth century the islands of the West Indies, unlike the American mainland, were seen as objects to be exploited rather than as colonies to be settled. Their early history is dominated by the 'pacification' and extermination of the native population, and the fierce naval rivalry between successive European powers. The introduction of the plantation system of sugar cultivation at the end of the sixteenth century, based on African slave labour, implicated the society even further in a cycle of deformed human relationships which left all parties morally and aesthetically maimed. Wilson Harris has called this syndrome 'victor-victim stasis', and an exploration of the way in which this has affected contemporary West Indian society is a central theme in his first four novels which form the *Guiana Quartet*.

Other West Indian writers have tried to interpret and describe the early history of the Caribbean. One of George Lamming's most recent novels, *Natives of My Person* (1972), examines the effect of the process of colonisation on European settlers of all classes. Though none of the crew of the ship *Reconnaissance* are known by the end of the novel to have reached the West Indies, the attitudes to authority and exploitation that they take with them are shown to be tainted already by the values of colonial society. Mittelholzer, in the *Kaywana* trilogy, explores the obsessions and fears of the quasi-historical van Groenwegel family, showing how these traits were exacerbated in a society organised exclusively for production, in which there were few social restraints on personal power or sexual gratification. Both Mittelholzer and Christopher Nicole, in his *Amyot* series set in the Bahama islands, succeed in recreating the uncertainty and lack of permanence of those earliest European settlements which were constantly threatened by the fluctuating balance of power in Europe and the hostility between first coloniser and native, then master and slave.

It was not until the end of the Napoleonic wars, when the Caribbean Sea was no longer of strategic importance to Europe, that the islands ceased changing hands and a degree of stability was established in the region. The territories which remained under British rule at the end of this period included the two mainland colonies of British Guiana (now Guyana) and British Honduras (Belize). Writers from both are considered West Indian, as they share with the islanders a common language and colonial history. The break with British colonial domination when it came affected the entire region, though each area produced its distinctive style of response. The first signs of this were in the early decades of this century when such men as Walter MacA. Lawrence and Norman Cameron in Guyana, C. L. R. James and Alfred Mendes in Trinidad, and Claude McKay, H. G. de Lisser and Thomas MacDermot in Jamaica began to write and encourage others to write poems and short stories dealing with local society.

Long before this the folk culture of the region had taken root. The African slaves brought with them a rich and diverse assortment of traditional myths, songs and religious beliefs which were passed on to their children, who incorporated into these traditions features of the European cultures they encountered. The vitality and flexibility of this folk tradition has ensured its survival to the present time in the religious cults of Pocomania in Jamaica and Shango in Trinidad, and in the steelband and Carnival of the southern Caribbean. Most important from a literary perspective were the creoles that the slaves evolved from their original languages and the European languages with which they came into contact. Two of the most distinctive were the French patois, spoken in the eastern Caribbean where French was for many years before the advent of

English the dominant European language, and the Jamaican patois, based on English and various West African languages. It was only when the social stigma attached to this indigenous culture was challenged that a literary tradition emerged which was no longer merely derivative of dated European fashions.

The European population of the West Indies always baulked at being identified as 'West Indian'. Most came as temporary settlers, to manage estates or make quick profits as pirates. A few were part of abortive labour schemes. Lionel Hutchinson's novel, *One Touch of Nature* (1971), describes the fate of the descendants of these peasant immigrants, known in Barbados as 'Red Legs'. Those Europeans who settled clung with determination to the mother country, quite unlike their North American counterparts. This tendency was aggravated after 1838, when Emancipation created a situation in which the term 'West Indian' lumped the creoles and free coloureds with the ex-slaves. Jean Rhys in *Wide Sargasso Sea* (1966) explores the neurosis which this confusion of identity must have produced among creoles. After Emancipation, whenever European workers were introduced as an alternative to African labour, they made the same haste to dissociate themselves from the black masses. Alfred Mendes's first novel, *Pitch Lake* (1934), follows the career of the son of a Portuguese immigrant in Trinidad, whose efforts to throw off his connections with the common people lead him to commit murder. In de Lisser's *The White Witch of Rosehall* (1929) the three major characters—Annie Palmer, her young lover Rutherford, and Rider, the alcoholic clergyman—are Europeans who have been defeated by various aspects of West Indian society. Their failure stems from their refusal to treat their West Indian experiences as constructive, and from their rejection of the part of themselves that had already responded to the culture of the slaves.

Historically, this fear of the black masses on the part of the ruling white elite can be seen most dramatically in the Morant Bay rebellion of 1865, one of the major events around which the Jamaican novelist V. S. Reid builds his novel *New Day* (1949). The uprising came at the end of a prolonged period of drought and continuous friction between the new class of black peasant farmers and the traditional white landowners. In the carnage that ensued, 439 people were killed or executed by the militia, including Paul Bogle, a Baptist minister, and a coloured Member of Parliament called George William Gordon. This event persuaded the Jamaican Legislature voluntarily to abrogate its responsibility for running the island in favour of direct rule from Westminster, where it was felt the newly emancipated blacks would have less influence.

Though in most British colonies white West Indians were a minority, their social and economic power made it natural for them to be in the forefront of the West Indian literary movement during its early stages. At the turn of the century, for example, it was possible for Thomas MacDermot, a white Jamaican, to capture the imagination of Jamaicans of all colours with his patriotic verses; his 'All Jamaica Library' was one of the earliest attempts to create a local literary tradition. Today white West Indians are a smaller, less powerful minority; many have retreated into a racially defensive position from which it has become increasingly difficult to create. The few writers who survive come typically from small islands or agricultural areas where their position has not until recently been seriously challenged: Ian MacDonald from rural Trinidad, Phyliss Allfrey and Jean Rhys of Dominica and Geoffrey Drayton of Barbados. Jean Rhys has expressed it in this way in a recent interview:

> I grew up with the feeling of being surrounded by alien people, but I liked many of them. Now they say that the English are devils, though their culture is derived from English culture; the horrors of slavery are constantly referred to but they leave out all the good.[1]

The opening decades of the twentieth century were years of serious economic crisis in the West Indies. A combination of hurricanes and drought wreaked havoc in the sugar industry which was already losing to foreign competition on the world market. In spite of high levels of unemployment, planters in Guyana, Jamaica and Trinidad imported East Indian indentured labourers, often at public expense, rather than pay wages high enough to ensure a continuous supply of local labour. The depression in the agricultural sector produced a flood of migration from the rural areas into the towns. De Lisser's heroine in *Jane's Career* (1914) was one of a virtual army of young girls who came to the cities in search of jobs as domestic servants. Not all of them had Jane's success. Many became prostitutes, living in the squalid barrack-yards to which West Indian writers from C. L. R. James onward have turned time and again as settings for their work. The pattern of rural dispossession leading to urban migration is a recurring theme in the work of West Indian authors. Often this departure from the land is associated with a sense of spiritual loss, as in Lindsay Barrett's *Song for Mumu* (1967).

Many men were forced to leave their islands in search of work. In Jamaica and the Leewards, the movement was mainly to the Panama Canal and the banana republics of Central America, or to Cuba and the United States as seasonal farm workers. In the southern Caribbean labourers also moved north to the Canal Zone, but there was another movement south, from Barbados, St Lucia and Grenada especially, to the Brazilian sugar plantations and to the Port of Spain waterfront, which was then a thriving trans-shipment port for the produce of South American countries such as Brazil and Venezuela. *Tropic Death* (1926), a collection of short stories by Eric Walrond, gives a grim picture of this search for work. Some of the stories are set in the West Indian territories from which the workers moved; others are set on the ships which transported them from place to place in their search for jobs. The third setting is Panama, where the wretchedness and squalor described seem only fractionally better than the starvation, disease and despair of the life portrayed in the islands.

The two major migrations of this period were the movement of workers to the Canal Zone and the United States, and the movement of West Indian troops overseas during the First World War. The Panama migration provided many West Indians with their first experience of the confrontation between labour and capital in a modern industrial world. It also brought them into contact with the American version of racial prejudice as well as American republican ideals, still relatively unpopular in the British West Indies. West Indians who went to the United States tended to settle there, so that their new experiences were transmitted home only indirectly—through the works of Claude McKay for example, whose involvement in the Harlem Renaissance was known and appreciated throughout the Caribbean. Most of the Panama immigrants, however, returned to the West Indies after their jobs in the Canal Zone were completed. Their influence on West Indian society was far-reaching. The rank and file members of Bustamante's trade union in Jamaica were all men who had received their labour baptisms in Panama. In Barbados and elsewhere 'Panama money' was used to educate a new generation of working-class children. Both Claude McKay in his novel, *Banana Bottom* (1933), and H. G. de Lisser in *Susan Proudleigh* (1915), comment on the phenomenon of the returned Panama worker, and the effect he had on the way of life and aspirations of his friends and enemies back home. His flashy clothes and jewellery were only the most obvious signs of a new demand among working-class West Indians for the right to leisure, luxury and educational opportunities.

The First World War produced a different confrontation. Thousands of loyal West Indians went overseas with the feeling that they were black English soldiers, prepared to fight in defence of an Empire to which they owed allegiance. In Jamaica, for instance, over 10 000 men volunteered. Once in the field they realised that in spite of their higher educational standards in some cases, they were treated as menials distinct from and inferior to troops from Canada, Australia and New Zealand. In an article written in 1932 in a Trinidadian magazine called *The Royalian*, H. C. Mentor points out that the West Indian troops stationed in Egypt became aware of the nationalist struggle being fought there. In Europe the troops stationed in France met black American regiments and France's Sengalese troops who by comparison to themselves seemed to be treated with respect. They were also exposed to the Marxist ideas behind the Russian Revolution which, in the words of the novelist Alfred Mendes who fought in France, seemed a straw of hope to be clutched 'in a drowning sea'.[2]

The war was a bitter disillusionment for many of the soldiers, and when they returned to the West Indies it was this group which led the attack on the colonial oligarchy. As one ex-soldier put it at a meeting of the Trinidad Workingmen's Association: 'If we can die for the white man against his German brother, we can die better for ourselves.' Both Cipriani, the first Trinidadian labour leader, and his popular successor 'Buzz' Butler were men who claimed their prestige from their war experiences. In Barbados another ex-soldier, Clennell Wickham, launched a weekly newspaper called *The Barbados Herald* in 1919. Its radical political stance and cultural interests anticipated and in some ways surpassed the movement which grew around the magazine *The Beacon* in Trinidad ten years later. Though the *Herald* did not produce as wide a circle of creative writers, the work of one West Indian poet, H. A. Vaughan, who was associated with the paper and later became Attorney General in Barbados, shows the same concern and involvement with the working-class struggle that characterised the later group in Trinidad.

The years of economic depression between the two world wars were a period of political and cultural ferment in the West Indies. None of the problems of the period before 1914 had been solved: unemployment rates were higher than ever. In 1921 work on the Canal was completed and the majority of West Indians still in Panama were repatriated. The East Indians who had traditionally constituted a buffer zone between the black masses and the white establishment in Guyana and Trinidad could no longer be depended upon to accept exploitative wages, and by the thirties the independence movement in India had generated a degree of political awareness among them that had until then been lacking. On the cultural side, the calypso had begun to emerge as a political weapon in Trinidad. Its style of cutting social satire was emulated in the editorials and short stories which appeared in contemporary magazines such as *The Beacon*, *Picong* and *Callaloo*. Toward the mid-thirties the first organised trade unions began to assume an increasingly political role as the leaders of popular discontent. The novel *Crown Jewel* (1952) by R. A. C. de Boissiere chronicles the movement from general but vague dissatisfaction with the system to positive social action within the trade union

movement among a wide cross-section of Trinidadians between 1935 and 1937. Many West Indian writers active at the
time participated in this social revolution. The Left Book Club
in Jamaica was one group which combined its literary activities
with a radical socialist stance in politics.

In 1935 there were unemployment marches in Trinidad and
Jamaica, strikes in British Guiana and disturbances in St Vincent over a rise in customs duties. The seriousness of the
situation was underlined at the close of the year when, in
response to a strike by coal hauliers in St Lucia—which was at
the time a refuelling point for British naval and maritime
vessels—a state of emergency was declared and a British
warship summoned. In 1936 the Italo-Abyssinian war broke
out. England's refusal to go to the aid of Ethiopia was seen as
the ultimate betrayal of the negro race. It is difficult to exagger-
ate the widespread cynicism about Britain which this incident
provoked. The Rastafarian identification with Selassie which
dates from this period is widely known, but popular sentiment
all over the West Indies was well in advance of world opinion
in its response to the Italian invasion.

During 1937 the storm broke. The oilfield strikes in
Trinidad were followed by widespread rioting in Barbados
over the deportation of the labour leader, Clement Payne.
Next came strikes in British Guiana and St Lucia, and finally
there were bloody riots in Jamaica. At the end of the year the
British Government appointed a Royal Commission to report
on the situation in the West Indies. Their report is one of the
most valuable contemporary documents of conditions in the
region. In spite of the painstakingly thorough assessment of
the situation which the Commission produced, its recommen-
dations tended to be palliative rather than radical, and even
these were delayed by the outbreak of the Second World War.
The full text of the Commission's report was not published
until 1945 for 'security reasons'. The same reasons were given
to facilitate the rounding up and detention of several Caribbean
labour leaders and journalists, including Alexander Bustamante who later became Jamaica's first Prime Minister, and
the writer Roger Mais.

These events in the late thirties and early forties must have had a profound effect on the West Indian writers of the fifties who were children or young adults at the time. George Lamming's *In the Castle of My Skin* (1953) is based on his childhood perception of the Barbados riots. Writing from differing class perspectives, both John Hearne in *Voices Under the Window* (1955) and Neville Dawes in *The Last Enchantment* (1960) use the changing attitudes to class and colour which these events precipitated as central themes in their novels.

From a literary perspective, the years between 1944 when Jamaica's new constitution was granted and the break-up of the West Indian Federation in 1962 were the most eventful decades in modern West Indian history. New trends had begun to emerge in West Indian society after the 1937 riots and the Second World War. The new black professionals were establishing themselves as a class with growing political power, and during this time literary and political developments were closely tied. Almost every publication in the area was fired by a new regional ideal which for a while transcended class and island barriers. A sense of pride in the history and culture of the Caribbean became fashionable as the new middle class tried to build up its own traditions. To understand these trends and the stimulus they gave to creative expression, we must first examine the forces which produced this new class to which practically all the writers of this period belong.

In a society where one group had traditionally monopolised the commercial, political and educational opportunities, only a few privileged outsiders could hope to achieve any real power or status. Ambitious parents willingly sacrificed their own comfort and social opportunities in order to provide their children with a chance of success. For the negro child, the best option had always been to win an 'exhibition' or government scholarship to one of the few good secondary schools, and from there to move into a white-collar job in the civil service or the teaching profession. Those who attained this goal were in a position to groom their offspring for the coveted scholarships to British universities which would guarantee them professions in law or medicine on their return. Dr Eric Williams, Prime Minister of Trinidad and Tobago, was one such 'schol' hope. His description of the ordeal of preparation for scholarship exams in his autobiography *Inward Hunger* tallies closely with V. S. Naipaul's fictional version of his similar experience in *A House for Mr Biswas*. By the time the East Indian indentured labourers entered the struggle for a better life, they stood a slightly better chance of succeeding by acquiring property or starting businesses with the capital they had saved during their indenture, and some of them chose to try first for commercial rather than academic success. Stories of miserly Indian farmers, such as the father of Beena and Kattree in Mittelholzer's *Corentyne Thunder* (1941), are part of West Indian mythology, but they tend to obscure the fact that for the East Indian indentured labourer as much as for the African ex-slave before him, a decent living for his children could only be obtained through a lifetime of self-sacrifice. Sam Selvon's character Tiger, who figures in *A Brighter Sun* (1952) and *Turn Again Tiger* (1958), is an example of an Indian peasant farmer involved in the double struggle for financial security and intellectual advancement.

All wanted their children to succeed, but one price for this success was often a truncation of family ties. The child who made good was usually thrust into a social circle that his parents could not enter or excluded from the society of his less fortunate peers. Edward Baugh has recognised this situation in his poem 'Small Town Story'.[3] The boy G. in Lamming's *In the Castle of My Skin* (1953) experiences a similar sense of alienation from his friends at the village school when he leaves to take up the place he has won at a secondary school. Like Naipaul, Lamming writes out of personal experience.

Often this divorce from the common people was encouraged by parents who had themselves been unsuccessful in reaching the highest echelons of their profession through some racial or educational disadvantage. They guarded their children jealously from what they considered were the degrading consequences of association with poverty and ignorance. Writing of his early childhood in St Lucia, Derek Walcott gives us this glimpse of himself and his twin brother, Roderick, watching a street meeting of the Salvation Army:

Like the long, applauded note, joy soared further from two

pale children staring from their upstairs window, wanting to
march with that ragged barefoot crowd, but who could not
because they were not black and poor, until for one of them,
watching the shouting, limber congregation, that difference
became a sadness, that sadness rage, and that longing to
share their lives ambition.[4]

Part of the early popularity and influence of Walcott's work
in West Indian literary circles must certainly have been due to
the fact that so many educated West Indians identified with the
struggle between opposing cultural influences which was from
the start a major theme in his plays and poetry. The Guyanese
literary magazine *Kyk-over-al* (1945–61) reflected this obsession among middle-class West Indians with their 'double
heritage'—the European traditions into which they had been
educated and the African-based folk culture of the class they
had left.

In politics, this mulatto self-image produced a new breed of
political paternalism in the fifties. Men like Norman Manley in
Jamaica and Grantley Adams in Barbados, who led two of the
first political parties, saw themselves as the appointed leaders
of the masses who on their own would have been incapable of
articulating their demands. A particularly unfortunate poem
by the Jamaican George Campbell, who was acclaimed at the
time for his championing of the masses, shows this attitude in
its least favourable aspect:

We want to identify ourselves with
Our people; come close to them and they
Come close to us. People how goeth your
World? Know you with pride in understanding
Or are there hard words in the dark: are you
Formless dust blown in the wind?
Bullets answered your gesture for wages
Sometime back; we give no cause for bullets
We shall lead you to a freedom that will
Elevate you from bullets, shall improve your
Mind.[5]

At its best, however, this sense of standing between the people and the oppressor produced the genuine concern and dedication which V. S. Reid ascribes to his prototype of the West Indian politician, Davie, in *New Day*; they were men who had not experienced hunger but had seen it at their door.

It was against this background that the literary and political experiments of the fifties and early sixties took shape. Foremost among these was the implementation of a federation of the British West Indies. This idea had been raised on various occasions in the past by British colonial administrators as a means of centralising and co-ordinating the government of their scattered West Indian territories. So far, however, the uneven political development of the individual territories and the disparity between them in size and natural resources had proved insurmountable obstacles in the face of fierce interterritorial rivalries which already existed. The shared experiences of two world wars had gone a long way to temper this insularity among working-class West Indians. The labour unions were among the earliest West Indian groups to canvas support for an independent federation; their efforts received the financial support of groups of West Indians resident in the United States who were already aware of the advantages of a corporate identity, and a West Indian federation was inaugurated in 1958—only to be disbanded in 1962, after Jamaica was allowed to reconsider its membership through a referendum.

For about ten years, from 1948 to 1958, the federal idea inspired some of the most memorable corporate efforts in the arts and cultural life of the West Indies. George Lamming estimates in *The Pleasures of Exile* (1960) that in those ten years at least a dozen West Indian writers had established themselves internationally with about fifty books to their credit between them. The University College of the West Indies was opened in 1949 and its extra-mural programme in these first years brought new life to many of the smaller islands where opportunities for sharing knowledge were few and far between. Magazines such as *Kyk-over-al*, *Bim* and the occasional *Focus* initiated an exchange of creative work and cultural information among West Indians which facilitated the cross-fertilisation of ideas and interests. Local writers began to gain an extra-

territorial audience for their work through inter-island publishing efforts such as the *Miniature Poets* series and the *Caribbean Voices* programme which broadcast a magazine of creative
writing to the West Indies from London between 1945 and
1958.

The occasion which best epitomised the spirit of the time
was the production in January 1952 in London of Walcott's
verse play, *Henri Christophe*. The play's cast included the whole
spectrum of West Indian talent then in Britain. The prologue
was written by George Lamming whose first novel, *In the
Castle of My Skin*, received a critical ovation when it appeared
the following year. The play was directed by Errol Hill, now a
successful West Indian dramatist in his own right, who later
wrote the first major dissertation on the Trinidad Carnival.
Another Trinidadian playwright, Errol John, played the lead
role. His own script, *Moon on A Rainbow Shawl*, won first prize
in the *Observer* drama competition in 1957 and was later
published by Faber. The rest of the cast and production team
reads like a roll of honour of leading West Indian artists and
intellectuals of the next two decades, many of whom were
students in Britain at the time. Reviewing the production for
The West India Committee Circular, one critic underlined its
significance:

> In the development of an indigenous culture in the Carib-
> bean (and no West Indian Federation can be really without it)
> no element is of greater potential importance than a West
> Indian theatre, for the theatre is the meeting place and the
> nursery of the arts. At the same time the initial obstacles are
> formidable. The three essential elements in the theatre—the
> playwright, the actor and the audience—must exist together
> if the theatre is to be a living reality in the life of the people.
> This condition has not hitherto existed in the West Indies.
> . . . There have certainly been writers, actors and audiences
> in the West Indies in the past, but not West Indian writers of
> West Indian plays for West Indian actors to perform to West
> Indian audiences. . . . In this critical stage of development of
> a West Indian theatre, the recent production of *Henri Chris-
> tophe* . . . is an event of the first importance. It was in every

way a West Indian production.[6]

The array of gifted West Indians who participated in the London production was itself indicative of the characteristic movement into exile of Caribbean writers that had begun when Claude McKay left Jamaica for the United States in 1912. Today most of the major published prose writers of the West Indies still live outside the Caribbean, though much of the inspiration for their work continues to come from the region.

One cause of this trend in the fifties was the widely reported success of Edgar Mittelholzer, George Lamming and Sam Selvon who all had novels published within three years of their arrival in London. The interest in the Caribbean which the flood of West Indian immigrants into Britain stimulated provided these writers with a British audience for their work and a chance of international recognition that few West Indian writers could have dreamt possible a generation earlier. Even after the first flush of success few writers returned to the West Indies to stay, as few could hope to survive as creative writers in a society where chronic unemployment for one quarter of the work force was still a reality, and the life of a writer was seen as an affectation in which only the rich or mentally ill could afford to indulge. In a sense, the exile of West Indian writers is an extreme form of the alienation which most West Indians have had to accept in exchange for the privilege of realising the highest ambitions of their societies. It has been argued, however, that the movement out of the West Indies was often necessary for the writer's creative development, as it helped to place in perspective the details of his relatively narrow but extremely intense experience of life. In an article called 'The Regional Barrier' written in 1958 for the *Times Literary Supplement*, V. S. Naipaul acknowledges the usefulness of residence in London as an aid to creative objectivity. He comments wryly on the ease with which he has slipped into the metropolitan mould of 'non-attachment': 'I am never disturbed by national or international issues. I do not sign petitions, I do not march. And I never cease to feel this lack of involvement is all wrong. I want to be involved, to be touched even by some of the prevailing anger.'

At the end of the article, Naipaul puts his finger on the problem which must have haunted all the West Indians writing in exile: 'And yet I like London. For all the reasons I have given it is the best place to write in. The problem for me is that it is not a place I can write about. Not as yet. Unless I am able to refresh myself by travel—to Trinidad, to India—I fear that living here will eventually lead to my own sterility; and I may have to look for another job.'[7] Eventually most of the major West Indian novelists living abroad were able to cross the regional barrier and write about their adopted country. Many of the works in which they do so are concerned with the theme of exile. In one group, which includes Selvon's *Moses Ascending* (1975), V. S. Naipaul's *Guerrillas* (1976), George Lamming's *Of Age and Innocence* (1958) and *Water With Berries* (1971), and Andrew Salkey's *Come Home, Malcolm Heartland* (1976), there is an almost Kafkaesque failure on the part of the exile to reconnect with the 'real' world of 'back home'. The characters remain throughout on the verge of return, struggling to understand their relationship to the metropolis as a necessary pre-condition to escape from it. Even in *Guerrillas* and *Of Age and Innocence*, both of which are partly set in hybrid, imaginary Caribbean islands, the metropolis remains the reality, and the returned exile seems incapable of seeing the society around him in any but the most general of stereotypes.

After the collapse of the Federation new schisms began to appear within Caribbean society. The fragile regional alliance between the professional middle class and the working class against the common colonial enemy was swept away by a new wave of elitism and national chauvinism in the West Indian territories which were granted independence after 1962. Rivalries between the islands became fiercer, and an atmosphere of bitterness and suspicion prevailed between old political allies, as each side tried to blame the other for the failure of the Federation while fortifying itself to deal with the new political reality. The American presence, which during the war had exerted a positive influence on West Indian thinking in relation to political independence from Britain, began to play a more sinister role in local politics. This was most marked in the case of British Guiana where foreign manipulation of the

Burnham–Jagan rivalry induced in 1962 some of the bloodiest scenes of racial violence in West Indian history between Africans and Indians. The horror and absurdity of this confrontation are reflected in the unusually compassionate tone of V. S. Naipaul's comment on the Burnham–Jagan split in his West Indian documentary, *The Middle Passage* (1962), and, at another level of involvement, in the note of despair in the poems in *Jail Me Quickly* (1963) by Martin Carter, whose radical political stance and deep commitment to the concept of a single Guyanese working class fighting for the same ends had landed him in political detention during the fifties.

While the Indian–African confrontation in Guyana is no longer as bloody an issue as it was in the early sixties, the East Indians living in the West Indies can no longer be characterised as the exotically dressed, quiescent community of which Claude McKay gives us glimpses in *Banana Bottom* (1933). In Trinidad and Guyana, persons of East Indian descent now outnumber those of African origin, and this situation has created new social tensions in both countries which West Indian writers have been among the first to attempt to interpret. Sam Selvon's first novel, *A Brighter Sun* (1952), is the earliest West Indian novel to isolate the Indian–African question as a major theme. Like Mittelholzer's *Corentyne Thunder* (1941) it also provides insights into the life of the East Indian farming community, but Naipaul's classic *A House for Mr Biswas* (1961) attempts to deal with a further stage of East Indian involvement in Caribbean society. In the world of the Tulsis, family and racial ties are used as weapons in the struggle for social advancement. Like Lamming in *Natives of My Person*, Naipaul turns the emphasis inward on one racial group and shows through the weaknesses and tensions of individuals within that group what its limitations are with respect to the wider society. Wilson Harris has subsumed what some observers see as a uniquely East Indian tendency to remain isolated from the mainstream of Caribbean society into a general consideration of the fragmentation of West Indian society which is for him a crucial legacy of the colonial past. In *The Far Journey of Oudin* (1961) his characters, though all of East Indian descent, span the range of human relationships between oppressor and oppressed to become a symbol for the whole community. In general West Indian writers so far have treated this area of racial tension as a problem which is the result of mutual ignorance and mistrust rather than the product of deep-seated animosities arising out of a history of fear or abuse of one group by the other.

The new racial and political tensions in the region after the break-up of the Federation and the granting of independence to Trinidad, Jamaica, Barbados and Guyana were paralleled by the emergence of new cultural features in West Indian society. Perhaps it is never accurate to describe a cultural development as 'new'. The West Indian literary tradition had always drawn its inspiration from the changing language and folklore of the region, and had even contributed to some of the changes. Sam Selvon of Trinidad and Louise Bennett of Jamaica, for example, have helped define the nature and range of their respective dialects by the use they have made of language in their work. But by the sixties changes in West Indian social structure had begun to affect the language and cultural orientation of the lower classes, and this development at the base of the society was to have important consequences for the classes it supported.

Side by side with the growing black middle class described earlier, a new class of dispossessed urban slum dwellers had developed. In Jamaica the Rastafarian sect became the symbol of one aspect of the challenge which this class represented to the new establishment. The sect was established after Selassie's coronation, which was seen by some of Marcus Garvey's followers as the fulfilment of a prophecy made by their leader concerning the redemption of the African race from bondage in the West. The Rastafarians saw Africa as their true home and, in many cases, refused to participate in any political or social action in Babylon—the term they used to describe modern Jamaican society and the rest of Western civilisation. After the Abyssinian invasion, they grew steadily from an eccentric fringe group of a quasi-religious nature (of which there were many at the time) to a mass movement that challenged the spiritual and social basis of post-colonial society. By the early sixties their beliefs and life-style dominated the cultural orientation of all the inhabitants of the 'dungle' and were passed on to similar groups of dispossessed West Indians in other islands and in London, Toronto and New York.

The Rastafarians' powerful speech rhythms and their rejection of the European heritage which an earlier generation of West Indians had tried so hard to accommodate attracted a new generation of writers who were no longer satisfied with the mulatto self-image put forward in the creative writing of the fifties. In Jamaica, the Rastas had a unique relationship with the University of the West Indies to which they often turned for support or justification when under attack from the rest of society. Their influence is consequently most pronounced in the work of Caribbean writers who have been associated with the University campus at Mona, Jamaica. Edward Brathwaite of Barbados and, to a lesser extent, the Jamaican Mervyn Morris, both well-known poets and lecturers at the University, are among the writers in whose work new stylistic developments can be linked to their growing understanding of Rastafarian ideas and speech rhythms. Another academic, Orlando Patterson, published a novel called *The Children of Sisyphus* in 1964 which attempts to place the Rastafarian experience within an existentialist framework. In the same year he also published a brief sociological study of the cult which in some ways clarifies the contradiction in his creative writing between his identification with the Rastafarians and his rejection of their doctrines as a viable philosophy of life. Writers as diverse as Roger Mais and J. B. Emtage, Sylvia Wynter and Derek Walcott, and John Hearne and Anthony McNeill have offered varying readings of the significance of this sect and the possibility of spiritual renewal which it offers West Indian society. One of the most recent contributions, *Ikael Torass* (1977), has come from Noel Williams, a Guyanese writer who was a student at Mona when the Rastafarian presence on campus excited most controversy between 1968 and 1971.

The attraction of Rastafarian ideas and speech was part of a wider process of racial assertion which swept through the Caribbean in the wake of the Black Power movement in the United States of America. West Indians from Marcus Garvey to the Trinidad-born Stokely Carmichael had made significant contributions over the years to the Afro-American struggle for civil rights and cultural recognition. Through his books *Home to Harlem* (1928) and *Banjo* (1929) Claude McKay is probably better known as a black American writer than a West Indian author. Thus, when the Black Power movement in America began to gain momentum, it was quickly taken up by West Indians in Canada and the United States and eventually transmitted to those still at home. Outside the context of racial minority from which the American movement emerged, the Black Power rallying cry of 'Power to the People' became the slogan of West Indians who felt that culturally and economically they had been betrayed by the new black elite. The first major confrontation which this movement produced was in Jamaica in 1968 when the deportation of the radical Guyanese lecturer, Dr Walter Rodney, sparked off a massive student demonstration that was quickly taken over by the general public, and ended in violent clashes between the people and the police. Andrew Salkey and Noel Williams have used this incident as a point of departure in their novels *Joey Tyson* (1974) and *Ikael Torass* respectively. Two years later in Trinidad, the Black Power movement was able to gain the support of the trade unions and offer a serious political challenge to the government of Dr Eric Williams's People's National Movement. This confrontation ended in an abortive army mutiny, the first of its kind in a former British West Indian colony. Together these incidents initiated a political re-awakening which affected almost every English-speaking West Indian territory and has already contributed to important shifts in foreign and domestic policy among the governments in the region.

One of the major repercussions of the mass movements of the seventies has been the renewed contact between Cuba and the rest of the West Indies. Culturally this political move was anticipated by the West Indian writers who belonged to the Caribbean Artists Movement in London in the late sixties such as John La Rose, Edward Brathwaite, George Lamming and Andrew Salkey. Salkey's *Havana Journal* (1971) records his impressions of the Cuban experiment and the cultural events connected with the Congress de Habana in 1968 which he attended, along with John La Rose and C. L. R. James. His *Georgetown Journal* (1972), written in 1970 after his participation in the inauguration of the Co-operative Republic of Guyana, is a useful gauge of the extent to which changes in the political climate in the West Indies had already begun to have a marginal effect on cultural attitudes in the region. The Cuban link has helped to draw West Indian literary criticism closer to Latin American traditions which, it has been argued, have too often been ignored in the assessment of the work of writers such as Wilson Harris and Denis Williams. C.A.M.'s role in the creation of this link has been crucial. Its magazine, *Savacou*, was one of the most influential publications to emerge from the flurry of literary activity which followed the Black Power crisis. Other publications which date from this time include *Bongo Man* and *Abeng* in Jamaica, *Moko* and *Tapia* in Trinidad, *Manjak* in Barbados and *Ratoon* in Guyana. Their names reflect the re-orientation of interest among West Indians in their language and history. This new interest was also reflected in the attempts to make communication through the spoken word rather than the printed page the object of stylistic refinement in Marina Maxwell's Jamaican 'yard' theatre and the experiments in oral delivery presented at Carifesta 1972.[8] Some of the new magazines encouraged a school of literary criticism which drew heavily on social relevance as a criterion for literary excellence. At its best this has produced the critical reassessment of the calypso as an art form and the revaluation of the importance of political commitment in the work of writers such as the Guyanese poet Martin Carter. Serious divisions have begun to develop though between writers and critics who place a heavy emphasis on such criteria and those who feel these are essentially outside the field of literary creation.

Now that literacy is no longer the exclusive domain of the middle class, writers are beginning to come forward who create from within the conditions they describe, rather than as outsiders championing adopted social causes. Rastafarian poets such as Ras Dizzy and Bongo Jerry, whose long poem *Mabrak* is already on its way to becoming a West Indian classic, have been able to communicate a quality of experience which on their own few outsiders would have been able to perceive. In a similar way, the social protest of reggae musicians such as Bob Marley, and some of the calypsonians of the eastern Caribbean, has become more self-conscious and careful of craft as their exponents discover the extent of their serious audience and the range of their own creative potential. A parallel exists between this development and the writing originating in metropolitan centres in Britain and America where a West Indian sub-culture has evolved. This includes the picaresque satire of Sam Selvon's *Lonely Londoners* (1956) as well as Austin Clarke's more recent short stories about West Indian immigrants in Toronto. Most of this new experience, however, has been channelled into poetry. The controlled anger present in Linton Kwesi Johnson's *Dread Beat and Blood* (1975) is a crucial element in the poetry of many second generation West Indian immigrants who feel frustrated by the limitations of their new societies.

Change is still the only constant in West Indian society. Often the scale of time and distance on which it occurs is so condensed that a chronological consideration such as this is misleading, as it tends to imply that one phenomenon has replaced another when in fact they co-exist. The cycles of change described in the thirties, fifties and seventies are still being repeated in the life and experience of individuals. In spite of their diversity, West Indian writers are held together by a background of trauma and promise which they share with the entire Caribbean community.

3   The Beginnings to 1929
by Anthony Boxill

Twentieth-century West Indian writing is more West Indian and less self-consciously imitative of English literature than is most of the writing done in and about the region in the eighteenth and nineteenth centuries. But surely Kenneth Ramchand has a point when he includes in his anthology, *West Indian Narrative* (1966), excerpts from Aphra Behn's *Oroonoko or the Royal Slave* (1678), Monk Lewis's *Journal of a West India Proprietor* (1834), Lady Nugent's *Journal* (1839), and Olaudah Equiano's *The Life of Olaudah Equiano* (1789). These works were all written by people who had spent some time in the Caribbean and who made very shrewd observations on the life and customs of the people there at a time when these people did not have much opportunity to write about themselves. Even if one does not try to make a case for these books as West Indian literature, it cannot really be denied that an acquaintance with these books would be an asset in understanding more recent West Indian writing. And if, as Arthur Drayton claims in his article 'West Indian Consciousness in West Indian Verse: A Historical Perspective',[1] West Indian consciousness developed not only in what was written by West Indians but also as a result of what they read, then it is necessary for a student of the region's literature to consider these early works very seriously.

There are numerous other descriptions of local life in books both of fiction and of travel by Englishmen in the eighteenth and nineteenth centuries. The best known of these are probably Michael Scott's *Tom Cringle's Log* (1836), Anthony Trollope's *The West Indies and the Spanish Main* (1859), Charles

Kingsley's *At Last: A Christmas in the West Indies* (1871) and James Anthony Froude's *The English in the West Indies* (1888). The tone of these books is condescending in varying degrees. Michael Scott sometimes can forget his sense of superiority when he presents some interesting aspect of Jamaican life in careful detail. At the other extreme Froude, even when he is making a valid point, is so offensively ethnocentric and so convinced that the black West Indian's only hope lies in being looked after by the Mother Country that it is difficult to see what contribution his writing could have made to the growth of West Indian literature. Yet in 1889, one year after the publication of his work, there appeared an impassioned rebuttal of it, *Froudacity*, by J. J. Thomas, a black Trinidadian. In his energetic defence Thomas makes one of the most positive early statements by a West Indian of the validity of his differentness. It is very significant that in this defence there is no sense of apology or inferiority.

More significant than these accounts of mere visitors to the islands is the writing that was done by West Indians themselves and by others who had lived in the West Indies for substantial periods. Drayton is impressed by the amount of literature that was produced locally by a society which had to contend with the burden of slavery. He believes that West Indian literature can in fact be traced back to the time when printing began in Jamaica, Barbados and Trinidad in the eighteenth and nineteenth centuries. Edward Brathwaite, the historian and poet, supports this view in a long, interesting article, 'Creative Literature of the British West Indies during the Period of Slavery'.[2]

In the introduction to his anthology, *Caribbean Verse* (1967), O. R. Dathorne traces West Indian poetry back to the eighteenth century. Perhaps most remarkable of all these critics and anthologists is Norman Cameron of Guyana, who in 1931 brought out the anthology *Guianese Poetry: 1831–1931* with an introduction by himself. Cameron did his work at a time when West Indian literature was not in vogue, and he saw the value of preserving some of this early writing for contemporary and future generations.

Drayton and Dathorne (Cameron's anthology restricted

itself to Guyana) seem to agree that a convenient place to start the examination of the development of West Indian poetry is with the work of Francis Williams, an eighteenth–century black Jamaican. He was a protégé of the Duke of Montagu, who sent him to the University of Cambridge to attempt to prove that a 'negro given the right circumstances could acquit himself as creditably as a white man'.[3] Williams wrote in Latin and composed odes to mark great occasions in Jamaica. His finest achievement seems to have been the ode dedicated to George Haldane when he arrived to assume duties as the Governor of Jamaica in 1759. This poem is preserved in its entirety in Edward Long's *History of Jamaica* (1774). Long, whose attitude was the opposite of that of the Duke of Montagu, finds many faults with the poem.[4] As one would expect, the ode is full of classical allusions and extravagant comparisons are made of Haldane to classical heroes, but the lines which seem significant are the references to Williams's colour: 'Minerva forbids an Aethiop to extol the deeds of generals'; and later on in reference to himself: 'Nor let it be a source of shame to you that you bear a white body in a black skin.' Here we find poignantly expressed the dilemma of many a West Indian that his colour makes him 'inferior' even when he has a sense of being able to understand and share in the culture of his white 'superiors'.

In the eighteenth century a number of light, satirical, topical poems were published in Jamaica, such as *The Politics and Patriots of Jamaica* (1718) and *The Election* (1788), both by anonymous authors, but the most important poem to appear about the West Indies was *The Sugar Cane* (1764) by James Grainger, an English doctor who practised for many years in St Kitts. There can be no doubt of Grainger's knowledge of and concern for the lives of the negro slaves because in the same year as his poem appeared he 'published a medical work on West Indian diseases especially designed for use in treating negro slaves'.[5] Grainger's poem is a strange mixture of sharply observed scenes, such as his description of the cutting of the cane, and an inability to understand what the feelings of the blacks must have been about their enslavement. He cannot see beyond their surface laughter. There is concern for them in the poem, but it is inevitably patronising. Joseph and Johanna Jones make a real attempt to see this poem in the context of its time: '*The Sugar Cane* may be considered for its time an "experimental" poem, attempting to dignify a humble subject by casting it in verse. Certainly it is a very early effort to view the region outside the bounds of travel narrative and arm chair romance.'[6] This is as kind an assessment as can be made of this poem although its historical significance is emphasised by the fact that it seems to have served as a model for two later poems, *Jamaica: a Poem in Three Parts* (1776) by an anonymous poet, and *Barbadoes and Other Poems* (1833) by M. J. Chapman, a white Barbadian doctor. Chapman makes the same kind of use as Grainger of his intimate knowledge of the West Indies and we find in his poem moving descriptions of landscape but little understanding of or sympathy for the plight of the slaves. Perhaps the most interesting item in his poem is his description, entitled 'The Dust', of the 1812 eruption of the volcano in St Vincent. Edward Brathwaite more than a hundred years later, no doubt inspired by this passage, entitles 'The Dust' his description of the effect on the people of Barbados of the eruption of Mont Pelée in Martinique in 1902. As effective as is Chapman's description of the eruption, its heroic couplets and its rhythms, even when one makes allowances for the poetic conventions of his day, make it quite clear that he does not have the same kind of feel for the rhythms and language of Barbadian life that Brathwaite shows in his version which uses free verse and deep Barbadian dialect.

This seems to have been the chief drawback of West Indian poetry of the eighteenth and nineteenth centuries—another example is William Hosack's *The Isle of Streams, or the Jamaican Hermit and Other Poems* (1876)—that most of the poets could not look at the life around them with West Indian eyes, experienced West Indians though they were. Instead they attempted to force the West Indian experience into the poetic diction and into the rhythms of English verse. Classical allusions abound and too often slaves are described as naiads or bacchantes.

This criticism is less true of the poetry produced in Guyana in the nineteenth century, probably because many of the Guyanese poets were black and understood better what it meant to be enslaved and oppressed. Simon Christian Oliver protests against the yoke and chains of slavery. Egbert Martin, the son of a tailor, wrote two books, *Poetical Works* (1883) and *Lyrics* (1886), under the pseudonym of Leo. Although imitative of English Romantic verse both in style and in subject-matter, he does manage to speak in his own voice occasionally in such poems as 'Twilight'. The religious poetry of Thomas Don, whose *Pious Effusions* appeared in 1873, reveals a great deal about the predicament of West Indians struggling against a background of slavery; as Norman Cameron puts it: 'The consolation of religion was one of their few possessions.'[7] Henry G. Dalton's descriptions in 'The Essequebo and its Tributaries' evoke the Guyanese landscape and distinguish it from that of the islands in ways that the literature of Guyana has continued to do. The overpowering immensity of the Guyanese landscape probably had much to do with encouraging Guyana's writers to find inadequate as models the nature poetry of Romantic and Victorian English poets.

Towards the end of the century S. E. Wills dared to abandon in some of his poems the eighteenth- and nineteenth-century English models and to write poems on local events in creole dialect. And Michael McTurk, whose pseudonym was Quow, wrote lively, if crude, dialect poems and fables in the press. The following lines from his short poem 'Query' are interesting because of Quow's experiment with dialect, but also because he has managed to suggest not only that the blacks questioned the culture and religion that was imposed upon them but did so with a sense of irony and humour:

> Da Backra one fo' go a hebben?
> Da Backra one fo' raise like lebben?
> Da wa' a-we po Negah do?
> Make a-we no fo' raise up too?
> Da we a Lamb—no see we wool,
> No make dem Backra make we fool,
> Dem sef a Goat, no'see dem hair,
> Dem no' wan' cut de 'tory fair.

Quow's poems and fables which appeared in the 'Argosy' in

the late nineteenth century have been collected in *Essays and Fables in the Vernacular*.[8]

The gradual discovery that standard English and the rhythms of English poetry did not always do justice to West Indian life is very important in the development of West Indian literature. It is encouraging to see the experiments with dialect that were carried out in Guyana at the end of the nineteenth century, but one must be careful to qualify them. As a rule dialect was used for comic sketches and for descriptions of low life. For elevated thoughts on nature and religion, the poets still tended to turn to the example of Wordsworth and Tennyson and to make extensive use of classical allusion.

The same observation might be made about the drama produced in the West Indies before 1929. Not many plays were written, the amateur dramatic societies preferring to rely on European classics, but the few which were written fall roughly into two groups. Norman Cameron tells us that in 1872 a Jesuit, Fr C. W. Barraud, wrote two five-act plays in the Shakespearean manner: *St Thomas of Canterbury* and *St Elizabeth of Hungary*. These were later published in 1892. Tom Redcam's *San Gloria*, a play about Columbus, falls into the same category, and although W. Adolphe Roberts in his *Six Great Jamaicans* claims that 'it could stand comparison with the work of any of the lesser Elizabethan dramatists',[9] it is difficult to see it as more than struggling for a grandeur which is Elizabethan rather than Jamaican. The other type of plays which tended to be written might appropriately be described as sketches of local life. These made no efforts towards grandeur or the heroic or tragic. Consequently they were less stilted and more lively, if less ambitious. An example of such a sketch is Sidney Martins's *Mrs Farrington's Third Husband* (1916).

Edward Brathwaite discusses some of the novels written in the West Indies during the eighteenth and nineteenth centuries: *The Adventures of Jonathan Corncob* (1787); *Montgomery, or The West Indian Adventurer* (1812, 1813); *Hamel, The Obeah Man* (1827); *Marley, or the Life of a Planter in Jamaica* (1828)—all by anonymous authors—and *Creoleana* (1842) by J. W. Order-son, a white Barbadian. Most of these, and one could mention many more, attempt to give a picture of what life was like for the white West Indian during the period of slavery. As Brathwaite points out, most of them were tracts against slavery full of high principled moralising. As novels, though, they are unconvincing because the protest remains on the level of principle and the authors seem unable not to be condescending to the slaves whose cause they wish to plead. The blacks in these books never achieve the kind of dignity that is accorded the whites, with the exception of Hamel in *Hamel, The Obeah Man*. In this novel the author makes a real attempt 'to enter into the imagination of at least a single slave' as Brathwaite puts it.[10]

For all their one-sidedness, however, these novels have a historical interest. It would be interesting, for example, to compare the religious moralising of *Montgomery* or *Creoleana* with that of Thomas MacDermot (Tom Redcam) in his two novels, *Becka's Buckra Baby* (1904) and *One Brown Girl and—: A Jamaican Story* (1909). The anti-missionary feeling and the tension between Christianity and obeah in *Hamel* might profitably be compared with similar themes explored by Claude McKay in *Banana Bottom* (1933) a century later.

At the end of the nineteenth century and the beginning of the twentieth a group of writers began to emerge who, though not convinced that West Indian society was ready to stand on its own, recognised nevertheless that it was different and that this difference from English society was not necessarily contemptible. The development of West Indian consciousness was probably helped by the interest that folklorists were taking in the culture of the region. The following list of publications suggests how busy these people were: Izett Anderson and Frank Cundall, *Jamaican Negro Proverbs and Sayings collected and classified according to Subjects* (1910); Martha Beckwith, *Jamaica Anansi Stories* (1924) and *Jamaica Proverbs* (1925); Graham Cruickshank, *Negro Humour, being sketches in the market, on the road and at my back door* (1905); Walter Jekyll, *Jamaican Song and Story* (1907); John Radcliffe, *Lectures on Jamaica Proverbs* (1859) and *Lectures on Negro Proverbs, with a preliminary paper on Negro Literature* (1869); and E. N. Woolford, *Sidelights on Local Life* (1917). Studies of West Indian language such as Thomas Russell's *The Etymology of Jamaica Grammar* (1868) and J. J. Thomas's *The Theory and Practice of Creole Grammar* (1869) must also have helped make some West Indians more aware of the structure and rhythms of the brand of English that had evolved in the islands. That these works brought to the attention of the reading public the way of life of the peasants and the poor cannot be questioned; that this fact affected the literature that was produced at this time is suggested by the new place that black peasants find in the early novels of de Lisser, and by the influence of Walter Jekyll on the work of Claude McKay. We get some idea of relationship of these two men in the moving portrait McKay paints of Jekyll as Squire Gensir in *Banana Bottom*.

H. G. de Lisser sums up in his book *Twentieth Century Jamaica* (1913) the growing sense of the texture of society as a whole and the sense of the distinctiveness of the Jamaican identity:

> What can be maintained at this point is that the Jamaican of any colour is not precisely like any other man; he is a Jamaican, and has characteristics that are common more or less to all his fellow countrymen. One is not born and brought up in a country for nothing. One does not read the same papers that one's fellows read, hear much the same sort of talk all the year round, come into close contact with all other classes of the people, eat the same food, and enjoy the same recreations, without one's mind becoming assimilated to the minds of one's countrymen.[11]

In an Author's Note to his third novel, de Lisser indicates how much it matters to him that his books should be made available to the Jamaican public:

> *Triumphant Squalitone* will, I hope, be published in England, as my other novels have been.
> There are many reasons for issuing local editions of my books. The best, from the Jamaican reader's point of view, is that he thus obtains the works much more cheaply than he otherwise could. The Colonial Editions of my previous stories, for instance, sell at half-a-crown per copy. And that is a price which, experience has proved, very few Jamaicans

can easily pay.

Now the only way in which a cheap edition of a book can be published in Jamaica is by making that book the medium of advertisements. The reading public of this country, there-fore, who have bought my books, owe it entirely to the merchants and business houses of Kingston that they have been able to do so at a low price.

It should be stated that this book is sold at fully fifty per cent below its cost of production. There is therefore no financial profit to its publishers.[12]

This passage tells much about the state of publishing in Jamaica at this time and about the financial status of the people. And it suggests the writer's strong sense of his community, his responsibility to it and his desire to communicate with it. It would be wrong to infer from this that de Lisser envisaged an independent Jamaica. In the first chapter of *Twentieth Century Jamaica* he explores the possibilities of Jamaica's future with either England, Canada or the United States. He does not consider independence or nationhood or any form of federa-tion with the other West Indian islands. His preference would be for 'a prosperous Jamaica directly owing allegiance to the mother-country'.

Tom Redcam (the pseudonym of Thomas Henry MacDer-mot which he devised by spelling his surname backwards), whose contributions to the development of Jamaican literature were begun in the decade before de Lisser, was not unlike de Lisser in the quality of his nationalism. 'His ideal was Jamaica within the Empire, but Jamaica as a recognised entity, and there was often to be found an unhappy note in his writings when he thought that his native country was being treated as a step-child', writes W. Adolphe Roberts in *Six Great Jamaicans*.

In 1904, after serving for a few years as assistant editor of the *Jamaica Times*, Redcam was appointed full editor. He used his position to influence and encourage writing in Jamaica. Roberts talks of the encouragement he received for his poetry, and points out that Redcam published McKay's early poetry and de Lisser's early articles. He was as convinced as de Lisser that the Jamaican's identity was distinct and that this needed to be reflected in a local literature. After becoming editor, Redcam launched the 'All Jamaica Library':

> In 'The All Jamaica Library' we are presenting to a Jamaican public, at a price so small as to make each publication generally purchasable, a literary embodiment of Jamaican subjects. Poetry, Fiction, History and Essays will be included, all dealing directly with Jamaica and Jamaicans, and written by Jamaicans, many of whom are well known to the public as successful writers. We hope to give readers something worth buying, and we hope all Jamaicans will support this attempt to develop neglected resources of mental and aesthetic wealth.[13]

These are thoroughly praiseworthy aspirations and it is a pity that they could not be attained. Only four works of fiction were issued by the Library: *Maroon Medicine* (1905) by E. A. Dodd under the pseudonym E. Snod; *Marguerite, A Story of the Earthquake* (1907) by W. A. Campbell; and Redcam's own two novels, *Becka's Buckra Baby* (1904) and *One Brown Girl and—: A Jamaican Story* (1909). The last-mentioned work was numbered 4 and 5 in the Library because it was the only full-length novel in the series; it also marked the end of this venture.

It is not hard to see why the 'All Jamaica Library' failed. There were probably financial troubles, but the difficulty of procuring good manuscripts must have been the underlying reason. None of the four works published was very good. Snod's *Maroon Medicine*, in spite of its occasional carelessness and errors in grammar, is the liveliest of the four. His central character, a Mr Watson, is a peasant who, though small and weak, outwits everyone with whom he comes into contact. He is a genuine Anansi figure. Campbell's *Marguerite* is a sentimental, moralising piece as are both of Redcam's novels.

But Redcam's novels must be considered briefly, not because of their success, but because his reputation as the father of Jamaican literature gives them an influence which Campbell's effort does not have. *Becka's Buckra Baby* and *One Brown Girl* are rendered lifeless by the sentimental didacticism of their author who shows little understanding of the art of the novel.

The first is a parable about love in which the heroine, Noel Bronvola, yearns to lay down her life for someone since her father sacrificed his that she might live. The story idealises this noble love while condemning the carnal love by which black women produce 'buckra' babies by white men. Becka, a little black girl who is given a white doll for Christmas by Noel, is killed in an accident while chasing a boy who has grabbed the doll. This situation allows Redcam to moralise insufferably. The book only achieves vitality when Redcam records a quarrel between a laundress, Mrs Gyrton, and her sister, Rosabella. These characters have an energy which not even Redcam's sentimentality can stultify.

The same is true of *One Brown Girl*. This longer work comes to life when the Jamaican black working–class characters are introduced, but the carefully arranged parabolic struggle of good, represented by three women, and evil, represented by two men, for the soul of the Brown Girl is quite unconvincing. Attempts to introduce Jamaican re-enactments of the parable of the Good Samaritan and the conversion of St Paul fall flat because they are so awkwardly handled. Long descriptions of landscape and passages about Jamaican history serve to suggest that Redcam has a sense of the importance of these things but not the imaginative strength to make them integral to the world he is attempting to create. However, for all the clumsiness of his fiction it is possible that de Lisser learnt something from his portraits of Jamaican peasants.

Redcam occupies a similarly influential position in the development of Jamaican poetry although his own poetry was much like his fiction in that it tended to be lifeless and imitative when he was struggling to evoke high ideals, and achieved vitality occasionally when he described the Jamaican folk accurately in the folk language. However, his dialect poems are not the ones that the school of poets which he encouraged chose to emulate. Consequently these poets suffer from many of his shortcomings. Their poetry is sentimental, imitative of Romantic and Victorian nature poetry, and strives too hard to seem elevated by using classical allusions even when such allusions are inappropriate to the subject of the poem. Many of the poets were women and their work can be found in an anthology, *Voices from Summerland* (1929), compiled by J. E. Clare McFarlane, who after Redcam was the most influential poet of that group. Many of the members of the group published volumes of verse: Constance Hollar, *Flaming June* (1941); Albinia Hutton, *Poems* (1912) and *Verses* (1932); Lena Kent, *The Hills of Saint Andrew* (1931) and *Dews on the Branch* (1933); Una Marson, *Tropic Reveries* (1930) and *Heights and Depths* (1932); Clare McFarlane, *Daphne, a Tale of the Hills of St Andrew* (1931); Arthur Nicholas, *Arcadia* (1949); and Tropica, *Island of Sunshine* (1905). Redcam's own poetry was collected posthumously in *Orange Valley and Other Poems* (1951). McFarlane's *A Literature in the Making* (1956) gives a somewhat uncritical account of the achievement of these poets.

The two best poets to have been encouraged by Redcam are undoubtedly W. Adolphe Roberts and Claude McKay, both of whom left Jamaica to go to the United States to become professional writers. Roberts's work in *Pierrot Wounded and Other Poems* (1919) and *Pan and Peacocks* (1928) shows a technical skill that is lacking in the work of the other Jamaican poets of his day but it is not distinctively Jamaican. McKay wrote two volumes of lively dialect poems, *Constab Ballads* (1912) and *Songs of Jamaica* (1912), before he left Jamaica, and two later volumes, *Spring in New Hampshire and Other Poems* (1920) and *Harlem Shadows* (1922). In the latter two books he gives up the energetic Jamaican language of the first two for an archaic poetic diction, and he is no longer content merely to observe and present. His passionate, powerful poems of protest against the racial situation in America are less marred by sentimental and archaic language than his nostalgic poems about Jamaica. However, it is not until his novels, *Home to Harlem* (1928) and *Banjo* (1929), that he begins to find a language which is capable of struggling with the dilemma he perceives in the lives of many a West Indian: the problem of preserving his identity as a black man in a world that is run by white standards. This psychological and linguistic quest finds its culmination in *Banana Bottom*, McKay's greatest work and a West Indian classic.

McKay's career is significant in another way, for he is the first major West Indian writer to have gone into exile to pursue his career. Others were to follow such as Jean Rhys and Eric Walrond, both very talented writers indeed. Rhys's first book, *The Left Bank and Other Stories* (1927), which contained some stories set in her native Dominica, indicates that the problem of identity explored by McKay applied just as poignantly to the white West Indian. Her fullest, most moving treatment of this theme is not accomplished until 1966 in *Wide Sargasso Sea*.

In *Tropic Death* (1926) by Eric Walrond we get a powerful picture of lower-class life not only in Jamaica but also in other West Indian islands and in parts of Latin America. His experiments with style and his use of dialect suggested that very good things would follow from his pen, but unfortunately nothing more of his appeared.[14]

The writers who remained published the odd novel or book of poems and never aspired to become professional. Frederick Charles Tomlinson, under the pseudonym Frederick Charles, published *The Helions; Or, The Deeds of Rio: A Political Comedy* (1903), a satirical, fairly amusing novel of political life in Jamaica to which de Lisser's *Triumphant Squalitone* seems to owe something. But Charles never wrote another novel. In Guyana the poet Walter MacA. Lawrence published *Meditations* (1929), and A. R. F. Webber wrote a novel, *Those that be in Bondage* (1917), which is a strange mixture of romantic sentimentality and protest against the treatment of East Indian indentured labourers on Guyanese plantations. Nothing more is heard from these writers.

There were, however, two writers who remained in Jamaica and because they were professional journalists managed to combine their careers with the writing of novels. One, Esther Chapman, is of only minor interest. She is an Englishwoman who spent much of her life in Jamaica. She was once a leader writer for the *Jamaican Daily Express,* and editor of the *West Indian Review*. Her novels—*Punch and Judy* (1927), *Study in Bronze* (1928) and *Too Much Summer* (1953)—explore in an exotic fashion the problems of colour prejudice and intellectual sterility in Jamaica.

The other writer who remained is, of course, H. G. de Lisser, editor of the *Gleaner*, the largest paper in Jamaica. His editorials kept his opinions before the Jamaican people for over forty years. He wrote ten novels, and in 1920 he founded an annual, *The Planters' Punch*, for which he often produced a full-length book. He adopted the policy of publishing his novels first in Jamaica then in England.

As W. Adolphe Roberts has pointed out in his foreword to *The Arawak Girl*, de Lisser's novels fall into three broad groups. *Jane's Career* (1914) and *Susan Proudleigh* (1915), his first two novels, deal with lower-class life in Jamaica. Next there are three novels which deal with the Jamaican middle and upper classes: *Triumphant Squalitone* (1917), *Under the Sun* (1937) and *The Cup and the Lip* (1956). The other five novels—*Revenge* (1919), *The White Witch of Rosehall* (1929), *Psyche* (1952), *Morgan's Daughter* (1953) and *The Arawak Girl* (1958)—are historical romances.

His first two novels are not only the most interesting from a historical perspective: they are his best work. Unfortunately the popularity of *The White Witch of Rosehall* has tended to overshadow them and too many critics have ignored these books. Kenneth Ramchand, however, has pointed out that '*Susan Proudleigh* is the first West Indian novel of emigration; *Jane's Career* is the first in which the central character, whose feelings and thoughts are explored in depth, is a Negro.'[15] Ramchand also points out the similarity in de Lisser's treatment of Jane and Michael Anthony's treatment of Francis in *The Year in San Fernando*. These two authors, different as they are in age and background, are amazingly alike in the way each describes a simple country person learning to cope with the complicated life of a city, and more importantly in the way each uses the treatment of domestic servants as a metaphor for the slavery of the West Indian past.

One wonders what made de Lisser turn from this kind of novel, which pulsated with the life of the folk, to his more shallow middle-class satires and ultimately to historical romance. The answer is probably that as he got older he became more conservative and lost his sympathy for people such as Jane and Susan. Even in *Jane's Career* one gets hints of this impatience in his ridicule of the behaviour of the people at Jane's wedding. *Revenge*, which deals with the Morant Bay rebellion of 1865, lacks the sympathy for the people that Reid demonstrates in *New Day* (1949). And in *The White Witch of Rosehall*, his best-known work because of its exotic and sensational treatment of the West Indian past, his white man is by far a superior human being to his black man, who is often depicted as treacherous and lacking in sensitivity.

One final point needs to be made about his fiction. All his novels are dominated by resourceful, vital women. Given the importance of women in the West Indian social structure, de Lisser must be credited with doing more than most West Indian writers to explore the effect of this dominant female personality on the West Indian psyche as a whole.

All the things for which West Indian literature is known and admired today can be observed evolving over a period of time. West Indian writers gradually abandoned their English models, experimented more and more with the language of the West Indian people, and concentrated more and more on trying to present to the people what was distinct and worthwhile in their lives. West Indian writers, such as McKay, Rhys and Walrond, began to go into exile and to produce very powerful work from there. West Indian characters, such as Susan Proudleigh, began to emigrate and to pursue the quest that Naipaul describes in *The Middle Passage*, and Brathwaite in his trilogy, *The Arrivants*.

4   The Thirties and Forties
by Reinhard W. Sander

The explosion of West Indian creative writing in the early 1950s came as a surprise to the literary establishment in England, where many West Indian writers had taken up residence and where their work was published. Apart from a few passing visitors with a general interest in art and literature, hardly anybody had taken notice of the developing creativity throughout the Caribbean in previous decades.[1] This growth was intimately linked with social, political and economic developments in the region. The origins of the literary movement in the 1930s and 1940s are essentially the same as those of the labour movement and of the nationalist political parties. Alfred H. Mendes has identified two major factors which motivated the writers of the 1930s:

> The first was, of course, the First World War where a large number of us had been abroad, and indeed, even those of us who had not been abroad were influenced considerably by what was happening in the world, and the second event was the Russian Revolution. Those, I think, were the two events in our lives at that time which drove us into writing about our islands.[2]

The world-wide Depression which led to social upheavals in the Caribbean in the late 1930s in turn motivated the next generation of writers. Whether consciously or unconsciously, West Indian writers were influenced by political events and contributed as exponents of cultural nationalism to the

45

struggle for independence.

A considerable part of West Indian literature in the 1930s and 1940s was published in little reviews which emerged in almost every territory. Barbados had its *Forum Quarterly* (1931–4), later resurrected as *The Forum Magazine* (1943–5), and its *Bim* (since 1942), edited by Frank A. Collymore; in Trinidad there appeared *The Quarterly Magazine*, edited by Austin M. Nolte, *Trinidad* (1929–30), edited by Alfred H. Mendes and C. L. R. James, *The Beacon* (1931–3, 1939), edited by Albert M. Gomes, *Youth*, published by the Trinidad and Tobago Youth Council, and *Picong* and *Callaloo*, edited by Jean de Boissiere; Grenada saw the *St George's Literary League Magazine*, edited by Robert M. Coard; British Honduras *The Outlook*, edited by Philip S. W. Goldson; A. J. Seymour edited *Kyk-over-al* (1945–61) in British Guiana, and in Jamaica Edna Manley edited four issues of *Focus* (1943, 1948, 1956, 1960), which took over from H. G. de Lisser's *Planters' Punch* (1920–45). In 1949 the University College of the West Indies added *Caribbean Quarterly*. The most significant of these magazines were *The Beacon, Bim, Kyk-over-al* and *Focus*.[3]

Almost all the writers who gained success in the 1950s had their first pieces of prose or poetry published in *Bim*. Edgar Mittelholzer, a regular contributor, made his first appearance in the February 1945 issue with a short story 'Miss Clarke Is Dying' and an article 'Of Casuarinas and Cliffs', and George Lamming followed in the next issue with his poem 'Image'. No. 9 (December 1948) marks the beginning of *Bim*'s role as a West Indian magazine. In the foreword we read: 'We take very great pleasure in introducing to our readers a group of five writers from Trinidad. Three of these, Messrs Telemaque, Herbert and Lamming, have been recently acclaimed as serious poets by Mr Swanzy, editor of the popular *Caribbean Voices* programme.' *Bim* No. 10 (June 1949) adds two further contributors from Trinidad: B. J. Ramon-Fortuné and Samuel Selvon, and features pieces by Gloria Escoffery and A. L. Hendriks from Jamaica, A. J. Seymour from British Guiana, and Derek Walcott and Harold Simmons from St Lucia.

Focus appeared only twice during the 1940s and was a purely Jamaican affair. It featured short stories, poetry, legends and short plays by writers such as John Hearne, A. L. Hendriks, John Figueroa, Peter Abrahams, Louise Bennett, Vera Bell, Claude Thompson, V. S. Reid, K. E. Ingram, Roger Mais, M. G. Smith, Basil McFarlane, Philip Sherlock, George Campbell, H. D. Carberry, Vivian L. Virtue and Cicely Howland. The *Focus* group was also closely related to the Little Theatre Movement in Jamaica, whose members wrote and performed Jamaican plays. The two short plays published in *Focus: 1948* were Cicely Howland's 'Storm Signal' and George Campbell's 'Play without Scenery'. However, it is significant that Edna Manley in her foreword comments that 'the Theatre Movement is urgently calling for Jamaican plays', and A. J. Seymour in 'The Literary Adventure of the West Indies' only discusses drama in a footnote, drawing attention to plays by Archie Lindo and M. G. Smith of Jamaica, Frank Collymore of Barbados, and N. E. Cameron and Basil Balgobin of British Guiana.[4] While there were few original plays, the theatre was alive. The Jamaican Little Theatre Movement had its counterparts in the Bridgetown Players in Barbados, the Whitehall Players in Trinidad, and the Georgetown Dramatic Club in British Guiana. These groups still depended largely on foreign material, but others, such as Sam Chase's popular theatre in Guyana and Beryl McBurnie's Little Carib dance group in Trinidad had already begun to experiment with alternative folk forms.

Kyk-over-al (1945–61) fulfilled a double role: it was clearly rooted in Guyana, but West Indian in scope and orientation. A. J. Seymour (born 1914) set the direction in his editorial in the June 1947 issue of *Kyk*:

This issue of *Kyk-over-al* looks out at the ferment of thought and consciousness in the West Indies and at the same time it looks at some of the historical associations laid away in the Ancient County of Berbice and its story. We're both at home and abroad, in our Country's past and in the historical future of the area. That is but fair when we remember that our Guianese community does not develop in isolation and that we are a unit in one of the future Dominions of the Empire.

Kyk was obviously inspired by the prospect of a West Indian Federation and ceased publication in 1961 shortly before the Federation broke up. It featured poetry and short stories by writers such as J. A. V. Bourne, A. J. Seymour, Wilson Harris, Frank E. Dalzell, Martin Carter, Horace L. Mitchell, Edgar Mittelholzer, Philip Sherlock and Frank A. Collymore. In general the short stories were imitative and hardly inspiring, but the poetry began to show a wider range of themes and quality, from Martin Carter's better forgotten 'Ode to Midnight' to A. J. Seymour's powerful 'Tomorrow Belongs to the People':

> Ignorant
> Illegitimate,
> Hungry sometimes,
> Living in tenement yards
> Dying in burial societies
> The people is a lumbering giant
> That holds history in his hand,

and to Wilson Harris's poetry which foreshadowed the linguistic skill and imaginative vision of his fictional work. Particularly memorable Harris poems are 'Green is the Colour of the World', and 'Savannah Lands' which he describes as

> Lands smoky with their dreams
> That drift across the world
> Like memories of ancient beauty dimly recalled.

Between 1945 and 1949 Harris published two short stories, a dozen poems and three critical essays in *Kyk*. These were perhaps the most significant contributions to the early issues of this magazine.

Kyk's significance lies in its pioneering efforts to stimulate a West Indian theory and practice of literary and cultural criticism. In an 'Open Letter to West Indian Writers' Seymour dealt with issues such as 'Why do we write? What do we and what should we write about? What shall we take from the U.K. and the U.S.A.?' He himself contributed essays on the pioneers of Guyanese poetry, Egbert Martin (1862–90) and Walter MacA. Lawrence (1896–1942), and others entitled 'Guianese Poetry', 'Sunlight and West Indian Poetry' and 'Poetry and Spiritual Values', which were followed by a special *Kyk* issue, April 1950, on 'The Literary Adventure of the West Indies'. Other contributors like the prolific N. E. Cameron wrote on 'Drama in British Guiana', 'Cultural Life in Jamaica', and Edna Manley on 'Art in the West Indies'. Aspects of culture like 'Painting in British Guiana' and 'The West Indian Family' were explored, and the features of West Indian speech were discussed in essays entitled 'On Writing Creolese' and 'The Language We Speak'. In the search for a Guyanese/West Indian identity, the preoccupation with history strongly entered the topics of discussion: 'Nineteenth Century Georgetown', 'Six Most Outstanding Men in B.G.'s History', 'The Story of Kykoveral', 'Guianese History', 'The Lost Guiana Boundary', 'The Buccaneer Governor'.

Even vaster in scope was *The Beacon*, a monthly magazine published by Albert M. Gomes (1911–78) in Trinidad from March 1931 through November 1933 (28 issues). *The Beacon* superseded the pioneering literary magazine *Trinidad*, which appeared only twice, in 1929 and in 1930, under the joint editorship of Alfred H. Mendes (born 1897) and C. L. R. James (born 1901). *The Beacon* devoted its pages not only to creative writing, but also participated actively in local, West Indian and world politics. In its editorials it denounced the Crown Colony form of government, reported and commented on the proposals for a West Indian Federation, followed India's struggle for independence and praised the Russian experiment in socialism. In outlook it was anti-capitalist and anti-ecclesiastical, bohemian and iconoclastic. Although it sold more than 5000 copies at the peak of its popularity, it received a hostile reception from the Trinidad middle class.

In its short career the magazine was involved in 'a libel action, frequent visits from the police, denunciation from the pulpit, pressure from both church and state, increasing opposition from the commercial community and chronic lack of funds'.[5] However, in spite of the hostility from powerful opponents the magazine survived for three years because of the single-mindedness and comradeship of the contributors. Among them were people who later rose to prominence in the labour movement and West Indian party politics: Albert Gomes, Ralph Mentor, C. A. Thomasos, Adrian Rienzi and C. L. R. James. Apart from contemporary politics, the *Beacon* group also showed a considerable interest in local and West Indian history. Articles in this field include: 'The Water Riots of 1903', 'Michel Maxwell Philip: 1829–86', 'With the West India Regiment in East Africa', and 'Trinidad: Then and Now', which foreshadowed two major historical works by Trinidadians, C. L. R. James's *The Black Jacobins* (1938), and Eric Williams's *Capitalism and Slavery* (1944). Other articles were concerned with the cultural origins of the majority of Trinidad's population. Those on Africa catered to the black population and attempted to create pride in the culture of the ancestral homeland; the special 'India Section' dealt with Indian philosophy, traditions and customs, and frequently focused on the activities of Mahatma Gandhi. The race question was discussed at length and sparked off quite a controversy among contributors and readers.

Both *The Beacon* and its predecessor, *Trinidad*, moreover, mark the emergence of West Indian short fiction. West Indian writing, the editors insisted, should utilise West Indian settings, speech, characters, situations and conflicts. They warned against the imitation of foreign literature, especially against the imitation of foreign popular literature, and turned down contributions which lacked 'authenticity'. They did in fact publish a solid body of short fiction that fulfilled their theoretical demands.[6] These short stories covered themes and material which set a pattern for the writers who contributed to Collymore's *Bim* and Edna Manley's *Focus* in the 1940s and for the novelists of the 1950s and 1960s. In 'Yacua', for example, Michael J. Deeble presents a historical romance, evoking the Amerindian past and the clash between European coloniser and Carib warrior. In 'Black Mother' Ernest A. Carr elevates the eruption of Mont Pelée in Martinique to the level of myth or legend. Here a black obeah woman pits her powers against white justice and white religion to free her son from prison. When the invoked cataclysm subsides, her son is the only survivor, and her magical carving becomes a god. In 'Boodhoo' by Alfred Mendes, 'The Tare' by W. R. H. Trowbridge and 'The Box' by Ernest A. Carr, the moral collapse of white men in the tropics is explored. 'Boodhoo' in addition treats the theme of racial miscegenation. A number of short stories such as C. L. R. James's 'Revolution' and Trowbridge's 'Filibuster' have their settings in Venezuela and are evidence of the writers' interest in Latin American affairs and political turmoil.

With the exception of Olga Yaatoff's and Kathleen Archibald's impressionistic pieces of Trinidad life, 'Gasoline Station' and 'Clipped Wings', the short fiction published in *Trinidad* and *The Beacon* is conventional in form. Mendes explained in 1972:

> We hadn't as yet arrived at that stage where we were so *avant-garde* as not to have a beginning and an end. This was to come later with George Lamming, Wilson Harris and others. James and I departed from the convention in the selection of our material, in the choice of a strange way of life, in the use of a new dialect. And these departures are still with our Caribbean successors.

Here Mendes is also referring to the group of short stories depicting the life of Trinidad's lower class in the 'barrack-yards', which he, James, Percival C. Maynard and C. A. Thomasos began to write. Disillusioned and repulsed by the hollowness of middle-class life, with strong socialist leanings, some of the writers quite naturally gravitated towards the life of the lower classes and 'took the material that [they] found in [their] backyards, so to speak, and used that material for fiction'. Mendes even went to live in a barrack-yard for six months to 'get the atmosphere, to get the sort of jargon that they spoke—the vernacular, the idiom'. As in James's 'Triumph', the writing that resulted was set in 'a fairly big yard, on either side of which run long low buildings, consisting of anything from four to eighteen rooms, each about twelve feet square', and it depicted the life of 'the porters, prostitutes, carter-men, washerwomen and domestic servants of the city'. With detached but sympathetic objectivity, James, Mendes, Maynard and Thomasos recorded the spiritual, moral and sexual values of their barrack-yard characters, and attempted to reproduce their dialect speech. They were particularly attracted to the life-style of kept women.

A good example of the social realism of barrack-yard literature is 'Her Chinaman's Way' by Alfred H. Mendes in *Trinidad* (1929). The kept woman in this short story is Maria, a young coloured woman with a 'voluptuous figure inherited from her half-breed Venezuelan mother'. She 'liked only those men who showed a desire to possess her, the men on whom she could depend for a living'. When the story begins, Maria is living with Hong Wing, a miserly Chinese shopkeeper, for whom she has a child. Before meeting Hong Wing, she had been 'husbandless' for more than six months, but her black friend Philogen, experienced in the arts of obeah, had bathed her in water prepared from rare herbs and roots, and the Chinaman soon became her new keeper. Now she again seeks Philogen's advice in ridding herself of Hong Wing, as she does not understand him and resents having to help him out in the shop in the evening. She is also interested in Dolphus, a black carter-man, but cannot leave Hong Wing because of the child, from whom she does not want to be parted. It particularly angers her that Hong Wing dislikes the child 'because of the milk bill he had to settle every month'. Philogen, the inevitable confidante figure in barrack-yard literature, immediately sympathises with Maria. She advises Maria to inform the police when Hong Wing sets out on his next opium smuggling expedition. Maria takes this advice, and the rest of the story depicts a tense and nervous Maria planning a new future but half suspecting that Hong Wing might escape the police net. In fact he does escape and takes terrible revenge by strangling her child.

In this, as in the other barrack-yard stories, no judgements are made by the author. To understand the life and actions of the barrack-yarders, the reader has to accept their assumptions as expressed in their language. It is no surprise that middle-class readers were shocked after reading 'Her Chinaman's Way', James's 'Triumph', Maynard's 'His Last Fling' and

Thomasos's 'The Dougla'.

Barrack-yard stories obviously made contact with the people, their problems, customs and beliefs, but it can hardly be said that they 'voiced the people's aspirations and anger'. This becomes clear when one contrasts the novels of C. L. R. James and Alfred H. Mendes with those of R. A. C. de Boissiere, who alone committed his writing to a radical analysis of social injustice. Mendes and James focused on the vitality and picturesqueness of lower-class life in their novels and played down the poverty and squalor that obviously existed. They reserved overt social criticism for their later political writing. These three writers were the only members of the *Beacon* group who published novels. They were also among the first to leave the West Indies for careers abroad. James left in 1932 for England where he published *Minty Alley* (1936), Mendes in 1933 for the United States where he published *Pitch Lake* (1934) and *Black Fauns* (1935), and de Boissiere in 1948 for Australia where he published *Crown Jewel* (1952), *Rum and Coca-Cola* (1956) and *No Saddles for Kangaroos* (1964). Only R. A. C. de Boissiere (born 1907) continues to write fiction.[7]

In Seymour's words Mendes's second novel, *Black Fauns*, 'gives the impression of an extended short story. The plot is subordinate to the authentic picture of Negro life in Trinidad in the barrack-yard.' Whereas in 'Her Chinaman's Way' and in other short stories Mendes concentrates on a particular incident in the life of a particular barrack-yarder, *Black Fauns* encompasses the barrack-yard as a community and presents a variety of characters. The female dwellers of the yard engage in discussions on religion, sex and politics, make love and quarrel with their male visitors, celebrate happy occasions and indulge in intrigues against each other. There is always excitement in the yard, especially when Snakey, the son of Ma Christine, returns from America to spend his holidays in Trinidad. A fierce battle for Snakey's attentions ensues between the sensuous Mamitz and the sedate but determined Martha. For a while Snakey succeeds in carrying on simultaneous affairs with both Martha and Mamitz, in fact using Martha's money to support Mamitz. Martha's violent attack on Mamitz when she discovers Snakey's infidelity is only one factor in the general holocaust which descends on the yard. As a visitor from a neighbouring barrack-yard remarks:

> Eh-eh, it looks like as if God vext with this yard in truth.
> Miss Et'elrida in jail, Miss Estelle in jail, nobody know what
> going to happen to poor Mart'a; Mannie in jail, Seppy dead,
> Snakey gone, Miss Mamitz in the hospital lying down like as
> if she dead, with her face all cut up and her bosom all cut up
> and a stab in her back—eh-eh, it is a good t'ing me an'
> Lestang ain' living here!

The novel ends when news about Mamitz's death is received in the yard, and the reader, as in most of Mendes's stories, is left to speculate about the final outcome.

It is obvious that barrack-yard writing contains an implicit attack on bourgeois society. A real social gap existed, however, between the writers and their barrack-yard characters. Mendes commented, 'There was this dichotomy. We were contradictions in terms'; but this dilemma is hardly reflected in *Black Fauns* and his short stories. In writing about an environment which was outside his own immediate social experience but which he could visit occasionally, Mendes has been open to the charge of literary 'slumming'. In James's *Minty Alley* the unease about this situation becomes in itself literary material. James introduces a middle-class character who from economic necessity has to find lodgings in a barrack-yard. The novel does not merely depict the events and characters in the yard—the progress of Mr Benoit's break with Mrs Rouse, and the hostility between Philomen, the East Indian servant girl, and Maisie—but it also explores Haynes's interaction with the barrack-yarders. The reader sees and hears only what Haynes does as he becomes more and more curious about the life of his fellow tenants. Haynes's role as eavesdropper can be compared with that of Mendes and James as writers. They are peeping through cracks in the middle-class wall that separates them from the barrack-yarders and capture glimpses of the excitement outside. For James and his black middle-class protagonist the wall is of 'thin wood', but it was perhaps less thin for Mendes and de Boissiere, creoles of Portuguese and French descent. Haynes in *Minty Alley* wavers between attraction to and disgust with the barrack-yard. He who 'had never since he was grown up kissed or been kissed by a woman' eventually overcomes his sexual inhibitions and enters an affair with the yard's flamboyant Maisie. This affair, and his gradual involvement as everybody's confidant (in spite of his inexperience the barrack-yarders have respect for him because of his education) mark the extent and the limit of Haynes's interaction. When Maisie leaves for America and Haynes returns to his middle-class environment, the temporary nature of his association with the lower class becomes evident. For a while Haynes 'went to see them fairly regularly, but after a time became rather amiss'; later he only remembers with nostalgia a way of life that was full of excitement.

The absence of lasting unions between male middle-class and female lower-class characters is even more evident in Mendes's first novel, *Pitch Lake*, which deals with the social aspirations of the Portuguese community in colonial Trinidad.[8] Like Haynes in *Minty Alley*, Joe da Costa, a Portuguese creole, is attracted to a lower-class girl. At the beginning of the novel he is about to break ties with her and with the Madeiran peasant origins of his father who keeps a rumshop in San Fernando. He joins his brother Henry and sister-in-law Myra in Port of Spain, and they help him climb the social ladder by initiating a match between him and Cora Goveia, a second-generation Portuguese creole. Although heavily influenced by social and racial snobbery, Joe at the same time falls for his brother's East Indian maid, Stella. As he is about to contract a prestigious marriage with Cora, Stella becomes pregnant. Fearing a scandal that would ruin his social chances, he resorts to murder.

The tragic ending of *Pitch Lake* and the ambivalent ending of *Minty Alley* stand in sharp contrast to that of *Crown Jewel* by R. A. C. de Boissiere. In this novel one of the central protagonists is André de Coudray, a French creole. Unlike Haynes and Joe da Costa, he succeeds in breaking through the social and racial barriers of his class by marrying Elena Henriques, the coloured daughter of a seamstress. This decision, which comes after his extended courtship of Gwenneth Osborne, the daughter of an expatriate English Chief Justice, is not merely a personal or social one. It is symbolic in the context of the novel as a whole and marks the culmination of André's growing political awareness. The union between André and Elena represents the alliance of a sensitive middle class with an awakening working class. André's development in *Crown Jewel* runs parallel to the growth of Trinidad's labour movement between 1935 and 1937. It is this political dimension which distinguishes *Crown Jewel* from both *Black Fauns* and *Minty Alley*.

Crown Jewel does not merely document the life of the lower classes. It voices their protest and shows them in active opposition to local and expatriate oppressors. Their point of view is represented by a number of labour leaders and politicians with whom André de Coudray is acquainted. These fictional figures are modelled on historical personalities: Boisson the Fabian socialist, for example, is based on Captain Arthur Cipriani, the French creole labour leader who after his return from military service in the First World War took up the cause of the 'barefoot man' in Trinidad. His opponent and de Boissiere's ideological mouthpiece, Ben le Maitre, is an interesting blend of Uriah Butler, the idiosyncratic leader of Trinidad's British Empire Home Rule Workers Party, and Jim Barratt, the Marxist leader of the Negro Welfare Association. Le Maitre's politics are those of Jim Barratt though most of the historical details of his life are drawn from Uriah Butler's career. The events in the novel (the hunger marches; the sporadic strikes defeated by the initial lack of solidarity among the workers, by scab labour and by police intimidation; the final upheavals in the oilfields) are also historically accurate. André's development from sympathetic observer to committed participant is, also paralleled by the development of Cassie, a maid at Chief Justice Osborne's, from subservience to militancy. She illustrates the active role of women in Trinidad's mass movement during the 1930s. Her marriage to Ben le Maitre at the end of the novel is as symbolic as that of André to Elena.

Other West Indian writers who published their work locally in the 1930s and 1940s have reached only a small audience and have for the most part dropped completely out of circulation.

Local publications include two novels, *Lalaja: A Tale of Retribution* (1944) and *Chalk Dust* (1945), by De Wilton Rogers of Trinidad; and collections of short stories by individual writers: J. A. V. Bourne's *Dreams, Devils, Vampires* (1940), published in Guyana, and from Jamaica Claude Thompson's *These My People*, Cecily Waite-Smith's *Rain for the Plains and Other Stories* (1943), Archie Lindo's *Bronze* (1944), R. L. C. Aarons's *The Cow that Laughed and Other Stories* (1944), and Roger Mais's *And Most of All Man* (1943) and *Face and Other Stories* (1942). Joint collections appeared in Trinidad—A. M. Clarke and R. C. Brown's *Short Stories* (1939) and Ernest A. Carr and A. M. Clarke's *Ma Mamba and Other Stories*. Among the early anthologies of short stories and poetry are *From Trinidad: A Selection from the Fiction and Verse of Trinidad, British West Indies*, edited by Albert M. Gomes in 1937, and *Papa Bois* (1947), which assembled some of the work produced by a group which met at the home of Judge Hallinan during the 1940s. Members of this group included Ernest A. Carr, Errol Hill, Neville Guiseppi, C. A. Thomasos, Barnabas J. Ramon-Fortuné, Edgar Mittelholzer and Seepersad Naipaul.

Of these Seepersad Naipaul is of particular interest. His contribution to *Papa Bois*, a piece on his father entitled 'They Named Him Mohun' would later inspire his own son, V. S. Naipaul, to write *A House for Mr Biswas*. Seepersad Naipaul, for whom English was an acquired language, also published *Gurudeva and Other Indian Tales* (1943) which was one of the first literary works by a West Indian of East Indian descent. In the 1976 modified and enlarged version of this collection, V. S. Naipaul points in his foreword to the influence these stories had on his own work, and characterises them as follows:

> They are a unique record of the life of the Indian or Hindu community in Trinidad in the first fifty years of the century. They move from a comprehension of the old India in which the community is at first embedded to an understanding of the colonial Trinidad which defines itself as their background, into which they merge.

They are an interesting companion to Mittelholzer's first

novel, *Corentyne Thunder* (1941), which depicts East Indian peasant life in Guyana.

The West Indian poets of the 1930s and 1940s, like most poets today, had even less of a chance of being published outside the West Indies. They contributed to the literary magazines discussed above or to the newspapers which began to feature indigenous poetry and short fiction: to the *Advocate* in Barbados, the *Chronicle* in Guyana, the *Gleaner* in Jamaica, and the *Guardian* in Trinidad. There is, however, a wealth of locally published material by individual poets. In Barbados there appeared Frank Collymore's *Thirty Poems* (1944), *Beneath the Casuarinas* (1945) and *Flotsam* (1948), H. A. Vaughan's *Sandy Lane and Other Poems* (1948) and William S. Arthur's *Whispers of the Dawn* (1941) and *Morning Glory* (1944); in St Lucia, Derek Walcott's *25 Poems* (1948) and *Epitaph for the Young* (1949), and Howick Elcock's *Alpha* (1949); in Trinidad, C. A. Thomasos's *Poems* (1939), Neville Guiseppi's *The Light of Thought*, and *Burnt Bush* (1947) by H. M. Telemaque and A. M. Clarke; in British Guiana, A. J. Seymour's *Over Guiana Clouds* (1944) and *The Guiana Book* (1948); and in Jamaica, Vivian Virtue's *Wings of the Morning* (1938), George Campbell's influential *First Poems* (1945) and Louise Bennett's *Jamaican Humour in Dialect* (1943) and *Miss Lulu Sez* (1949). Before A. J. Seymour published *The Kyk-over-al Anthology of West Indian Poetry* in 1952, most territories had produced their own anthologies. These include J. E. Clare McFarlane's *A Treasury of Jamaican Poetry* (1949), N. E. Cameron's *Guianese Poetry: 1831–1931*, J. R. Casimir's *Poesy: An Anthology of Dominican Verse* and A. M. Clarke's *Best Poems of Trinidad* (1943). Another publication along similar lines is the *Anthology of Local Indian Verse* edited by C. E. J. Ramcharita of Guyana.

The West Indian poets of the 1930s found it much harder than the prose writers to break with metropolitan conventions.' Unlike the short fiction, the poetry published in *The Beacon* is alien, imitative and uninspiring. The same could be said for most of the poetry published by the Poetry League of Jamaica, whose members included Constance Hollar, Lena Kent and Albinia Hutton. Its founder, J. E. Clare McFarlane, for example, opened his 'Villanelle of Immortal Love' with the lines

> Love will awaken all lovely things at last.
> One by one they shall come from the sleep of Time,
> Bearing in triumph the deathless dreams of the past.

More promising and talented among its members were Vivian Virtue and Una Marson whose work, though dependent on borrowed tradition, began to show an awareness of contemporary poetic techniques and attitudes.

In the 1940s some poets virtually leapt from sterile imitation to exciting innovation. Foremost among these was Martin Carter, whose conservative 'Ode to Midnight', cited earlier, is clearly anachronistic in both form and content. His 'Death of a Slave', however, published only a few years later, is firmly rooted in the West Indian experience, experiments with new forms, and attempts to capture Guyanese speech rhythms:

> in the dark earth
> in cold dark earth
> time plants the seeds of anger
>
> this is another world
> but above is same blue sky
> same sun—
> below is same deep heart of agony.

Like Carter in Guyana, Jamaican poets such as George Campbell, M. G. Smith and Basil McFarlane, all members of the *Focus* group, were fired by the same spirit of nationalism. They shared the new awareness of history, of social and political injustice, and turned to the folk for their material and medium of expression. Poems such as George Campbell's 'History Makers'

> Women stone breakers
> Hammers and rocks
> Tired child makers
> Haphazard frocks

and Philip Sherlock's 'Pocomania'

> Black of night and white of gown
> White of altar, black of trees
> 'Swing de circle wide again
> Fall and cry me sister now
> Let de spirit come again
> Fling away de flesh an' bone
> Let de spirit have a home'

are notable examples of this trend. At the same time the first dialect poems by Louise Bennett appeared. In them she makes use of Jamaican dialect to depict the humour and wisdom of the folk.

A large portion of West Indian poetry in the 1940s explored the West Indian landscape; poets such as A. J. Seymour, Harold Telemaque and Frank A. Collymore evoked the authentic natural qualities of their surroundings. A further step was taken when an attempt was made by West Indian poets to present universal experiences through West Indian imagery. The Honduran Raymond Barrow succeeds in doing this in his poem about dawn:

> Dawn is a fisherman, his harpoon of light
> Poised for a throw—so swiftly morning comes:
> The darkness squats upon the sleeping land
> Like a flung cast-net, and the black shapes of boats
> Lie hunched like nesting turtles
> On the flat calm of the sea.

With the publication of Derek Walcott's two volumes of poetry at the end of the 1940s, West Indian poetry was well on its way to matching the pace set by West Indian fiction. It had reached the phase where, in Seymour's words, 'the land in which the people live and move and have their being, begins to assert its presence and to supply the dynamic necessary for developing the new voice'.

Two West Indian writers living outside the region during the 1930s and 1940s were Claude McKay (1889–1948) and Walter Adolphe Roberts (1886–1962).[9] Both were Jamaicans and left for America in their early twenties. They came from differing backgrounds: the white creole Roberts from an upper-class family, McKay from a black peasant family. Both maintained a life-long interest in the West Indies and recalled the scenery of Jamaica with nostalgia in their poetry. The majority of their fictional works deal with aspects and problems of their adopted country, and reflect the writers' racial and social origins. Three of Roberts's novels—*Royal Street* (1944), *Brave Mardi Gras* (1946) and *Creole Dusk* (1948)—record the steady decline of French creole culture in Louisiana during the nineteenth century. The trilogy begins with the influx of French refugees from Haiti who strengthen creole traditions, continues with their heroic participation in the American Civil War, and ends when they lose their identity and marry into Anglo-American families. McKay's collection of short stories, *Gingertown* (1932), deals with life in the 'Negro Metropolis'. In *Banjo* (1929) he moves to the seafront of Marseilles in France and describes its drifting population of blacks from Africa, America and the West Indies. These works are expressions of a black counter-culture in America and of the Pan-African movement in the black world as a whole.

McKay's only novel with a West Indian setting is *Banana Bottom* (1933). Bita Plant, who has been sent by white missionaries to further her education in Britain, rebels against alien values on her return to Jamaica and actively asserts her cultural origins. Roberts's novel with a Caribbean setting is *The Single Star* (1949). Like his Louisiana novels it is also a historical romance. Its action takes place during the Cuban War of Independence (1895–8) and focuses on the involvement of Stephen, a creole Jamaican, with the Cuban rebels, one of whom is Ines Cardona. At the end of the novel, Ines chooses to remain in her native Cuba rather than marry Stephen and follow him to Jamaica. The theme of Cuban nationalism relates this novel indirectly to the movement for independence in Jamaica during the 1940s.

It was another Jamaican, V. S. Reid (born 1913), who dealt directly with the issue of West Indian nationalism.[10] His novel, *New Day* (1949), shows that Jamaica's history was not one of subservience but involved active resistance to colonial oppression. On the other hand, it clearly advocates a cautious and reformist approach to change. Garth, the new nationalist leader, relates the 'false start' of the 1865 rebels to the present when he compares them to fledglings who flapped their wings too heavily: 'So mother bird clipped them. For our own good, she said. She was probably right. They would have flapped us into trouble.' *New Day* captures the ambivalence of the nationalist movement. At the same time it reminds us of the ambivalent position held by West Indian writers in the 1930s and 1940s; although they recognised the need for change, they had not yet fully succeeded in breaking with the traditions and modes of thinking which they had inherited from their colonial masters.

5   The Fifties *by Sandra Pouchet Paquet*

It is now commonplace to identify the 1950s as the decade
when West Indian literature emerged as a recognisable entity.
Kenneth Ramchand has documented that some fifty-five
novels were published between 1949 and 1959 by twenty
different writers.[1] In this decade, Derek Walcott established
himself as a poet with three volumes published in quick
succession: *25 poems* (1949), *Epitaph for the Young: XII Cantos*
(1949) and *Poems* (1953). Flanking this effort were the varied
contributions of poets like Edward Brathwaite, Martin Carter,
Frank Collymore, Wilson Harris, George Lamming and E. M.
Roach. West Indian drama also witnessed an upsurge of
creativity. At the end of the decade, Errol Hill boasted that
despite a high mortality rate, some 'twenty-seven serious
dramatists' were operating in and out of the West Indies.[2]

These achievements were all the more remarkable because
there were no publishing houses in the West Indies that could
support this outburst of creativity. Small presses, like the
Pioneer Press of Jamaica, were inadequate to the task.
Moreover, there was as yet no significant reading public in the
West Indies educated to support a literary movement. Encouragement came primarily from the B.B.C.'s *Caribbean Voices*
(1945–58), and from three local publications: *Bim* (Barbados),
Kyk-over-al (Guyana), and the occasional issues of *Focus*
(Jamaica). Limited opportunities at home prompted many
artists to seek a more receptive environment abroad, and to
win the support of an international audience until such time as
an appreciative West Indian response could be realised.

Accomplishments in fiction, poetry and drama were not isolated phenomena. There was a similar movement in painting and sculpture. Folk arts were receiving unprecedented attention from scholars and enthusiasts alike. Institutions important to the arts were founded: the Little Carib Dance Company in Trinidad, the Jamaica School of Arts and Crafts and the National Dance Theatre Company of Jamaica. Beryl McBurnie, Olive Lewin, Olive Walke, and later Rex Nettleford, were shaping a new public response to indigenous culture. Calypso was flourishing, and steelband was steadily gaining acceptance as a folk art with similar claims on the imagination and loyalty of the general populace.

In all of these arts the primary focus was on West Indian society, on self-discovery and self-definition. Most of the artists of the 1950s were ground-breakers who took themselves seriously. Their sense of mission became a criterion for succeeding generations of West Indian writers. This twin dedication to their art and to their society is an important aspect of artistic achievements which were both preceded and paralleled by a tremendous growth in political and social awareness in the colonial Caribbean. In 1956, Elsa Goveia's *A Study on the Historiography of the British West Indies* added a new dimension to the earlier work of C. L. R. James[3] and Eric Williams[4] regarding a West Indian re-evaluation of the region's history and potential. All were major steps in challenging the attitudes of an inherited colonial relationship to Great Britain.

On the level of practical politics, this new sense of history and the ensuing search for alternatives to colonial rule were rapidly gaining popular support. The Cuban revolution made a fearful hero of Fidel Castro. A new nationalism militated for independence from Crown Rule. Guyana was cruelly divided by racial strife and ideological differences, and the rest of the English-speaking Caribbean cringed with fear of a new 'communist' threat. Yet, there was hope for a unified community under the West Indian Federation even after this was rejected by Guyana in 1956. And all the while, in a continuous stream that began in the late forties, West Indians emigrated to Great Britain in search of jobs, education and the glamour of the metropolis. Unconvinced by the potential of an independent Caribbean, they flocked to the Mother Country in great numbers.

The political and social movements of the decade are an important frame of reference for evaluating the literature of the fifties. Despite the voluntary exile of most of the writers published at this time, they were characteristically concerned with the structure and values of Caribbean society. Even Samuel Selvon, reputedly the least political of them all, was carefully examining the process of change and its attendant crises in novels like *A Brighter Sun* (1952) and *Turn Again Tiger* (1958).

This emphasis on the West Indian writer and his society was at issue in one of the first competent attempts to evaluate the literature of the fifties, when Edward Brathwaite found it necessary to divide West Indian writers into 'the Emigrants and the Islanders'.[5] Brathwaite worried that the writer's physical disconnection from his roots would interfere with what he identified as the responsibility of West Indian fiction, namely 'an exploration and mapping of the physical, social, moral and emotional territory that is ours'.[6]

It was left to George Lamming to state the case for the artist in exile. He argued that, despite their exile, West Indian novelists of the decade remained essentially rooted in the experience of the West Indian peasant majority: 'The substance of their books, the general motives and directions are peasant.'[7] Lamming confirmed Brathwaite's assumptions about the writer's responsibility to his community but used a more political language: 'That is the real question; and its answer can be the beginning of an attempt to grapple with that colonial structure of awareness which has determined West Indian values.'[8]

As these writers wished, the literature of the fifties is demonstrably sensitive to the general social condition. More often than not, the exploration of the private self or of the individual experience is tied to an exploration of the interdependence of private and public worlds; to an exploration of the individual's relationship to the inherited structure of values that dominates his society. Since discussion of the works of the more established West Indian writers is outside the scope of this essay, it is left to consider the contributions of writers like V. S. Reid,

Roger Mais, John Hearne and Andrew Salkey of Jamaica,
Martin Carter and Jan Carew of Guyana, and the late E. M.
Roach of Trinidad and Tobago.

V. S. Reid's first novel, *New Day* (1949), is a seminal work,
important for its pioneering use of a modified Jamaican dialect
and its highly selective use of Jamaica's political history. In
1956, Samuel Selvon would also use a modified Trinidadian
dialect in *The Lonely Londoners*, another successful experiment
in the lyric appropriateness of dialect as the language of narration in West Indian fiction. But Reid's dialect is different. He
carefully recreates the cultural and literary influences of the
King James Bible on Jamaican speech. Later, George Lamming
and Roger Mais would explore these influences to suit their
own contexts, but Reid's dialect is a calculated celebration of
the Jamaican landscape and people; it is 'a dialect with a sense of
mission'.[9]

In *New Day*, Reid goes back to the 1865 Morant Bay
rebellion in order to establish a historical, political and cultural
context for the events of November 1944, when Jamaica won a
guarantee of self-rule from Great Britain. Reid makes this
turbulent period in Jamaican history the organising framework
for his account of the fortunes of the Campbells, a fictional
Jamaican family who are actively involved in the events of both
1865 and 1944. Reid uses the Campbells, a predominantly
white family of mixed European and African ancestry, to
individualise both his sense of the character of the Jamaican
people, and the continuity in the island's experience. *New Day*
breaks fresh ground in the West Indian writer's involvement
with history—its distortions, its betrayal and its creative
potential.[10] Reid is not concerned with historical accuracy so
much as with exploring the evolution of Jamaican society in
terms of an individual family's response to social and historical
pressures.

New Day makes positive statements about the combined
power of an illiterate, poverty-stricken plebiscite, and a socially responsible, light-brown middle class educated to organise
an effective resistance against the injustices of colonial Jamaica.
But Reid's second novel, *The Leopard* (1958), has a very
different focus. On a much reduced canvas involving only

three major characters, Reid attempts an 'African' novel in which the multiracial inheritance of *New Day* is portrayed as a curse on white, black and mulatto alike. Set in Kenya during the Mau Mau rebellion, Reid's romantic evocation of Nebu, the African freedom fighter, contrasts with his portrayal of the Gibsons as a decadent white colonial presence, and with Toto as the tragic mulatto who is the physically and spiritually crippled product of Europe and Africa. Reid's emphasis is on an emotional rendering of the relationship between the African father and his mulatto son. While Reid's racial stereotypes are an unfortunate simplification, structurally they allow him to keep the novel's argument absolutely clear, as he explores the intricacies of racial and cultural tensions in a colonial situation.

As a novel about the Mau Mau rebellion, *The Leopard* suffers from comparison with a work like Ngugi's *A Grain of Wheat* (1967). But it is an important first in West Indian fiction, that the West Indian's relationship to Africa be pursued on a level other than that of African survivals in the Caribbean. Reid identifies a common plight in a shared colonial relationship to Great Britain, and moves closer to the perceptions of other West Indian writers regarding the crises that attend a multi-cultural society with a history of colonial rule.

In 1952 and 1953, three major first novels were published: Samuel Selvon's *A Brighter Sun* (1952), George Lamming's *In the Castle of My Skin* (1953) and Roger Mais's *The Hills Were Joyful Together* (1953). Each contribution significantly widened the scope of the West Indian novel. Set in rural Trinidad, *A Brighter Sun* explores the New World experience of Trinidad's Indian community in a state of transition, growing away from their beginnings on the sugar plantation and confronting an inevitable process of creolisation and urbanisation. Lamming's *Castle* is also concerned with change as the feudal structure of the plantation system gives way to the pressures of organised labour and the first stirrings of an independence movement. The concomitants of such change are displacement, dispossession and alienation, all of which Lamming embodies in a careful balance between autobiography and island history.

Roger Mais's *Hills* has certain features in common with *Castle*: an elaborate symbolic structure; common themes of alienation and dispossession; an emphasis on the community experience rather than on individual fortunes; even the crude transposition of the techniques of playwriting into a fictional context. But the differences are as remarkable. While Lamming describes the disruption of life in a village on the periphery of Bridgetown, Mais focuses on the anguish of slum life in Kingston. His themes are not of disrupted life but of frustrated life, and where Lamming explores the anguish of change, Mais explores the tragic dimensions of stasis.

In *Hills*, Mais limits himself almost exclusively to the inmates, as he calls them, of a Kingston yard. These are Kingston's sufferers: a seemingly random collection of the stereotypes bred by poverty and underprivilege. Mais describes the multifaceted constriction of these wasted lives. The dominant image in the novel is appropriately that of a prison from which there is no escape. The yard is a sun-baked, desert-like environment in which life is stunted, malformed and diseased. This is in direct contrast with the promise of life and growth symbolised by the verdant hills and mountains that tower over Kingston. In a carefully worked parallel with Kingston's prison, Mais makes the point that the yard is not an accidental prison but one that is maintained as such by those who have freedom and power.

There are some positives in Mais's depiction of the horrors of rapid and uncontrolled urbanisation. He recognises the will to survive and the will to escape the humiliations of the prison: in Surjue's criminal gamble; in the desperate love of Rema and Surjue; in the generosity of Ras; in the community spirit that surfaces from time to time to rescue individuals from each other, or from the world outside. But in *Hills* all is ultimately futile.

In Mais's second novel, *Brother Man* (1954), the setting is still the Kingston yard but his emphasis shifts from the group to the tension between the group and the gifted individual. In this novel, it is the tension between the vulgar pattern of deteriorating life in the slum and the creative force that opposes it. The Messianic theme is fully developed in obvious parallels between Christ and the Rastafarian John Power, alias Brother Man. Mais identifies the Rastafarian as a healing force that derives from the squalor of the yard. The casually drawn figure of Ras in *Hills*, the bringer of peace and comfort who is none the less powerless to rescue the inhabitants of the yard from their fate, is now a major force for spiritual and moral regeneration. What is important to the gifted individual versus the group conflict here is that John Power survives the fickleness of the mob that alternatively supports and tries to destroy him. But John Power survives because of the devotion of a small community of faithful. He does not survive as the isolated, detached figure he is for most of the novel, but comes to terms with his need of others in Minette: 'He saw all things in a vision of certitude, and he was alone no longer.'

The tension between an independent spirit and the need of supporting personal relationships is a central concern in Mais's third novel, *Black Lightning* (1955). Set in a small Jamaican village where life proceeds at an idyllic pace, and where freedom of choice and movement is part of the challenge of everyday life, the novel describes the tragedy of Jake, village blacksmith and sculptor. Jake pursues an impossible ideal of independence both in his life and his art. This sets him on a self-destructive course that is at odds with the rhythms of life around him. Jake is unable to accept the suffering, dependence and need that persist in his sculpture of the biblical Samson. In a crude analogy with the biblical myth, Jake's wife deserts him and he is reduced to a state of self-pitying dependence through blindness. When Jake eventually kills himself, the novel carefully apportions responsibility for his death, not on a negligent or unappreciative community but on an unresolved tension within the artist himself.

Though *Black Lightning* is crudely flawed, till that time no other West Indian writer had given the dilemma of the West Indian artist and his relationship to his community such exclusive treatment. This had been an important theme in Lamming's *The Emigrants* (1954); subsequently it proved a preoccupation of Lamming's novels and the works of other writers as well—among them Walcott, Harris and Brathwaite.

John Hearne, the Jamaican novelist and a close friend of Roger Mais, published his first novel—*Voices Under The Window*—in 1955, the year of Mais's death. By the end of the decade, Hearne had published three others: *Strangers at the Gate* (1956), *The Faces of Love* (1957) and *The Autumn Equinox* (1959). Hearne readily acknowledges Mais's influence: 'Mais taught me how to write, how to see essentials; that much of writing is rejection.' Hearne also acknowledges the power of Conrad, Faulkner and Hemingway,[11] though it is perhaps the latter who weighs most heavily on both Mais and Hearne.

Hearne tells a good story in clean, uncluttered prose. His novels have a spirit of adventure independent of the exclusiveness of focus discussed here. The common distinction applied to his fiction is its middle-class versus peasant focus. At the centre of his novels is the middle class by birth, money, education, colour and aspiration. He writes about this class with a keen appreciation of its style, values and vulnerability in a society that is poised to challenge its inherited scale of influence. Hearne rests his case on 'the good ones': those who qualify as sensitive to moral nuances, however private the moral code; those who have the courage of commitment to an ideal outside the self, whether this be embodied in an individual, a cause or a certain style of conduct; those who have a certain capacity for heroic gesture of the Hemingway variety.

Despite his fidelity to the West Indian landscape and the West Indian middle class, Hearne continues to argue that he is not primarily interested in social commentary.[12] Yet the social commentary is always there, often suggesting a neglected context for his examination of various themes, and sometimes confusing the issue. For instance, *Voices* is about the private and public failures of Mark Lattimer, a politician who is mortally wounded while rescuing a child from the crush of a riotous mob. Hearne furnishes enough detail to make the politics of the situation convincing. Mark fails because he is finally unable to bridge the alienation imposed by his middle-class colonial upbringing. He is incapable of the commitment Hearne symbolises in the 'fat ugly girl who was a communist, and who had once been very zealous in the Catholic Church'. But as Hearne insists, in *Voices* politics is 'just a useful peg on which to hang the coat'.[13] Accordingly, despite conflicts of race and class raised in the novel, the issue of Mark's failures dissolve rather weakly into a celebration of the style of Mark's dying—a stoicism of the stiff-upper-lip variety, which Hearne identifies with Mark's middle-class breeding and military training.

In *Stranger*, Hearne's bias is more explicitly stated as he examines the merits and demerits of political commitment against the values of the landed gentry in Cayuna, his fictitious Caribbean island. Hearne embodies the values of this class in the Brandt family and their 200-year-old plantation. He depicts Brandt's Pen as administered in a benevolently feudal fashion. Its owner, Brandt, is a man of unshakeable integrity whose strength is his capacity for love and loyalty: 'a man to whom friendship means more than political allegiance'. It is against the values that Hearne invests in Brandt and his property that the limitations of political commitment are explored in two declared communists: Roy, Brandt's best friend, and Etienne, a deposed dictator. Both are committed to destroying what Brandt's Pen stands for and both are presented as lesser men, partly because Hearne identifies them as bent on a course of destruction versus the endurance and continuity associated with Brandt's Pen. It is not that Roy and Etienne are unworthy characters, for they are capable of great personal sacrifice, but in them Hearne posits a waste of life rather than a potential for growth and fulfilment.

As in *Voices*, Hearne sidesteps the political and social issues he raises in the novel. Communism is not evaluated in relation to the novel's Queenshaven slums but in relation to the private code of ethics and middle-class durability depicted in Brandt's Pen. Hearne actually uses Brandt's Pen to affirm rather than challenge stereotypes of the country-bred 'coolie' and of the poor, desperate and black in Queenshaven.

In *Faces*, Hearne restates his defence of Brandt's Pen. The novel evaluates the Brandt's Pen ideal of plantation life and sturdy British wives through the eyes of Andrew Fabricus, a dispossessed member of Cayuna's agricultural middle class. The central value in Fabricus's life is his cousin's property, Brandt's Pen: 'For me it was one of the places where the life of my country had been cast and carefully nourished. Whatever people had done since then, nobody had been able to make anything so efficient, so beautiful, and so enduring.'

The argument in favour of Brandt's Pen is established through three characters. Margaret, brown and passionate, is loyal to Fabricus's dream of re-establishing his lost inheritance. Rachel, his former mistress and current employer, is a dark-skinned mulatto and representative of the crudest merchant instinct that attempts to buy its way into social respectability. Jojo Rygin is brown, headstrong and bursting with creative energy. Rygin challenges Brandt's Pen as something dead, a monument to the past, but Hearne depicts Rygin's passion as anarchic and self-destructive. At the end of the novel Hearne makes his point: Rachel is dead, Rygin is in prison on a murder charge, while a healthy son born to Brandt and his British wife assures the continuity of the Brandt Pen ideal.

The scale of sympathies that informs *Stranger* and *Faces* is in no way challenged by *Equinox*. In this novel, Hearne weighs the human wreckage of devotion to a cause against the immediate rewards of working personal relationships. Set in Cayuna with Castro's revolution in progress in neighbouring Cuba, the plot revolves around the love of Jim Diver for Eleanor Stacey. He is a pro-Castro Cuban-American and she is a brown Cayunan heiress with a Brandt's Pen connection. Hearne portrays Diver's commitment to the revolution as a weakness of character. The preferred alternative is Nick and Eleanor Stacey's commitment to deep personal ties.

Hearne's judgement is implicit in the sad, quixotic Pierre Auguste, the wasted relic of a lost Haitian cause. Pierre Auguste's dereliction testifies to the waste of Diver's commitment and the good sense of the Stacey's comfortable domesticity, which Hearne makes secure against the influence of decadent continental American and Cayunan rebel alike.

Another Jamaican novelist to publish in the 1950s is Andrew Salkey. *A Quality of Violence* (1959) examines rural Jamaica in a state of physical and spiritual crisis. The time is the devastating drought of 1900 and the peasants have turned to the Pocomania cult for relief from their distress. Salkey sets the adherents of this cult in opposition to a brown, Bible-fearing minority of small landowners. The leaders of the cult are defeated eventually by a combination of their own fraudulent excesses and the wit of their opposition. But the cult survives under the new leadership of a trio of ganga-smoking disciples with a taste for blood and violence. It survives in the imaginations of the children who freely combine the myths and rituals of Christianity and Pocomania in their secret games. It survives more pervasively in Salkey's evocation of Haiti as the place where the Bible-fearing Marshalls will go to escape the drought, and where voodoo dominates.

The novel may be compared with two earlier Jamaican novels: McKay's *Banana Bottom* (1933) and Mais's *Brother Man* (1954). *Violence* offers another evaluation of the nature and power of Afro-Caribbean religions that is similar to McKay's sensational dismissal of Pocomania in *Banana Bottom*. But Salkey takes his cue from Mais in the scope of his treatment and in a symbolic evocation of the environment. The drought is 'the drought of their faith on the land, and the drought of rational action'. However, it is unfortunate that Salkey's evaluation rests on the popular perception of Pocomania and voodoo as a 'black art'. Even the sustained parallel with Christ's passion and death on Calvary stresses the cult's potential for violence and irrational action rather than its framework of authentic religious belief.

In the 1960s Salkey turned to a different kind of fiction that Brathwaite would justifiably compare with Hearne's and Naipaul's.[14] V. S. Naipaul of Trinidad and Tobago had established himself as a major new talent with three novels published in the 1950s: *The Mystic Masseur* (1957), *The Suffrage of Elvira* (1958) and *Miguel Street* (1959). A less prolific writer, whose efforts have paled beside the achievements of more established West Indian writers, is Jan Carew of Guyana.

In 1958 and 1959, Carew published two novels: *Black Midas* and *The Wild Coast*. The impact of the vast continental landscape is everywhere in evidence in the language and bias of these novels, as is the varied racial and cultural composition of Guyanese society. These were to prove significant features of the novels of Wilson Harris as well but nowhere does Carew anticipate Harris's experimental approach. Carew's novels are highly conventional adventure stories of frontier life in Guyana, which none the less reflect the thematic interests of other West Indian writers. In both novels Carew explores what he calls 'shadows of the past' in the El Dorado myth, slavery and colonialism.

In *Black Midas*, the shadows that pursue Aron 'Shark' Smart, the novel's picaresque hero, are Shark's father, the legendary 'diamond king' and pork-knocker, and Shark's white 'god-father', Beauchamp, who also made a fortune in diamonds. Carew condemns his hero to a compulsive re-enactment of their successes and failures in the deep bush. In the city of Georgetown, Shark must also contend with the lingering authority of a white colonial presence. Georgetown watches as Shark buys a 'white man house'; 'We were all conscious of the white man who owned this house, of his presence in it. He had gone away but he had left a strange atmosphere behind him, forcing us to act as if he was listening all the time.' In *The Wild Coast*, the emphasis shifts to Guyana's brutal slave history, an inheritance that resurfaces in the warring bloods of the mulatto and the santantone. The hero, Hector Bradshaw, is torn between the call of the deep bush and his slave ancestry and the Eurocentric values of the great house and his middle-class colonial education. He is the exemplary 'divided child' of West Indian literature.

Carew's passionate depiction of the Guyanese landscape and its impact on the language and character of the Guyanese people is the best part of these novels. Carew's undoing, if it can be so described, lies in an uncritical and often indulgent use of racial myths. In *Black Midas*, Pancho's character is explained in terms of his racial mixture: 'Both the Indian and the Negro were forest people, but the former could match their moods to the brooding silence of a forest twilight, while the latter had an easy laughter to hide their sadness.' Carew frequently indulges in such shallow evocations of the primitive. In *The Wild Coast*, the African wind dance is a 'shango bacchanal', and the singing of the shango drums is 'savage'.

Despite a thematic and structural interest in the conflicting values that inform contemporary Guyana, there is surprisingly little in these novels that reflects the racial and political strife that divided Guyana in the fifties. Not so with Martin Carter, poet and political activist, who made the anguish of that decade the very substance of his poetry.

Until *Poems of Succession* (1977), Carter was best known for *Poems of Resistance* (1954) and *Poems of Shape and Motion* (1955). Earlier works include *The Hill of Fire Glows Red* (1951), *The Kind Eagle* (1952) and *The Hidden Man* (1952). At first Carter's poetry celebrates the historical necessity for revolution and the creation of a new, post–colonial society. The poet enters a dialogue with the frustrations, the chains, the brutality of the past, and projects a future that would liberate the tortured spirit of Guyana:

> I come from the nigger yard of yesterday
> leaping from the oppressor's hate
> and the scorn of myself;
> from the agony of the dark hut in the shadow
> and the hurt of things;
> from the long days of cruelty and the long nights of pain
> down to the wide streets of tomorrow, of the next day
> leaping I come, who cannot see will hear.
>
> (*Poems of Resistance*)

The poet listens to the 'tongueless whispering' of the long buried slave and drinks 'from the calabash of my ancestors'. He identifies the progressive 'march of men' despite an inherited burden of hunger and nakedness and misery. Yet Carter is sensitive to the vulnerability of 'a dream to save the world':

> Who comes walking in the dark night time?
> Whose boot of steel tramps down the slender grass?
> It is the man of death, my love, the strange invader
> watching you sleep and aiming at your dream.
>
> (*Poems of Resistance*)

In *Poems of Shape and Motion*, there is a shift in tone from the rhetoric of defiance and hope to images of doubt and hesitation:

> I was wondering if I could make myself
> nothing but fire, pure and incorruptible.

Here the revolution itself has become an onerous burden;
resistance and action have not realised a revolutionary's
dreams. Carter's confidence in the inevitable march of progress adjusts to images of uncertainty:

> I walk slowly in the wind
> I walk because I cannot crawl or fly.

There is a sharp contrast between the poetry of Carter and
that of Eric Roach of Trinidad and Tobago. Published primarily in *Bim*, Roach's poetry offers little that is innovative in style
and language. But in the 1950s, when many writers were
leaving for Great Britain, Roach stayed with a sense of commitment to new directions in the Caribbean:

> Remember the cadences of island patois,
> Old men's goatskin drumming,
> Young men's tin percussion,
> The sun's rose ruddy in our blood,
> The wine excitement of our island women;
> O man, your roots are tapped into this soil,
> Your song is water wizard from these rocks.
>   ('Letter to Lamming in England', 1952)

For Roach the artist had a public responsibility to his community, present and past. Painter, poet and sculptor are charged
with the responsibility to speak for both slave ancestors and
their survivors in the New World. Roach saw his African
origins as a source of creative energy at the heart of Caribbean
life:

> I claim their strength and their affranchised pride,
> Reopening stubbornly the dead well
> Of history of our wretched race that fell
> Through utter hell to man's last degradation.
> Deep down in the deep seam the water's clear
> And clean from the black rock of Africa.
> There are bards there and craftsmen, heroes, kings,
> And dark ecstatic dancers throng the kraals.
>   ('The Fighters', 1953)

Roach extolled the values of the African peasant majority in the Caribbean: their will to survive; their 'courage, strength and kindliness'. His dominant images were drawn from their world in which cycles of growth and fruition balance decay and death.

After a long silence in the sixties, Roach spoke with a new voice; despair and disillusionment dominated his poetry until his suicide in 1974. But in the fifties, Roach's poetry announced the values of a peasant and African inheritance and sought to give a poet's direction to the idea of a West Indian people.

V. S. Reid, Roger Mais, John Hearne, Andrew Salkey, Jan Carew, Martin Carter and E. M. Roach all attest to a variety of Caribbean voices as opposed to a predictable uniformity. Their territory, race, class, education, ideological commitment and a host of other factors contribute to their diversity. However, as with the more established West Indian writers of the fifties, they are bound together as an identifiable community of artists by their common concern for the spiritual and social condition of the West Indian people. Whatever the individual bias, their works consistently strove for new levels of self-awareness in a time of social and political change. They explored the Caribbean's New World self and psyche, and initiated much of the process of self-exploration that distinguishes West Indian literature.

6   Since 1960: Some Highlights
by Edward Baugh

The 1960s opened auspiciously with the publication of Wilson Harris's *Palace of the Peacock*. Harris made his impact at just the right moment, charting important new directions for the West Indian novel, and helping to fill the gap caused by the silence or temporary decline of those novelists who had brought West Indian writing to world attention during the 1950s. In 1959 a very accomplished first novel had appeared, *A Quality of Violence*, but none of Andrew Salkey's subsequent novels is nearly so worth preserving, although his most recent, *Come Home, Malcolm Heartland* (1976), is a lively, up-to-date variation of the themes of exile and the metropolitan Black Power, revolutionary movement—a sibling to George Lamming's *Water With Berries*. After Harris, of the new novelists to have emerged since 1960, the ones of most considerable achievement—judged on the basis of a combination of quantity, quality and distinctiveness—are Michael Anthony, Austin Clarke and Garth St Omer. There are others of whom one particular novel stands out, notable among these being Denis Williams's *Other Leopards* (1963) and H. Orlando Patterson's *The Children of Sisyphus* (1964). And even more important than these are two novels that have been the only ones published so far by their respective authors—Lindsay Barrett's *Song for Mumu* (1967) and N. D. Williams's *Ikael Torass* (1976). A special place must be reserved for Paule Marshall, the Barbadian American, whose *The Chosen Place, The Timeless People* (1969) is alone enough to put her in the front rank of West Indian novelists, even though her earlier work, coupled with the fact that she is a native of the United States, had not much qualified her to be considered a West Indian novelist at all.

A second auspicious event of the sixties was the appearance of Derek Walcott's *In A Green Night* (1962). Here at last was an indication that a major poet was emerging out of the English-speaking Caribbean, and that the reputation of West Indian literature was not to be left entirely to the novelists. Soon Walcott was consolidating that achievement, fulfilling the precocious promise with which he had begun to excite a few local literati from his eighteenth year. By the late sixties, when Brathwaite made his international debut, stimulating partly by the fact that he had brought poetic *form* into such close identification with West Indian black experience, poetry was at centre stage. Playing a supportive role to Brathwaite and Walcott, there came a clutch of poets, mostly younger than they (except for A. L. Hendriks, whose first volume, *On This Mountain*, did not appear until 1965, when he was forty-three), whose work is accomplished and serious: Wayne Brown, Anthony McNeill, Mervyn Morris and Dennis Scott, to name those who have had volumes published. The even more recent emergence of young poets who write predominantly about, and in the accents of, the urban 'sufferer', and who create in terms of oral rather than written communication, has sustained the increase in the appeal of poetry within the region. One thinks, for example, of Linton Kwesi Johnson's *Dread Beat and Blood* (1975) and Orlando Wong's *Echo* (1977).

About drama, unfortunately, little can be said, since very few texts have been published in the period under survey and even fewer of that number are of much merit. The notable exceptions are Walcott's four plays in *Dream on Monkey Mountain and other plays* (1970), Errol Hill's *Man Better Man*,[1] Barry Reckord's *Skyvers*,[2] Michael Gilkes's *Couvade* (1974) and Roderick Walcott's *The Banjo Man*.[3] In respect of productions, only Walcott has had any considerable region-wide exposure. But dramatic writing has made notable progress during the period, the major dramatists so far being the Walcott brothers, Reckord and Trevor Rhone. The last-named has laid claim to his own little world, with his comic—sometimes tragi-comic—exposure of urban, mainly middle-class Jamaican manners and morals. Reckord has ranged more widely, an ebullient, iconoclastic prophet, willing to be reckless in his craft in order to deliver some urgent, unequivocal social message, dictated by his muse of common sense and reason.

From the publication of his first novel, Michael Anthony has been a controversial figure, although he is of all West Indian novelists the one least interested in controversial matters. If one says that his best work has the clarity and luminosity of a shallow stream, this is not to disparage it but only to define its limitations and the nature of its appeal. Anthony attempts nothing grand, and is hardly concerned with 'messages'. As a rule, he eschews great historical or political events and broad or packed social canvases. In his latest novel, *Streets of Conflict* (1976), he makes a half-hearted attempt at the themes of social and racial injustice. But the 'big' event of the novel, the 1969 student riots in Rio de Janeiro, seems to be used mostly to give spurious depth to a very inconsequential love story. Everything is treated superficially, and Anthony's failure suggests that his talent cannot thrive away from the very Trinidadian, autobiographical, particularised subject-matter of the work on which his reputation rests: *The Games Were Coming* (1963), *The Year in San Fernando* (1965), *Green Days by the River* (1967) and his collection of short stories, *Cricket in the Road* (1973).

Concentrating on a careful recreation of the humble, ordinary life of the rural and semi-rural Trinidad of his youth, Anthony refreshes our awareness of the significance of the ordinary, and of how, in its simplest, homeliest motions, the heart can touch so much that is at once elemental and complex. His memory-sharpened evocations of particular place and time verify some basic, universal truths of the human condition. At the same time, by being so true to time and place, he naturally captures some of the realities and nuances of West Indian social relationships, but without any interposing zeal of anger, protest or ridicule.

His records are as objective as the loving eye of memory will allow them to be. Consequently, in his limited way, he affirms the presence of his folk as *persons*, rather than using his novels as *arguments* for that presence and personality. So, for example, whereas a novel such as *In the Castle of My Skin* is of far greater

scope and depth than Anthony's novels, the latter's boy protagonists are more real, exist more completely in their own
right, than Lamming's G.

Anthony's simple, lucid, economical, self-effacing style is
ideally suited to all the ends of his art, which seems at one and
the same time so unpremeditated and so careful. In *The Year in
San Fernando* and *Green Days by the River*, the style is perfectly
adapted to reflecting the consciousness, sensitivity and self-
awareness of the boy protagonists, opening gradually, almost
imperceptibly, to the touch of experience and the world. These
novels are as much about the quiet marvel of that unfolding as
about anything else.

Childhood and adolescence are the subjects of a comparatively high percentage of West Indian novels, most of them
more or less autobiographical. Apart from Anthony's and
Lamming's, one thinks particularly of Ian McDonald's *The
Humming-Bird Tree* (1969), which bears very sensitive witness
to the deep divisions of race and class in the Caribbean. No
doubt the imaginative discovery of one's own world and sense
of identity (or uncertainty about it) tend, especially in the West
Indian context, to be most vividly illuminated by the light of
childhood impressions. Certainly, in retrospect, the West
Indian experience of school, a favourite literary topic, seems to
provide a paradigm of the historical tensions and conflicts
within culture and society.

In *Amongst Thistles and Thorns* (1965), Austin Clarke made a
worthy contribution to the West Indian literature of childhood. This account of a Barbadian boyhood, which also
showed Clarke's potential as a comic writer, was composed,
like his first published novel, *Survivors of the Crossing* (1964), in
the shadow of Lamming's *In the Castle of My Skin*. But
Survivors was a failure, crudely propagandising, over-
ambitious and rather hysterical in its angry, implausible narrative of a latter-day uprising on a Barbadian sugar plantation.
Amongst Thistles and Thorns, memorable enough, is a decidedly
lesser work than *In the Castle of My Skin*. A convenient
illustration of this can be had from a close comparison, in
context, of two very similar 'set-piece' episodes, descriptions
of typical 'old-time' canings by brutal elementary-school

headmasters.

It is in his Toronto trilogy—*The Meeting Point* (1967), *A Storm of Fortune* (1973), *The Bigger Light* (1975), supported by his collection of stories, *When He Was Free and Young and He Used to Wear Silks* (1971)—that Clarke lays claim to his own territory. These three novels are about West Indian, chiefly Barbadian, immigrants in Canada, the attendant clash of cultures and the sense of disorientation and alienation; about the psychological pressures and how the situation in which the immigrants find themselves heightens their problems of self-realisation. Like Selvon's 'lonely Londoners', Clarke's immigrants are working–class, a significant fact, because it is by this class that West Indian cultural patterns are most vibrantly and unashamedly preserved in exile. With the Toronto novels, Clarke helps to consolidate the development of a distinct, sizeable area of West Indian literature. The white metropolis, whether London or Toronto, now provides an important, authentic extension of West Indian society. This development is remarkable because no other body of creative writing produced by transplanted minorities in the western world has addressed itself so directly to the experience of the exile.

Clarke's touch may not be as consistently sure as Selvon's but he covers more ground and is more 'serious'. He does not operate completely within the comic mode but blends that with the mode of protest. The blend or the transitions from one mode to the other are sometimes infelicitous; sometimes, disturbingly, Clarke even seems to patronise or laugh at the characters on whose behalf he is enlisting our sympathy and anger. Sometimes the characters seem to act more as handy vents for the author's feelings than out of their own inner dynamic. Especially in *The Meeting Point*, Clarke forces the tone too much by resorting to the sensational. He can also fall victim to the temptation of 'style'. For example, speaking of a Barbadian woman who makes an embarrassing display of herself in 'testifying' before a white congregation, he says: 'Gertrude rose, red as a rose in a dress, and said aloud, as if her whole body was a resort in which the Spirit was rejuvenating.'[4]

But Clarke's achievement is substantial, a valuable contribution to the literary presentation of the black man in the white world. And whereas in Selvon the white world is present more or less as the given background, Clarke directly confronts the Canadian conscience with images of itself. Another of his achievements is in taking women as major characters in the trilogy, indeed as the protagonists of the first two parts. His is a complex portrayal of woman—more particularly West Indian woman—by a male writer; he now seems like something of a pace-setter for a recent trend in West Indian writing. One thinks, for example, of two unpublished plays by Reckord, *A Liberated Woman* and *The Witch*, Walcott's play, *The Joker of Seville*, and Brathwaite's *Mother Poem* (1977).

In Clarke's *The Bigger Light*, cultural alienation is integrally bound up with the theme of personal and sexual alienation. The book is a sensitive study of the breakdown of a marriage, of sexual need, uncertainty and self-centredness. Among the most telling scenes are those in which Boysie, in bed with his wife, suffers through the perfunctory, monosyllabic moments of casual-tense, awkward physical proximity without any real communication or any sexual fulfilment.

Boysie's failure to communicate with Dots (to some extent her fault) is part of Clarke's fascination with the problem of language, as communication and as power, one of the main areas of similarity between *The Bigger Light* and Selvon's *Moses Ascending* and an area of special interest for West Indian writers. Boysie, bent on establishing a new Canadian identity for himself, assiduously writes letters to Canadian newspapers and magazines, thereby actively expressing his will to identify with his new country. He cherishes the few letters that are pub-lished. But, written in an uncomfortable, flawed English, laughable in its cliché-ridden literary pretentiousness, the let-ters serve mainly to highlight his loneliness and cultural dilem-ma. The only persons we, or he, ever see reading them are the friends or acquaintances to whom he shows off the clippings.

He realises that to feel secure in a particular world, one must master the language of that world. His situation makes him increasingly conscious of language. He feels that he is given a revelation when a Canadian undergraduate introduces him to 'something called language' and to 'a social conscience version of language'. He sets out to master 'this new language', but in

the excitement and difficulty of explaining his revelation to
Dots, he slips back into his native 'Bajan' English. His pursuit
of the new language involves a blurring and, in terms of his
West Indian-ness, a lessening of his social conscience. He is
scandalised when Dots responds in broad, loud Bajan to his
attempts to explain to her his new ideas and sensitivity.
Towards the end of the novel, as he drifts more and more
inward, he wanders into a cathedral; this sets him off into
reverie, recollecting the Anglican cathedral in Barbados; the
theme of language is at once enacted and stated in a passage
which sums up his malaise and the history of it:

> There were actually people inside this cathedral talking!
> Now, back home in Barbados, you couldn't talk in church.
> Not *talk*, you had was to whisper in the white man church
> back there, boy! . . . Talk? In the white man church, god-
> blindyou, and let a police come and throw a couple o'
> bull-pistle lashes in your arse, and then lock-up your arse for
> talking in the presence o' God? . . . anyhow, no man would
> be such a gorilliphant to have *talk*' even on the doorstep o'
> that big powerful cathedral . . . and the Lord Bishship that
> man with the fat red face and the big belly, rolling-off them
> words offa his tongue in the prettiest Kings and Queens
> English and Latin from the Classicks, so blasted sweet that
> everybody who ever heard him, and those who didn't have
> the privilege to have hear' him, but only hear' 'bout him
> through hearing and talking, man, that Lord Bishship from
> up in England could talk more prettier than the six o'clock
> news 'pon the BBC radio! That was a Lord Bishship! And
> that was a cathedral![5]

And this is the man who has to be introduced, in Canada, by a
young Canadian, to 'something called language'!

All the themes meet in that passage, including power and
freedom and identity and culture and race. One of the things
which the passage helps us to see is that Boysie's departure
from Barbados is a kind of liberation, even though it is there
that he is most truly himself. It helps to persuade us that a
return to Barbados would not be a viable way out of his

dilemma. This option is neatly closed off by Clarke when, at the end of the book, he has Boysie receive a letter from a friend who has returned home but who feels that he cannot remain there because he sees through and cannot adjust to the 'fraudulence' of the post-independence Barbados. The friend's letter provides the cue for Clarke's recent novel, *The Prime Minister*, a satirical look at contemporary Barbadian politics.

The condition of alienation at home is nowhere given more rigorous scrutiny than in the novels of Garth St Omer. Indeed, the problem becomes obsessive with him, each new work being, as it were, a fresh attempt to find the perfect fictive expression of it. All the protagonists, whatever their differences of colour, status or achievement, are the one protagonist, unflinchingly worrying-away at his *angst*, incessantly turned, and turned inwards, on a tight little circle around his 'centre of self'. When on occasion he escapes from the paralysing home environment, it is only to find that he takes the paralysis with him.

The St Omer protagonist is afflicted by the 'will to meaning' in a world that seems more absurd the more closely it is scrutinised. His alienation is compounded of the problems of guilt, choice and responsibility. He envies what he despises, and treats brutally the women who, attracted by the 'aristocracy' of his anguish, compliantly bare their selves to him—which only makes him more angry with them and with himself. The battle of the sexes is given a frightening reality. Sex as weapon and snare is seen as a leading component of the web of frustration and meaninglessness, both a factor of, and a momentary, unsatisfactory release from, the pressures of 'small-island' society: poverty, class, race, respectability, the fierce competition for 'success' in a situation of very limited opportunity, and, pre-eminently with St Lucian writers, the Church.

The confusions and restlessness of St Omer's protagonists are recorded in a spare, undemonstrative, tautly-muscled style, which by its very nature conveys an important part of the author's vision. To expose their innermost selves with such cold, 'objective' precision is not only a kind of consolation against the burden of self-awareness but also a mark of their heroism such as it is, the only possible heroism left them, to accept unflinchingly the burden of self. At the beginning of *J–, Black Bam and the Masqueraders* (1972), one of the main characters says,

> When what I write is less memory than examination and evaluation, there is an orderliness and a sequential lack of haste that suits me. I sit then and write for hours forgetting myself, pleased with the feeling of control over what I write about events which once overwhelmed me. The orderly pace of my reflections and of my thoughts reassure me.[6]

So the very act of recording his self-scrutiny as precisely and unsentimentally as possible provides a form of release from self ('forgetting myself'). And, in spite of what he says, the orderliness extends to the passages of memory. All the protagonists experience the clinical pleasure which John Lestrade experiences in *A Room on the Hill* (1968): 'From his memory he had exhumed corpses of his old self, probing them with the scalpel of his new awareness, lifting his motives delicately out of their integuments to look at them.'[7]

Although the St Omer protagonist can seem self-indulgent and irresponsible, it can be argued that he is being true to a 'higher' responsibility, that of an uncompromising will to face truth and to question all motives, a responsibility which includes that of accepting, without excuse or self-pity, the blame for failure to fulfil the 'lesser' responsibility. And it is even possible to feel, as he 'progresses' from novel to novel, that he has been moving, almost imperceptibly, with slow, excruciating agony, towards a positive shouldering of the 'lesser' responsibility. We may read in these terms Peter Breville's relationship with his wife Phyllis, from *Nor Any Country* (1969) to *J–, Black Bam and the Masqueraders*. The very fact that he will not turn away from the reality of his unbearable, brutal, mutually bruising and degrading relationship with Phyllis can be seen no less as an assertion of responsibility than as a failure of will. And one may even feel that slowly, painfully, some little light of happiness is leaking into that terrible darkness. Peter's choice, in spite of all the unhappiness and cruelty it has caused to others as well as to himself, ultimately seems more admirable than that of Paul (his older brother, but really his soul–twin). Paul is the one who never left home, nor fulfilled any of his early promise. He gradually withdraws into feigned madness, as a sort of defence mechanism, both to protect himself against his sense of failure and to cultivate his contempt for his environment. On the face of it, Peter and Paul represent twin choices which are equally valid and equally futile but Peter's is more admirable, more heroic even, because it accepts the pain of involvement with other people.

Anthony McNeill, Mervyn Morris and Dennis Scott have, like the Trinidadian Wayne Brown, enriched the stream of West Indian poetry by their tough intelligence and rigorous craftsmanship. Brown's achievement so far (*On the Coast*, 1972) has been weakened by an obvious and pervasive debt to Walcott. But he shows evidence of an individual personality, and his 'Noah' is one of the very finest poems to have come out of the West Indies.

McNeill, Morris and Scott all attained their poetic majority in post–independence Jamaica, and their work reflects that situation. In Brathwaite and Walcott, we are conscious of the traumatic, determining colonial past and background; it is a focus of attention and a condition of the poets' self–definition. In the younger writers, these things are accepted as history; the definition of self and society presumes, broadly speaking, that the past has been looked at, and proceeds from there. The focus is much more comprehensively a matter of here and now; we are now on our own. The poem 'No Sufferer', which con-. cludes Scott's *Uncle Time* (1973), indicates the two broad areas of concern within which these three poets work and the necessary connection between the two:

No sufferer,

but in
the sweating gutter of my bone
Zion seems far
also. I have my version—
the blood's drum is

insistent, comforting.
Keeps me alive. Like you.
And there are kinds of poverty we share,
when the self eats up love
and the heart smokes
like the fires behind your fences, when my wit
ratchets, roaming the hungry streets
of this small flesh, my city . . .

Like McNeill and Morris, Scott is concerned about the grim
actuality of Jamaican society (an extreme version of the basic
condition of West Indian society), aware of his own privileged
position in the society and of the possibility of explosive
confrontation. But the act of reaching out compassionately to
the social 'sufferer' is validated by a concern, an invitation, for
self-scrutiny. There is an affinity between the tattered, lonely
dignity of Scott's 'old Ras' ('Squatter's Rites'), 'scratching his
majesty/among the placid chickens', 'king of a drowsy hill',
and the Icarus figure (the poet) of 'Visionary', who 'stumbles
headlong against the sun':

> wounded
> and wilful he
> beats to home,
> . . . the stubborn
> heavy pounding of that
> one wing wonderful.[8]

Similarly, the imagery of strenuous physical effort, of physical violence, of bruised, maimed bodies, helps Scott to convey
distinctively not only the quality of urban Jamaican poverty
but also the nature and responsibility of the poet and the
creative act, as in 'Bird of Passage':

The poet is speaking.
The window reflects his face.
A bird crawls out of the sun. Summoned.
Its wings are like tar.
That is because it is very hot.

The poet sweats too.
There is a beak at the back of his throat—
the poem is difficult,
his tongue bleeds.
That is because the bird is not really
dead. Yet.
Clap a little.

The wry, self-mocking, deliberately anti-climactic yet strangely menacing ending is a Scott hallmark. So too is the surrealist use of imagery and the almost tactile sense of rhythmic architecture. In its movement, the poem, displacing space and time, is like some dancer, creating a design as he moves, freely yet with a rigorous control, so that our appreciation of the grace of his movement is inseparable from the feeling of tension and effort which issues in that grace. This quality in 'Bird of Passage' is achieved partly by the use of short, simple sentences, a blunt, plain diction, and emphatic pauses subtly varied.

Fascination with bird imagery is another distinctive, richly suggestive motif of *Uncle Time*. The bird which crawls out of the sun in the last-mentioned poem has a counterpart in 'For the Last Time, Fire', an apocalyptic vision of the social confrontation which Scott fears as all too imminent and immanent in West Indian society, a future version of the slave rebellion. This poem displays most of Scott's particular strengths.

That August the birds kept away from the village, afraid:
             people were hungry.
The phoenix hid at the sun's centre and stared down at the
             Banker's house,
which was plump and factual, like zero.
Every good Banker knows
there's no such bird.

But the phoenix, brooding with a laconic menace at the heart of fire, is the unifying, controlling symbol of the frightening reality that the poem enacts, the 'terrible beauty' which is about to be born at the close.

The sense of danger is suggested from the outset by the unhurried movement of the poem, the flat, matter-of-fact way in which some of the harshest details are stated, understated even: 'people were hungry.' When the destitute woman, repulsed by the Banker, miscarries, she leaves 'a slight trace of blood on the lawn'. When they can take the oppression no longer: 'the villagers counted heads, and got up.' And so: 'one night there were visitors, carrying fire.' There is savage irony here, the holocaust being indicated in a tone suggestive of the polite rituals and empty manners of high society. The poem is totally compelling on the level of the fable. 'All things prepare the event' with a chilling logic. It is as if the *dramatis personae*—the Banker, 'Mrs So-and-so the Banker's wife', the Banker's edgy dogs, the starving woman, the villagers, the phoenix—are caught in a 'slow dance on the killing ground'. The quality of a solemn dance, of ritual, runs through Scott's work whether the theme be violence or praise. In Scott's love poems, this dance of He and She, moving apart or together, takes on the quality of wordless, slow-motion explosions of marvel.

Scott has also been justly hailed as a pathfinder in the use of dialect for serious poetry, his most famous piece being the title poem of *Uncle Time*; but the two other dialect pieces in the collection—'Construction' and 'Grampa'—are also fine. In these poems, Jamaican dialect realises something of its potential for 'serious', quietly reflective, lyrical utterance. These poems are instances of the increasing and increasingly subtle use of the vernacular in West Indian poetry, Brathwaite's being the most considerable achievement to date. Another version of the new subtlety is seen in Scott's 'No sufferer', where, apart from the very Jamaican use of 'sufferer', the poem comes to a pointed, yet naturally realised vernacular end by the simple substitution of 'I' for 'me'.

Some of the current subtlety in the use of dialect is exemplified by Mervyn Morris, who uses the vernacular in a variety of situations, as in 'I Am the Man' (*The Pond*, 1973), when he wants to evoke the pent-up rage of the 'sufferer' and the threat which it holds for the privileged:

I am the man that build his house on shit
I am the man that watch you bulldoze it
I am the man of no fixed address
Follow me now

The dialect here is, on the surface, minimal—a matter of substituting 'that build' and 'that watch' for 'who builds' and 'who watches'. But these apparently slight substitutions radically affect the whole mood and colour of the stanza, as they affect the pronunciation and intonation of the whole, thereby asserting the dramatic presence of the imagined speaker. The repeated 'I am the man . . .' pattern, which runs throughout the poem, builds up to a drum-beat insistence.

In 'For Consciousness' (*Shadowboxing*, 1979), the dialect acts as a mask, through which Morris makes a sharp satiric comment on the post-colonial situation in the West Indies and on the windier pretensions of the 'consciousness' movement—black consciousness, political consciousness, 'roots' consciousness and so on. At the same time, by making his observations through the mouth of a dialect-speaking persona of a seemingly peasant background, Morris suggests that the common people are able to see through the frauds of the new 'consciousness' and the deceptions of apparently radical change. The poem captures the aphoristic power of the grass-roots wisdom of the folk: 'Plenty busha doan ride horse/an' some doan t'ink dem white.' But there is a further level of interest in that the consciousness of the persona is only part of the poem's total consciousness.

Ol' plantation wither,
factory close down,
brothers of de country
raisin' Cain in town.

The speaker is hardly likely to be aware of the Cain/cane pun and even less of the disturbing level of suggestion in the pun, the suggestion of the superficiality and hypocrisy of the fashionable 'brother' label and salutation, the suggestion of the latent violence and treachery of the 'new plantation', of brother rising up against brother in the confusions of 'consciousness'. A further level of deliciously ironic resonance is in the hint of the Stephen Foster-type 'darky' song ('Swanee River')—a hint which comes not only in the reference to 'ol' plantation' but also in the rhythm of the piece.

Good sense and wit are prime virtues of Morris's work. He cultivates a keen irony. He refuses to be boxed into positions of monolithic intolerance and unquestioning, to be told how to think, to dance blindly to every passing street-band. His refusal to run with 'the pack' is all the more real because he acknowledges so fully the frightening power of the 'keen discriminators'[9] and the 'thought-inspectors',[10] the 'new powers [which have] enslaved us all'. His indictment of the self-righteousness of the new thought-manipulators is validated by his vigilance against any self-righteousness within himself. He knows that if there are traps all around us, there are traps enough within each single self. So when the boy summoned up the courage to look into 'The Pond', in which 'swam galliwasps and nameless horrors', what he saw was 'his own face peering' back at him. Morris's 'Narcissus' is not the beautiful youth who was so smitten by his own reflection that he fell into the pool, drowned and was rewarded by being turned into a lovely flower. He is the man who, fearful to acknowledge and accept his other, darker self, tries to strangle it but is in turn destroyed by cowardice when he realises that he cannot 'destroy that other self'. So 'he shrank into a yellow-bellied flower'.[11]

The tone of protective but healthy self-mockery in Morris is achieved partly by the deliberate, near-parodic use of simple, traditional stanza-patterns, with rhythm and idiom wilfully, playfully skirting the edge of cliché. While this manner can seem too easy, lacking, for instance, the strenuous, compelling rhythmic texture of Scott, the reader will be deceived if he fails to see that this manner is part of the poem's meaning.

Between Morris's 'Journey[s] Into the Interior' and his sensible, acerbic comments on the world outside, lie his love poems. Here he makes a valuable, rare contribution, by his exploration of married love and the demands of family life—not a popular area of poetic interest. Here again, his honesty with himself is an aspect of his artistic integrity. In 'Family Pictures', after detailing sensitively the love with which child and wife ensnare and harry him, but which he needs and which makes a king of him, he goes on to witness to the need for his private space, the 'desire to be alone . . . in spite of love'.

The private space that Morris claims as a right has its difficult, frightening features—the difficulty and fright of self-knowledge. The private space which McNeill describes in *Reel from 'The Life-Movie'*[12] is characterised by a sort of existentialist terror and sense of abyss. If for argument's sake one were to place poets on an imaginary line ranging from, at the one end, those who observe life to, at the other end, those who suffer it, the author of *Reel* would be among the latter. Of course all worthwhile poets do both; most are somewhere in the middle of the line. But McNeill's work bares and bears the raw nerve-scars of one who has looked into the 'Black Space' (title of the concluding, apocalyptic poem in the volume). In that poem, which integrates personal, social and universal concerns, the themes of interracial warfare (black and white) and the possible nuclear suicide of the human race are inter-fused. The poem conveys its nervous energy, its feeling of things always eluding man's control, a very modern anxiety and urgency, partly by the use of imagery drawn from twen-tieth-century technology, the Frankenstein robot which our world has invented and which threatens our humanity. The imagery of computers ('Ciphers went quite ecstatic/ Programmed to go berserk') and of the impersonal electronic marvels of the mass media works, in *Reel*, together with the imagery of the drug (counter-) culture ('angel' and 'needle' and 'spliff') to record the malaise of a 'turned-on', 'hyped-up', 'hooked', 'freaked-out' age. But this very twentieth-century, Americanised scene is also given a convincingly local dimen-sion, whether in theme, idiom or image. In 'Musks', for instance, the predatory forces which circle man's spirit, pa-tient, ruthless, are imaged in the repulsive (though deceptively graceful and easy-going in flight) John Crow, the Jamaican turkey-vulture, a deep and popular symbol of death and devil-work in the Jamaican mind. In an introduction to *Reel*,

Scott suggests that these 'scavengers . . . function as a finely-worked metaphor for the poor' of Jamaica.

The soul-scapes which the poet's expressively 'jumpy' *Reel* discloses are mostly scenes of anguish and extremity, of life itself as 'dread', to use a recent, already hackneyed yet still powerfully charged Jamaicanism (from the Rastafarian sub-culture), which McNeill uses with telling discretion. In 'Flamingo', the poet sees himself in the image of the exotic but comical bird. The major persona in these poems, in whatever guise, is that of sufferer, loner, outsider, whether the would-be suicide at midnight poised on top of a 'high-rise' office build-ing in the empty heart of downtown Kingston ('Who'll See Me Dive?'); or the 'Suicide's Girlfriend', who steps back from the edge of the abyss, back

> into her life given over
> again to fiancé and cops
> strung under the building like nets
> to retrieve whatever was left.

Or Don Drummond, whose music voiced the 'hurt/which captured [him] nightly into/dread city'. In the 'Rasta' poems, McNeill's loners are buoyed up by a dream of community which can heal the hurts, so that Drummond, for example, is seen as a spiritual leader who can 'let we lock conscious when wrong/and Babylon rock back again'.

The question of maintaining one's balance (sanity, 'cool') is a central preoccupation of the poetry in *Reel*, as in the balance between the latent hysteria or rage and the simple yet strict quatrains and octosyllabic lines in which some of the poems are written. Within a fairly conventional prosodic framework, McNeill exercises great rhythmic flexibility, achieving a very 'natural' voice, blunt yet sophisticated, relaxed yet intense, constantly engaging by the many home-grown and very modern verbal subtleties. And the 'charge' which the poetry carries comes to us partly through the sense that the precarious balance is constantly in danger of explosive disruption, a disruption which might be ambiguous, either joyful release or destruction, break-out or breakdown, the limitless space and freedom which is also terror, the abyss.

7 Edgar Mittelholzer
by Michael Gilkes

Edgar Mittelholzer (1909–65) is an important West Indian writer because he was a pioneer, the first of his generation to emigrate to the U.K. to make a serious career of writing novels. His dedication to his art was fierce and the list of his published work is impressive: twenty-two novels, a short 'fable', a travel book, an autobiography and numerous articles, short stories and poems. Brought up in the colonial backwater of New Amsterdam, Berbice County, British Guiana, considered eccentric because of his individualistic beliefs (he adopted Zen Buddhism as his religion when he was only nineteen), the young Mittelholzer determined to become a writer against all the odds and to grow 'rich and famous by writing novels for the people of Britain to read'.[1] This was more than an idle boast, for he endured twelve years of receiving only rejection slips from British publishers before one of his novels, *Corentyne Thunder*, was accepted. Even then, with success beckoning, he refused to relinquish his ideal of authorial integrity. The publishers had suggested that he use a *nom de plume*, since, because of the war, German-sounding names were distasteful to British readers: Mittelholzer promptly refused.[2] Success had to be on his terms. An austere, often prickly middle-class individual, Mittelholzer had few hobbies or close friends, dedicating most of his energies to the business of writing. The *Kaywana* trilogy alone,[3] which spans a historical period of 337 years, is proof enough of his extraordinary ability to organise a wealth of detail in a story of epic proportions; and it is for his twin talent for total dedication and story telling that Mittelholzer is most frequently praised. In spite of his success, however, much of his work is regarded as sub-literary, the work of a novelist *manqué*. Edward Brathwaite, writing of Mittelholzer's contemporary, Roger Mais, might almost be summing up a case against Mittelholzer: '[He] never became the master of a sufficiently convincing technique to make what he had to say into an effective work of art.'[4]

But the real importance of Mittelholzer's work in the development of West Indian fiction lies in another direction: in its pioneering concern with the problem of identity, what Denis Williams has called more accurately 'the lack of assurance of the indwelling racial ancestor'.[5] For although the attempt, in the novel, to identify and proclaim clearly the uniqueness of a West Indian society and way of life began with earlier writers like Claude McKay, C. L. R. James, and Alfred Mendes in the 1930s, it was Mittelholzer who first raised the question of psychic imbalance and the resultant *angst* of identity which is the most central and urgent theme of West Indian literature. Deeply conscious of his own 'hybrid' pedigree, Mittelholzer, the swarthy son of a near white, negrophobe father, seems to project in his work a dualistic fear of 'inner division'. He says in *A Swarthy Boy* (1963) that he felt as if:

> Two elements have always lived within me, side by side and in restless harmony. . . . The Idyll Element dreamed of a peaceful, sylvan situation. . . . The Warrior Element listened always to the sound of the Conflict . . . perpetually ready to resist, to repulse, to do battle to the death with any foe that might appear. *Greensleeves* weaving through the sword motif from *The Ring*.

He sedulously developed what he regarded as the 'Germanic' side of his nature (with its insistence on strict routine, discipline and strength of will), cultivating a taste for the pessimistic philosophy of Schopenhauer and for the heroic, 'Teutonic' resonances of Wagner's music, nourishing what was to become a highly oppressive super-ego. Even as a young man Mittelholzer was aware of a deep disharmony within himself and was constantly on his guard against melancholia and morbidity. The insistent note of despair in his novels is already present in the diaries of 1932–36: 'A very sombre week. The artificial necessity of living' (16 January 1932) is a typical entry. He read widely and tried different 'philosophies' (rather like a hypochondriac trying different medicines) in an attempt to cure his tendency towards melancholia, but apparently with little success. 'The impulses of the Flesh returned' runs the entry for 8 October 1932. 'Mastered them up to present'; depression returned, however (aggravated by a hopeless love affair), culminating in his attempted suicide on the night of 14 May 1936.

This, then, is the pattern which seems to have run through Mittelholzer's life, and the lives of almost all the principal characters in his novels: the attempt and failure to reintegrate, by effort of will, an inherited psychic disunity, leading, in turn, to despair and an obsession with death. In his first published novel, *Corentyne Thunder* (1941), one sees this 'divided consciousness' already at work. Geoffry Weldon, the son of a wealthy mulatto (but European-looking) plantation owner and a Guyanese Indian peasant, is torn between loyalty to his father, who wants him to go abroad to study, and his love for the Corentyne coast and Kattree, an Indian peasant girl to whom he is related. *Corentyne Thunder* is important because it is the first novel to deal with Guyanese peasant life and also because it is the first, though muted, appearance in Mittelholzer's fiction (in the character of Geoffry Weldon) of the theme of division of consciousness.

In *Corentyne Thunder* Mittelholzer is very much the young, would-be colonial author, 'writing novels for the people of Britain to read'. The novel's frequent historical and geographical glosses are clearly concessions to the metropolitan reader's ignorance of the book's ethos. Ramgolall, Mittelholzer explains, 'lived on the Corentyne coast of British Guiana, *the only British colony on the mainland of South America. . . . He was an* East Indian *who had arrived in British Guiana in 1898 as an immigrant* indentured to a sugar estate' (my italics). Introducing Geoffry Weldon, Mittelholzer suggests the inner resources of his character by direct authorial comment, but in so doing strikes an excessively portentous note:

He had power, a deep, tight-locked power that, one felt, might make a terrible whirl of damage, like a cyclone, if unlocked without warning. Seeing him, one thought of a coppery sky and a dead-smooth sea—the China Sea of Conrad—and a falling barometer.

These infelicities of style and technique are the exception rather than the rule, and Mittelholzer's characters, though lacking in depth, nevertheless retain their credibility for the reader.

It is one of Mittelholzer's achievements that he is able to present with gentle irony, considerable insight and economy a graphic picture of the process of 'creolisation' at work in the Hindu peasant community of the Corentyne. In the character-isation of Baijan he catches exactly the brash, energetic tone of the man determined to make his way up the social ladder—an older, less introverted Mr Biswas: 'I hear Dr Matthias buy over ol' Mrs Clyde' house, eh? Good place, you know. One o' dese days I got to own a house like dat.' In his big 'two-storey house wid de red roof', Mr Ramjit with ostentatious generosity calls: 'Charlie boy, make you'self useful in deh an' bring out some biscuits an' soft drinks fo' Beena an' Kattree an' de ol' man. Keep deh mouth' occupy till breakfast time':[6] while 'Miss Elizabeth Irene Ramjit' plays 'Backerollee, from de tales of Hoffman' on the piano for guests who feel increasingly uncomfortable and intimidated by the opulence of a living-room crowded with furniture and thick rugs on the floor, on the polished surface of which Beena has already left faint, accusing toe-prints. Made to feel exposed, awkward, out of place, Ramgolall, Beena and Kattree do not enjoy their visit. Later, at Baijan's Anglican church wedding, their naturalness asserts itself in the face of all the bourgeois clutter of flowered hats, white gloves, iced cake and champagne. At the reception they understand neither the forced gaiety nor the pompous, wordy speeches; when the parson makes 'a queer sign with his hand', intoning '*In nomine patris et filii et spiritus sancti*', their incomprehension is complete. On the way home, Ramgolall is sick in the car. The drift away from the land has already begun, however, and cannot be reversed. When Ramgolall dies of shock and grief after he discovers that his canister has been rifled, his death is symbolic of the passing of another, older way of life: for the canister has contained not only his hoard of coins, but also a whole past existence:

> In it lay stored away all the troubles and pleasures that life had brought him: kicks and angry words from the overseers, his first marriage—riot and the shooting by the police, Pagwah festivals, the death of his first wife and that dark day when his eldest son had got killed in a dray–cart accident.

Big Man Weldon, however, is, unlike Ramgolall, almost completely alienated from the land which for him is little more than a pleasant, or occasionally unpleasant, view from the window of his speeding car. He remains totally committed to the colonist's 'external' view of the land as a means of wealth through conquest. The fact that Geoffry has inherited his father's 'European', boldly outward-looking attitude as well as his mother's peasant sensibility has helped only to widen the already present division within his consciousness, so that he rejects the land and the life of the peasants while recognising at the same time that these things are a vital presence from which he is excluded. In fact, the character of Geoffry and the significance of his relationship with Kattree provide what is perhaps the most interesting focal point in the novel, for he and Kattree are made to represent the two parts of what later becomes a familiar dichotomy in Mittelholzer's work: Intellect/Spirituality versus Emotion/Sensuality. Kattree and her sister, Beena, are the embodiment of natural beauty and goodness, as yet untainted by the outside world. Geoffry is strongly attracted to the natural, physical vitality of Kattree and the Corentyne, but at the same time longs for the outer world of ambition and culture. This is, of course, the familiar theme of the conflict between Nature and Nurture, with Kattree in the role of Noble Savage; it is also a foreshadowing of what is now a much-discussed and well-documented problem: the Caribbean artist's crisis of identity—his need for roots within the context of his own landscape as well as for the cultured, metropolitan atmosphere in which his art can grow and flower. It is a dilemma that still faces the Caribbean writer, and

that makes possible the apparent paradox in which the successful Caribbean writers (with few exceptions) live and work
abroad, mainly in Britain, but quarry their material from
within a Caribbean consciousness. That the need for access to
publishing houses was not by any means the most important
reason for the exodus of writers which began shortly after
Mittelholzer's departure for England in 1948 is attested to by
the comments of the writers themselves. What most of the
Caribbean writers seemed to have in common, in the nineteen-
fifties and early sixties, was the desire to 'get out', as Lamming
puts it in *The Pleasures of Exile*, to leave the Caribbean so as to
avoid the atrophy of creative talent which remaining might
bring about. Mittelholzer records a recurring nightmare, the
feeling of being 'trapped' by one's origins: 'And then, with a
shudder, I would awake to find myself in Bagshot, Surrey, or
in Montreal, Canada, or on the Maxwell Coast of Barbados,
and the relief would be tremendous.'[7]

Geoffry's crisis of identity embodies a split between two
ways of life, but reveals at the same time another, more
disturbing aspect—an inability to reconcile intellectual and
physical urges. Against Kattree's unaffected sexuality his own
guilt-ridden condition appears neurotic: 'There are so many
things one would like to root oneself away from but just can't.
Where sex is concerned especially. That's what makes me want
to commit suicide sometimes, you see.' It is this aspect of
Geoffry's inner division which predominates and which is
ultimately responsible for his cynicism and rootlessness. In
Geoffry Weldon one recognises the prototype of the virile
Mittelholzer hero whose fear of spiritual atrophy leads to
deliberate sexual repression and a preoccupation with occult
science and Eastern mysticism in an attempt to enter 'into the
pure spirit of the Higher Plane'.[8] The need to find a solution to
the conflict between Flesh and Spirit is the driving force behind
Gregory Hawke of *Shadows Move Among Them* (1951), Hubertus Van Groenwegel of *The Harrowing of Hubertus* (1954), Mr
Holme of *The Weather in Middenshot* (1952), Brian Liddard of *A
Tinkling in the Twilight* (1959), Garvin Jilkington and Lilli
Friedlander of *The Jilkington Drama* (1965) and Sheila Chatham
of *The Aloneness of Mrs Chatham* (1965). Geoffry Weldon is the

first of many Mittelholzer characters who, faced with an almost irreconcilable inner division of consciousness, are drawn 'like a piece of wood moving towards the centre of a whirlpool'.

The cry of the goat-sucker, which in *Corentyne Thunder* is an integral but unremarkable feature of the landscape:

> and once a goat-sucker, lying flat on the road a little way ahead, said: 'who–you?' and flew off in swift silence

is seen, in retrospect, as the first, perhaps unconscious, stirring of the theme of psychic divison: the 'zweideutigkeit' felt by the hero of *Uncle Paul* (1963) and indeed by Mittelholzer himself.

Most of Mittelholzer's later themes are already present, in embryo, in *Corentyne Thunder*. Big Man Weldon's gruff, practical attitude to life, his rough, planter's philosophy:

> The damned world wants reorganizing. That's what's wrong. Less talk about morality and religious myth and more simple, practical common sense

is heard again in the later work, where (especially in the 'English' novels) it acquires the compulsive, dogmatic tone which eventually led to the publishers' repeated rejection of Mittelholzer's work. The sense of the Guyanese past, of life on the old Dutch plantations and the legends born of a violent history of slavery, is present in the description of Dr Roy's house, Vryheid, which was 'built in 1827 by a Dutch planter, Mynheer Vanderhyden, whose tombstone may still be seen in the backyard'. It is Mittelholzer's double sense of the violence and mystery of the past with its residues of legend and racial admixture that pervades the *Kaywana* trilogy and *My Bones and My Flute* (1955), and creates the charged, hallucinatory world of *Shadows Move Among Them*; but the intolerable inner conflict of the individual—the division of consciousness which afflicts the young Geoffry Weldon, forcing him to consider suicide as the only possible solution—is the most notable (and the most disturbing) theme in *Corentyne Thunder*, and finally emerges as the central theme of the later novels.

This is also the conflict within the heroine of *The Life and Death of Sylvia*, a novel published in 1953 but completed by 1948,[9] and revealing close similarities of style and plot with the unpublished 'Angela Vimiero',[10] which Mittelholzer had intended as a sequel to *Corentyne Thunder*. In *Sylvia*, Mittelholzer portrays the complex life of the colonial middle class to which he himself belonged. Sylvia is the daughter of an English architect and a lower-class Guyanese woman of African and Carib Indian extraction. At the sudden death of her father, who, involved in a *liaison sexuelle*, is murdered by a jealous rival, the Russell fortunes begin a steady decline. The rascally solicitor, Mr Knight, who by destroying the promissory note in his name held by her father (he finds the note in a drawer of her father's desk) is able to foreclose on their mortgage, gradually reduces Sylvia, her brother David and her mother to poverty. Sylvia is forced to look for a job, since Mr Knight's offers of help are barbed with lewd suggestions, but finds herself no less exposed and threatened by dissolute, lascivious employers. In spite of the occasional support and help of friends, Sylvia, whose moral integrity will not allow her to accept the values of a corrupt society, drifts helplessly towards destitution, until, suffering from starvation and pneumonia, she dies, a lonely rejected figure in the house of a childhood friend.

The novel can be seen as an indictment of the New Amsterdam and Georgetown societies through which Sylvia moves as a tragic heroine. But Sylvia's tragedy is also a projection of the author's preoccupation with the psychological effects of genetic 'taint'; the real tragedy lies not so much in society's cruel rejection of the heroine as in her own destructive psychic disorientation, the result of inherited characteristics: the Caribbean condition of racial admixture. Sylvia is a tragic figure not only because she is an innocent victim of a coercive, philistine society, but also because (and this is the more significant reason) of her own irreconcilable inner division, her mulatto inheritance: 'She saw herself as two beings—one ugly and deformed, the other lovely and striving to be good and clean.' She is torn between an obsessive desire for sexual experience and an instinctive chastity, between the demands of social acceptability and personal integrity, and ultimately between life and death. Sylvia struggles as much against an oppressive, racially divided society as against her own ambiguous feelings—the familiar dualism of spirit and flesh—so that while at one level the book is an indictment of the class-structured, colour-based hierarchy of the colony (one of the novel's strengths is the way in which cumulative, entirely convincing detail is used to evoke this atmosphere), at a deeper psychological level, operating as it were through the heroine's 'divided consciousness', the novel manages to be both a celebration and a denial of sexuality.

Sylvia's unhealthy, ambivalent attitude to sex is only one expression of her psychic and genetic imbalance. The 'division of consciousness' in Mittelholzer's work often took other, as it were, allotropic forms, appearing for example as a conflict between good and evil (*My Bones and My Flute*), material and spiritual (*The Wounded and the Worried*, 1962) or between the individual and society at large (*The Aloneness of Mrs Chatham*). In *Sylvia*, the main conflict is between strength and weakness—a subject that held a continual fascination for Mittelholzer. Milton Copps, who is (like Milton Woodsley of *My Bones and My Flute*) another of the author's self-portraits—his fierce individuality and his love of Wagner's music and Nietzsche's philosophy are enough to indicate this—recognises that Sylvia's internal conflict stems from something more than an Oedipus complex:

> Heredity, let's assume, has inflicted upon her a streak of weak character which, no matter what environmental influences have been at work, cannot be suppressed. Despite all efforts on her part, it continues to push up its head, because it happens to be a legacy from dear Mother.

This is the familiar Mittelholzer thesis which is worked out in elaborate detail through the *Kaywana* novels: an inherited strain of coloured ('bad') blood inevitably precipitates a 'weakness' or 'taint' of character which, unless heroically resisted, is finally destructive to the psyche.

If the undermining presence of a personal obsession often

prevents Mittelholzer from achieving a truly creative art, then the extent to which he was able to view his inner conflicts objectively and to incorporate them without setting up undue strain within the novel is, I suggest, a valid measure of the success of his writing. The novel in which this associative attempt appears most successful is *A Morning at the Office* (1950). The novel had been written by 1948, before he left Trinidad to settle in England, and its publication brought him immediate recognition as a West Indian novelist of importance.[11] Like *Sylvia*, the book is an unsparingly honest and penetrating appraisal of a typically hierarchical, colour-based, colonial society. The 'office' itself is a microcosm of the West Indies, whose formal pattern of racial and social degree is reflected in the way the multiracial staff is organised: the white manager at one end, insulated by the frosted glass door of his private office; the black messenger at the other, separated by a wooden barrier from the central area with its coloured, East Indian, Chinese, French and Spanish creole workers. This compact framework, structural as well as symbolic, reflects the author's tight control and deliberately objective view of his material within a precise time-scheme (6.56 a.m. to noon of one morning). Mittelholzer examines the colonial West Indian situation, simultaneously revealing the historical 'shadows' which have conditioned and created the characters' present responses and indicating the direction and shape such a society might take in the future. The daily lives of all the characters are shown to be burdened with a past that is responsible for the frustrations and prejudices that create racial snobbery, resentment and lack of self-respect. Mittelholzer sees the process of social emancipation in the West Indies as dependent upon the recognition of the black West Indian's claim for respect as an individual: Horace Xavier, the black messenger, finally rejects the barrier of colour and class and asserts himself by giving up his job and storming out of the office. The author, however, sees this as only a beginning: 'If the West Indies was to evolve a culture individually West Indian it could only come out of the whole hotch-potch of racial and national elements . . . it could not spring only from the negro.'

The novel is successful not only in its combination of

sensitive characterisation within an accurately observed social milieu with a plot which underlines the need for the full and compassionate integration of different peoples and cultures; but also in its deeper, most complex theme of the need for psychic balance as a starting point. For the characters in *A Morning at the Office* are linked together not only by their involvement, within the narrow confines of office and island, in the West Indian colonial situation; they are also united at a deeper, more personal level by a shared psychological impediment. This is the inner frustration which the central 'Jen fairy-tale' contains in an allegorical form, and which produces (in the white Mr Murrain, as well as in other characters) the sensation of being 'trapped in the skin'.

Even in the epic *Kaywana* trilogy (a working-out of the theme of strength versus weakness par excellence), there is an attempt, in spite of lurid descriptions of violence and sexual depravity, to establish a balance between the two sides of human personality: between the physical and spiritual selves. The middle book of the trilogy, *The Harrowing of Hubertus*, is in fact mainly a study of the introspective character of Hubertus van Groenwegel, who is deeply aware of his own lack of psychic integration. To Mittelholzer, the sexual and racial conflict and the resultant mixing of bloods involved in the violent slave past of Guyana, in which his ancestry actually took root, must have seemed a natural choice for what was to be his *magnum opus*. The trilogy represents an imaginative (though factually and chronologically accurate) reconstruction of the social and political history of Guyana from the early seventeenth to the middle of the twentieth century and, within this framework, the epic saga of the growth and development of the van Groenwegel family tree.

But the *Kaywana* trilogy is not only an epic, imaginative record of the peculiar social and historical reality of Guyana, a national novel; it is also a prodigious, pioneering attempt to examine the cultural and emotional ambivalence which is a heritage of the West Indian past. By embodying the conflicting claims of history and heredity within the violent, ambiguous fortunes of the van Groenwegel family, Mittelholzer, like Nathaniel Hawthorne, attempted to exorcise the ghosts of the past, and at the conclusion of the *Kaywana* trilogy might almost be saying, with Hawthorne:

> Let us thank God for having given us such ancestors; and let each successive generation thank Him, not less fervently, for being one step further from them in the march of ages.[12]

Hawthorne's ironic puppet-show, in which the New England 'heritage' is seen to be ambiguous, has a great deal in common with Mittelholzer's *Kaywana* trilogy; the puppeteer's remarks remind us of Hubertus van Groenwegel's ambivalent regard for the family name: an attitude which lies at the heart of the *Kaywana* novels. Divided within himself, Mittelholzer sought in his work both to examine and to identify this 'two-ness'. As a result, he is generally, to an extraordinary degree, emotionally involved in his fiction, so that it is never safe in reading his work to accept a superficial estimate (even if it appears to be Mittelholzer's own) of events or characters.

The progress through the trilogy of the ancestral 'blood' of the van Groenwegels reflects Mittelholzer's enduring preoccupation with 'two-ness' and the need for psychic integration. The pattern which evolves may be summarised as follows: an inherited strain of 'bad blood' produces an inner division (strong/weak, spiritual/sensual) which if unchecked leads to degeneracy and the death-wish, but if resisted can be channelled and redirected to good ends. The novels' historical framework serves mainly as a vehicle for the author's real concern with what is in effect a personal and psychological malaise, and Mittelholzer projects onto the events of the Guyanese past, with its burden of violence and sexual guilt, his own sense of inner conflict of allegiances. Part African slave, part white slave-owner, Mittelholzer deliberately fragments his personality, as it were, allowing these two conflicting elements of his psyche to act out their opposition to each other in terms of strength versus weakness or (in Hubertus's case) spirit versus flesh. It is precisely because Mittelholzer is himself involved in this way that the novels' 'moral purpose' appears to be undermined by intractable, contradictory impulses. But, as a closer reading of the novels' ironic purpose reveals, the author is aware of this conflict of opposites; in fact, this is his main concern and gives a centrifugal unity to the work, for these irrevocably opposed forces are the expression of an indivisible whole. In *Kaywana Blood* (1958), when Adrian van Groenwegel, Dirk's son, plays his own piano composition, his description of the piece reveals it as a musical allegory which summarises the dualistic theme of the trilogy itself and reveals the author's deliberate contrapuntal approach:

> 'It's loose in form', said Adrian, 'but there are two twin themes, the one sad, the other gay. One is symbolic of the strong and the other of the weak, and they keep intermingling and—and warring with each other . . . and eventually the strong one takes command near the middle of the piece, and the other one seems as if it's going to die away, but suddenly it comes back into its own, and another warring takes place. Then towards the end you hear them both interlaced, and both are being resolved in a perdendosi.'[13]

Mittelholzer's 'two twin themes', therefore, like his characterisation of Dirk and Graham van Groenwegel as 'strong' and 'weak', constitute an artistic rendering (whether conscious or unconscious) of a psychological theory: that a balanced union of the strong/male and weak/female principles alone can bring about psychic and social health. Mittelholzer's own awareness of inner conflict between the male and female aspects of his personality would certainly seem to have provided the background to his lasting obsession with strength and weakness. And in his characterisation in presenting, for example, Hendrickje as a 'phallic', power-seeking female, Graham as an excessively soft or matriarchal male and Dirk as overly masculine and hard, Mittelholzer has, with some insight, suggested both the symptoms and the inevitable result of a perversion of the patriarchal or matriarchal principles and revealed his overriding concern with psychic balance.

Like Alfred Desseau, the hero of *A Tale of Three Places* (1957), Mittelholzer saw himself as belonging naturally to the Old World culture of Europe and considered his Caribbean background too restrictive and limiting. From 1962 onwards his novels deal exclusively with English characters in an English setting. His characters' relationship to English society now becomes his main theme, and his heroes tend to insist dogmatically on what are obviously their author's own extreme right-wing views. Mittelholzer seems to be writing these 'English' novels in an attempt to impose his views on English society which, to his essentially Victorian cast of mind, must have seemed too left-wing, too liberal to command his respect and allegiance. The novels of this period are all, in a sense, a protest against the effeteness of the society which he has now adopted as his own, and for the health of which he now feels a certain filial anxiety. His heroes, meanwhile, become fatally self-alienated and develop an almost pathological arrogance towards society. Acceptance by the parent culture of England had to be on his own terms, and when this was clearly not forthcoming—publication difficulties began in earnest with *The Piling of Clouds* (1961)—the dogmatic authorial voice became almost hysterically insistent. Rejection of his novels meant rejection of himself by English society and the books were, at their deepest level of meaning, a protest at this 'unreasonable' course of action. The result of this sort of conflict on a person as psychically unstable as Mittelholzer was almost bound to be tragic. Novels like *The Piling of Clouds, Uncle Paul* and *The Aloneness of Mrs Chatham* are really little more than thinly disguised sermons on religion, art, politics, and crime and punishment. *The Piling of Clouds* was rejected by five publishers and *The Aloneness of Mrs Chatham* by fourteen, before being finally accepted. What had begun as the young writer's desire 'to become rich and famous by writing novels for the people of Britain to read' eventually became a personal invective against political liberalism and 'the cloying syrup of welfare-state ease'.[14]

Among Mittelholzer's later novels, *The Aloneness of Mrs Chatham*, which appeared between the publication of *Uncle Paul* and *The Jilkington Drama* (1965, published posthumously), is of special interest for several reasons. Mittelholzer himself considered it to be one of his most serious books; the novel certainly embodies most of his deeply-held views on sex, transcendentalism, politics and English society.

But while society's rejection of the principal male character (who has dedicated himself to exposing what he regards as its weak, left-wing liberalism, its 'will to rot') is a main concern in the novel, there is also another, more temperate—though no less familiar—theme: the preservation of psychic balance, through a process of withdrawal ('aloneness') and self-discovery. These two themes are yoked uneasily together in the main characters, Charles Harpenden Lessier ('Harpo') and the heroine, Sheila Chatham, and represent the two impulses which run throughout Mittelholzer's work—one masculine, disruptive, militant, aggressively individual, the other feminine, quietly introspective, concerned with inner peace and 'wholeness'. They recall once again the two elements which Mittelholzer had said 'have always lived within me, side by side and in restless harmony';[15] their interaction provides the main interest, as well as the major disharmony, in the novel. The book's dogmatic, assertive style almost occludes the introspective theme of 'aloneness', which appears ill at ease in the context of Harpo's violent outbursts against the 'effeteness' of English society.

Interestingly enough, *The Aloneness of Mrs Chatham* represents the final version of a work Mittelholzer had begun several years earlier. An examination of the six manuscripts which have recently come to light reveals the change in Mittelholzer's approach to his art as he revised and recast the work.[16] One sees the novel undergoing a 'hardening of the arteries', as it were, and the shift in emphasis away from an associative art, related to a Caribbean scenario, towards the development of a dogmatic, proselytising fiction involving English characters in an English setting. In the published version, the author's views on the deterioration of English society are given a central place. The main theme of the early version (set in Barbados) is Mrs Chatham's struggle to keep her psychic balance, torn between her liking for the sensual, attractive Alva Lessier (a West Indian from St Lucia) and his deeply religious brother, Herbert. The inner conflict of the heroine is conveyed with perception and tact; there is no hint of the moralising so evident in the later, 'English' version.

Mittelholzer, as a literary pioneer, may be compared with

Nathaniel Hawthorne or Charles Brockden Brown, the nineteenth-century American novelists. But when Mittelholzer's work is seen as an attempt, at a deeper psychological level, to resolve a 'division of self' of which he was himself aware, and which he often deliberately chose as his theme, then the importance of his novels becomes clearer. For they reveal a significant facet of the development of West Indian fiction where (as in V. S. Naipaul, George Lamming, Wilson Harris, Denis Williams and Garth St Omer, for example) the theme of psychic disintegration is central. Mittelholzer's work embodies and illustrates in a remarkable way the dilemma implicit in the whole body of Caribbean literature: 'that wrestling contradiction of being white in mind and black in body'.[17] It is a dilemma out of which, paradoxically, much of the vigour and originality of Caribbean writing derives, since it continually forces the artist to make 'creative use of his schizophrenia'.[18]

8 Samuel Selvon *by Michel Fabre*

Selvon's *A Brighter Sun*, published in 1952, five years before V. S. Naipaul's *The Mystic Masseur*, introduced the great period of Trinidadian novels which continues to this day.[1] Born in 1923, the son of a dry goods merchant, a descendant of an Indian immigrant and the half-Scottish, half-Indian daughter of an overseer on a cocoa plantation, Samuel Selvon had a somewhat limited education because he had to work early; he had, however, become quite proficient in literature while at school. A voracious reader, he saw writing as a medium for self-discovery and self-realisation; he began, accordingly, with poetry and journalism. Poetry he has professionally given up because it entails no remuneration although he still indulges in it privately. Journalism helped him find an outlet for the short stories he had written while serving in the West Indian branch of the Royal Naval Reserve during the Second World War. Many of these stories were accepted by the B.B.C. after Selvon came to England in 1950. He became a professional writer in 1954, largely due to the success of his first novel.

A Brighter Sun is set in Trinidad. This *bildungsroman* deals principally with the personal, social and racial coming of age of a newly-married Indian who leaves his peasant family in the Chanaguas sugar-cane area to settle with his wife Urmilla in the suburban Barataria community. The major theme is initiation into manhood and into a measure of intellectual and social awareness through the lessons of experience and through dogged efforts at self-education. Tiger's story is set in the wider context of the island and connected with the comparable evolution of neighbouring couples like creole Joe and Rita Martin, with the result that his personal destiny is also seen in historical perspective. The narrative focuses on the protagonist's awakening to the requirements of a multiracial society under neo-colonial domination and on the limitations necessarily caused by his background. Comedy mingles with suspense and satire with local colour. Bonds as well as tensions appear between the groups in the community. East Indian prejudice against blacks is voiced: 'Nigger people all right but you must let creole keep their distance.' So is self-deprecating creole behaviour: 'Is so we black people can't get on. Why we creole can't be like Indian, quiet and nice?' Yet such attitudes are slowly eroded by a new solidarity which challenges traditional ways. The quest for egotistic progress and the temptation of associating with whites are denounced by Tiger who, after his wife gives birth to a still-born son, violently insults the two doctors, one Indian, one black, who had refused to go out in the rain to help her. Selvon reverses the stereotype by having an English doctor perform efficient and cheap service, yet when Tiger is kept waiting by a creole store-girl because a white lady happens to enter the shop, folk speech again emphasises everyday reality: 'White people is God in dis country. . . . Black people like we don't stand a chance. Don't mind, as long as you ain't white, dey call you black, wedder coolie or nigger or chinee.' The consciousness of the community is revealed accordingly, with the narrator at times explaining that 'things are so in Trinidad'.

The building of a road by the Americans at the naval base changes the landscape and destroys the community's garden-plots, yet it also enables Joe to earn good U.S. dollars and Tiger to learn from the friendly but paternalistic Yankees; the scene when he invites his bosses for a dinner at home is a masterpiece of satire at American insensitiveness to foreign culture. Economic development by a foreign power, the novel seems to imply, does not benefit the natives and, a year after completion of the Churchill-Roosevelt highway, fights start between U.S. servicemen and local residents. By the time the Americans leave, Tiger has learnt a good deal about himself and his country. He builds a house, sends his wife to

Chanaguas to recover and becomes reconciled with the Martins whose friendship he has come to value. He has reached some sort of wisdom, when he exclaims: 'You don't start things over in life. . . . It not as if you born all over again. Is the same life.' He laughs at the thought of going back to the canefields yet he remains a farmer at heart. In the concluding paragraph, looking at the sky he thinks: 'Now is good time to plant corn.'

Tiger's closeness to nature largely accounts for his balance yet he desires to understand the scheme of the universe and is never content. Not wanting things to happen to him unwittingly, he buys a book about road-building when the surveyors come. His intellectual reaching out is coupled with half-formulated mysticism: 'When big things happen,' he tells Sookdeo, 'I does go out and look all about the hills and the trees and the sky and them. And I does get a funny feeling, as if strength coming inside me. That must be God.' Conveyed by the limited, half-articulate perception of such protagonists to whose vision the narrator limits himself, the social and political message of the novel is implicit: within the emerging popular consciousness there is a groping among the exploited for interracial unity against those in power, whatever their colour.

Selvon faced the problem of conveying this message to a double audience. Writing for the wider European public as well as for his fellow Trinidadians, he had to create a literary language suited to cultural particulars while creating a bond of sympathetic immediacy with foreign readers unconversant with West Indian culture who sometimes required nearly anthropological information. The traditions of the eighteenth- and nineteenth-century British novel also influenced Selvon to make a handful of half-related stories coalesce into a 'proper' plot, although he may have felt spontaneously more akin to the Trinidadian style of spinning yarns and telling stories in the more authentic calypso tradition of the folk. He further attempted to set individual change within the larger context of Trinidadian events and the even larger framework of a world in turmoil during the war. Such is the function of the opening paragraphs in each chapter, which heap up occurrences—economic, military, personal and anecdotal. Contrary to Dos Passos's 'newsreel' technique, such episodes are more contrapuntal than explanatory. Individual fate may be part of the general trend of history but it is often cut off from it through personal insignificance or geographical isolation. The historian's organised vision is thus challenged by the jumbled accumulation of experiences which constitutes the web of common existence. The fall of a 'mad nigger' can be reported in the same breath as wartime measures with no hierarchical importance being implied between the events. Only towards the end, with Tiger's growth in awareness, does the choice of events become more symbolical, the irrelevant being winnowed out of the narrator's conscience.

A problem of tongue and tone also posed itself in the use of the third-person narrator. By translating Trinidadian customs, flora and fauna into easily accessible terms, the narrator remains somewhat detached. His use of standard English makes him stand apart from the small people—Chinese, creole or Indian—who resort to various brands of local dialect or 'corrupt' forms of often mispronounced English. The distinctiveness of each sub-group's linguistic peculiarities is somewhat emphasised as in the hilarious episode of Sookdeo's selling Ramdhin a half-blind donkey. When Ramdhin complains, Sookdeo can retort: 'But me tellam. Me say him fat but him don't "look" well. Yuh don't understand when me talkam good English give yuh?'

Written somewhat quickly after the favourable reception of *A Brighter Sun*, *An Island Is A World* (1955) is a more ambitious, a more socially-oriented and politically-conscious novel. Its topical interest becomes clear when one recalls that a federation of the West Indies was then under discussion and its articulateness is all the more aesthetically fitting as it deals with a better-educated segment of the Trinidadian population. The novel explores varied responses to the divisive tensions and to the lack of clear cultural identity that plague the island. As in *A Brighter Sun* contrastive delineation is used, setting off middle-class Foster against lazy, rum-addicted Johnny, an Indian who waits for the Big Invention that will make him rich.

Retrospectively, Selvon considers his second novel 'more as a draft of a work I was not quite geared to write at the time and which I did not develop sufficiently'.[2] He feels more hesitant now to write about such a huge and complex country as the United States because he knows it better, although his 1954 sojourn there lends as much credibility to Rufus's response to the ice-bound, provincial Midwest as Selvon's London experiences do to Foster's impressions. Stylistically, the novel evinces a clever but sometimes artificial use of contrastive devices; for instance, the opening chapter parallels Foster's and Johnny's visions of themselves in the morning; chapter 10 ends with Andrews asking: 'Marleen, will you marry me?', while chapter 11 begins with Rufus answering Sylvia: 'How can I marry you?' *An Island Is A World* shows a wider linguistic range than *A Brighter Sun* by also using American English, and a slightly pompous and stilted variant of the Queen's English which Foster apparently delights in employing for satirical effect. The narrator remarks: 'Foster spoke proper English when he felt like it, using local dialect for emphasis and contrast.' In the course of a debate with his cousin, Foster notes that they use broken English only when they find themselves losing ground.

Dealing with West Indians in London, their bewilderment in the metropolis, their unending search for homes, jobs and women, and the hostile politeness of the British, *The Lonely Londoners* (1956) came out two years after George Lamming's polemical treatment of the same theme in *The Emigrants*. Selvon uses a loosely-knit plot structure which allows him to string barely-related sketches in a fashion similar to Claude McKay's *Banjo*, 'a story without a plot'. Selvon depicts the fun-loving aimlessness of West Indians in contrast to the cold, uptight seriousness of 'old Brit'n'.

Although the novel is full of pinpricks at English prejudice, the West Indians' loneliness and nostalgia for their islands never turns into bitter denunciation of segregation and racism. There is self-analysis alongside the nostalgia: 'I does wonder about the boys, about how all of us come up to the Old Brit'n to make a living and how years go by. . . . I ain't no place at all. Is still the same way, neither forward nor backward. . . . Sleep, eat, hustle pussy, work. . . . Look how it is, these Jamaican fellars who only here for two-three years save up enough money to send for their family and I ain't have one cent in the bank.' No wonder Moses dreams of going back home to sleep under a tree and dig his toes into the warm sand of a sunny beach; London is a cold hell,

> a lonely miserable city, if it was that we didn't get together to talk about things back home we would suffer like hell. Here is not like home where you does have friends all about. . . . Nobody in London does really accept you. They tolerate you but you can't go in their house and eat or sit down and talk. It ain't have no sort of family life for us here.

This is not the biting mood of calypso but the bittersweet feeling of the blues, when one laughs to keep from crying.

Selvon refrains from exploring the underlying reasons for the presence of West Indians in England. He ascribes their exile to a lack of stable political and cultural identity. Possibly because he was himself looking for an answer, both in personal and ideological terms, Selvon did not pursue his depiction of the expatriate scene further at the time but he returned to Trinidadian sources and conflicts with *Turn Again Tiger*.

The Lonely Londoners is an impressive achievement in style, with its mellow, humorous, mildly satirical tone. Modified West Indian dialect is used for dialogue and narrative passages alike. Yet, whereas linguistic variations serve realistically to differentiate ethnic groups in *A Brighter Sun*, the major opposition now arises from the tension between standard English and modified dialect. Although each protagonist retains typical Jamaican, Trinidadian or African cultural habits, their common syntactic usage, slang words and phrases make them stand out from the dignified remarks of a British spinster or the sociological jargon of a London newspaper reporter. But more important, Selvon's problem lay in reducing the distance between the European reader and the characters; he managed this by having the narrator also speak modified dialect subtly interwoven with standard English in lyrical monologues. To take an example, the opening descriptive paragraph with its slow rhythm provides information the way a Conan Doyle opening might, fog included, but the elision of verbal compounds, the changing of 'there was' into 'it had', the omission of articles, the use of 'fellars' towards the end are sufficient to create an in-group feeling while enabling the non-Trinidadian reader to become part of the group of 'chosen listeners'. According to Selvon, such technique was largely the result of inspiration:

> I had wonderful anecdotes and could put them into focus but I had difficulty starting in straight English. These were entertaining people but I could not move. Then I started both narrative and dialogue in dialect and the novel just shot along. It was not difficult to understand because I modified the dialect, keeping the lilt and rhythm but somewhat transformed, bringing the lyrical passages close to standard English. You don't want to describe a London spring in dialect form, this is straight poetry.[3]

All in one sentence without punctuation, the eleven-page concluding rhapsody on spring in London is remarkable for the lyrical quality of its language as it gradually emerges from everyday dialect; the reader, having by that time picked up enough dialect through repetition and connotation, is able to appreciate the discarding of it. Later in the novel the end of the narrator's meditation on the changing of seasons is pure poetry: 'In the grimness of the winter, with your hand plying space like a blind man's stick in the yellow fog with ice on the ground and a coldness defying all effort to keep warm, the boys coming and going . . .'

Turn Again Tiger (1958) is a somewhat unexpected sequel to *A Brighter Sun* when one remembers Tiger's implicit refusal to return to Chanaguas at the end of the first novel. When Tiger is asked by his father to oversee an experimental cane project at Five Rivers, he finds himself involved in rural exploitation again, though only as a time keeper. He now is armed with the literacy and social consciousness acquired at Barataria and he can step back and analyse the situation of field-workers who suffer from varying degrees of underdevelopment because of their total dependence on the cane industry. With Five Rivers as a belated example of the long tyranny of King Cane, the novel explores this serfdom as a legacy of the colonial past. In this circumscribed world, a strict hierarchy prevails from white supervisor downward to overseer, Chinese shopkeeper and illiterate Indian labourers.

The novel opens with the planting of cane and closes upon its harvesting. Tiger goes through this season in hell with a resolve to explore and transcend the memory of a life forgotten, of exploitation symbolised by the overseer with horse and whip. Tiger, however, cannot act differently from the other field-workers when it comes to the attraction of Doreen Robinson, the overseer's wife, the temptress who bathes naked in the river when he comes across her. He flees from the taboo she represents and his defeat becomes self-destructive—he neglects his duties, destroys his books, performs demeaning tasks for her—until she later consents. But then he has to resort to violence in his mind—their sexual encounter is a rape for him, utterly devoid of tenderness—in order to free himself by reversing the violation historically inflicted on coloured women. Tiger's symbolical cleansing in the pool shows his expurgation of the weakness in himself that remained vulnerable to the white woman as representative of white power.

More than a private crisis, Tiger's conflict stands for the psychological plight which plagues the island as a lingering sequel of colonisation. Similarly, the father-son opposition stems from their different conceptions of a worker's nature. Tiger is filled with joy when his father, a wonderfully expert foreman but too ready to kowtow to whites, regains self-confidence and dignity at harvesting time. Conversely, through daily contact with field hands, Tiger loses his feeling of superiority. Other characters also gradually assume more importance: the Chinese shopkeeper triumphs over Singh who had taken his wife in the canefield; More Lazy, the itinerant entertainer, is redefined as a harvester; Old Man Soylo, a former foreman who hated cane since his son had been a victim of burning it before harvest, becomes Tiger's mentor and finally rejoins the community again. Traditionally cast as subservient to the male world, women are now recognised as forces in the community. No longer a child bride, Urmilla competently supports her husband and emerges as a strong, sensitive personality even more aware than Tiger. She becomes a symbol of fertility; at the end of the novel Tiger computes the many benefits of the season: 'Urmilla was bearing another child, perhaps the greatest thing of all.'

Selvon seems to answer the question, once so eagerly posed by Foster, of one's debt to one's origins, by advocating involvement in the daily life of people and shared struggle for dignity as well as better social conditions. Creolisation and self-education at Barataria had somewhat estranged Tiger from his roots; he never renounces his growth of awareness but, in the canefield, he acquires a humbler sense of belonging and a new psychic integrity which will enable him to become a community leader upon his return to the city. A true ritual in rebirth, his season in the cane fields brings him further from the cycle of anguish historically linked with cane and prevents him from perpetuating the cycle of exile.

Tiger's relation to his folk origins is never romanticised; on one hand, a balance is created between the sympathetic rendering of the hero's inner life and the essentially comic depiction of episodes involving minor characters. Comedy enhances objectivity and precludes idyllic exoticism. On the other hand, as Sandra Paquet very accurately remarks, Selvon's aesthetics are close to the calypso tradition with its delight in melodrama, its male chauvinistic view of women and its preoccupation with racial stereotypes. His very style is akin to calypso rhetoric, wit and anecdote. This calypso tradition becomes part of the novel's anti-romanticism, not only in such episodes as Otto's waking up from a dream to find all the village women massed before him, which creates delight through reversal of his fantasies of sexual power, but also through the role of More Lazy, the typical calypso raconteur whose every adventure is made into a ballad.[4]

As in the preceding novels, a wide-ranging, modified dialect prevails instead of strict, naturalistic, linguistic accuracy. Interestingly, narration and dialogue are derived exclusively from a character's possible range of experience with the result that the thoughts and inner lives of white people remain opaque. One never knows, during Doreen's involvement with Tiger, what the white woman thinks; one only infers from what Tiger

observes because the narrator definitely belongs to the Trinidadian, not the European, universe. This allows the narrator to
merge easily with the protagonist's own consciousness, re-
inforcing cohesion in points of view and sympathy for Tiger's,
and the field-workers', outlook.

The Plains of Caroni (1970) is Selvon's only novel to have
been written wholly in Trinidad. While home on a Gug-
genheim Fellowship, Selvon was commissioned by the Tate &
Lyle Company to write on sugar production, it being
'Agricultural Year'. At the end of a six months' stay at
Tacarigua, he surprisingly completed a novel treating of
peasant opposition to mechanisation. When the new cane
harvester arrives, Romesh, fresh from the university, is the
only one to welcome it. His companions and his family oppose
it. His uncle Balgobin, a champion of cane-cutting, damages
the engine beyond repair with his 'poya'. Unions and parties
side with the people, and the press play the old story of men
against machine for all it is worth. The Company's efforts to
modernise are checked for a while.

As important to Romesh as his social concern, however, is
his discovery about himself. Seeta, his overly possessive,
ambitious mother involves him with Petra whose white skin
she sees as a token of success. When the police investigate,
Balgobin is safely stowed away. To prevent Romesh from
talking, Seeta discloses that he is Balgobin's son, not his
nephew, a prearranged marriage having prevented Balgobin
from marrying her. Nearly mobbed as a 'white Indian', Romesh makes a narrow escape thanks to Petra who seems willing
to take his destiny in her hands, and they emigrate to London.
Besides social strife and family near-melodrama, Selvon treats
of the new coloured ruling class, its aspirations, its foibles and
of tourist-like 'Trinfashions' that lead to coining such words as
'trinfare', 'trindrink', or 'the Commu-Demo-Afro-Indo-
Trinworkers'.

Those Who Eat the Cascadura (1972) is more remarkable than
The Plains of Caroni. Selvon treated no other plot in so many
different forms: he first published a short story in Trinidad in
the forties; then a novella later collected in *Ways of Sunlight*;
then a play which was broadcast by the B.B.C.; finally a novel

using as background the village life he had shared at Tacarigua in 1969. The novel is noticeably different from the story, both in plot and perspective. In the short story, the first-person narrator is the overseer of the Franklin cocoa plantation at Sangre Grande. He repeatedly asserts his neutrality as an observer; he trusts the whites and suffers in silence when his beloved Urmilla falls in love with an English friend of Franklin's, Johnson, whose life is threatened by a mysterious ailment, and who has come to rest in Trinidad. Johnson becomes interested in such folk superstitions as Papa Bois, the guiablesse or soucouyants about which old Sookdeo, the Indian watchman, is an authority. He even climbs an immortelle tree in search of a corbeau's egg for a lucky charm.

The full-sized novel makes many points more believable or explicit. Gary Johnson is a writer researching into West Indian folk ways, which enables Selvon to explore obeah in a nearly anthropological fashion without falling into exoticism. The major change comes from making the Indian overseer, Prekash, into a major protagonist so jealous of Johnson that he attempts to rape Sarojini. Interracial sexual rivalry is emphasised but in a more romantic atmosphere than in *Turn Again Tiger*, due in part to the important role of local colour in such scenes as 'dancing the cocoa' or the playing and disputing between Sarojini and her mates, not to mention the romance between the girl and Johnson. The supernatural is also stressed through the impressive figure of Manko, the village obeah-man whose predictions are fulfilled although he uses his powers to alleviate some evil. Quite adroitly, Selvon uses the love rivalry as symbol and the hurricane as metaphor in order to connote wider social tensions on the estate ironically called Sans Souci.

The topic of interracial marriage is often treated in Selvon's fiction. The Jamaican Brackley continues dating Beatrice although he is not accepted by her British family in 'Waiting for Auntie to Cough'. In *The Lonely Londoners* Moses sums up the situation: 'They go back home with English wife, and what happen? As soon as they get there, the places where the wife could go, they can't go. Next thing you hear the wife horning them, and the marriage gone puff.' In *Turn Again Tiger* Boysie returns with an English wife to Barataria; the community hardly dares speak to her, so strong is the colonial legacy which made the white woman into an untouchable goddess.

I Hear Thunder (1963) treats of a similar situation: Mark, who has joined the Royal Air Force, returns home a doctor with a white wife. This causes much gossip and the female section of the community is flustered. Mark's own mother, a washer-woman full of dignified good sense, is awed by her English daughter-in-law whom she can only call 'Madam'. She refuses to leave her familiar environment in Success Village in order to share her son's new, large house; Mark's social achievement estranges him from his mother. More generally, the novel explores the predicament of someone educated away from home and returning after a period of growth and trials abroad. With his big job in San Fernando, Adrian is to some extent Frank's local double and both are contrasted with the native figure of Ramdeem, who has never attended school and re-mains awestruck by the mysteries of education. When Frank tries to re-identify with his people, his having married Joyce compounds his difficulties and their marriage, although not actually destroyed, suffers. Borrowed from a nursery rhyme, the title evokes the ominous rumblings of a distant storm, symbolising the hardships to be weathered in the course of the novel.

Experimenting in dialogue and dialect, *The Housing Lark* (1965) resorts to the style and characters found in *The Lonely Londoners* and was meant to be a funny, farcical novel about the working and housing conditions of the black immigrants in London. In *Moses Ascending* (1975) the identification of the first-person narrator with Moses, whose personality has already been revealed and defined in *The Lonely Londoners*, allows Selvon to appeal directly to the reader, whom he sometimes addresses as 'Dear R.'. The personalised styles of speech which distinguish the protagonists and their idiosyn-cratic traits make the comedy complex. Although there is more of a plot than in *The Lonely Londoners*, if only because Moses is the centre of all events, the story is less important than its treatment. After years of living in basements, Moses has ascended to the top floor of his derelict house in Shepherd's

Bush where he indulges in writing his memoirs while Bob, his white Man Friday, looks after the tenants. Problems arise when Black Panther militants use the basement as their head-quarters, with beautiful Brenda adding the spice of sex to the flourish of politics; or when Faizull, an elusive Pakistani ten-ant, illegally shelters Indian immigrants who slaughter sheep in the backyard. 'Honest' Moses accepts corruption like any other man but later loses his ill-gained money in a generous move to pay bail for a black militant who turns out to be a fraud. His 'kind conscience' also prompts him to relinquish the top floor to Bob and his wife after he has been caught *in flagrante delicto* in the bathroom with her.

Selvon's treatment of such good-humoured episodes is full of irreverent asides and it accurately records the changes that have occurred in London since the early days of coloured immigration in the fifties. A valuable social document, the novel is enjoyable. But its aesthetic interest comes, in my opinion, from the sophisticated appropriation by 'colonial' writing of a literary style formerly reserved to the British-born. Moses's speech is a blend of outdated, stilted phrases with Caribbean syntactic turns which define him as a senior expatriate in contradistinction to the colloquialisms of other blacks or the rhetoric of the Panthers. Yet, beyond veri-similitude, Selvon also attempts a distinctly subversive effect. Take a paragraph like:

> '*Kay sir rah sir rah*', as the Japanese say. It was a motley trio Faizull shepherd into the house. I have seen bewitched, bothered and bewildered adventurers land in Waterloo from the Caribbean with all their incongruous paraphernalia and myriad expressions of amazement and shock, but this Asian threesome beat them hands down.

Here, through Moses as a writer-of-memoirs, Selvon as a novelist claims the right to depart from the naturalistic ways of using English usually prescribed to non-British writers by paternalistic literary critics. Selvon does not assimilate into the European mainstream; he explodes it, he subverts it. Whereas reviewers tend to consider *Moses Ascending* as a mere sequel to

The Lonely Londoners, it represents a unique attempt, along the lines of post-modern fiction, to unite the iconoclastic techniques of the West and the iconoclastic techniques of the calypso in order to liberate Trinidadian fiction by negating the monopoly of the 'great tradition'. This is really a 'novelist's novel', refined to the point of indulging in pun, parody and allusion in the same breath. Just listen to Moses:

> 'I am not an ignoramus like you,' I say, beginning to lose my cool.
> 'You think writing a book is like kissing hand? You should leave that to people like Lamming and Salkey.'
> 'Who?'
> Galahad burst out laughing. Derisively, too.
> 'You never heard of them?'
> 'I know of Accles and Pollock, but not Lamming and Salkey.'
> 'You see what I mean? Man Moses, you still living in the Dark Ages! You don't even know that we have created a Black Literature, that it have writers who write some powerful books what making the white world realize our existence and our struggle.'

Who is right? Outdated Moses still lost in British manufacturers' advertisements, or Galahad praising Caribbean social realism? The double irony shows that Selvon has gone a long way beyond the aesthetics of *A Brighter Sun*.

A pioneer in Trinidadian fiction, quick to exploit the topical tensions of his time and render them in striking, accurate literary terms, Sam Selvon has moulded the folk tradition of the Caribbean into a recognised literary form, somewhat in the way Ralph Ellison used the blues in *Invisible Man*. Throughout his novels, he has achieved a convergence of the written and oral modes in Trinidad, largely by bridging the gap between local creole and accepted standard English. He has extended that form to accommodate the European tradition. His preoccupations with language are contemporary; he is still creating new ironical tools fitted to the demythification of solemn postures, be they imperialistic dictates or frozen modes of expression which prevent the spirit from moving in harmony with fundamental emotions. Selvon's humanistic vision extends beyond social concern, whether explicit or muted; it centres on the essential worth of the individual within the community.

9   George Lamming *by Ian Munro*

Barbados-born George Lamming is the most outspoken nationalist of the generation of West Indian novelists who grew to maturity in the turbulent 1930s and 1940s. His six novels chronicle the sweep of West Indian history, from the colonial setting of *In the Castle of My Skin* (1953) through the achievement of independence in *Season of Adventure* (1960) to a post-independence uprising in *Water With Berries* (1971). His most recent novel, *Natives of My Person* (1972), is the culmination of his work, reaching back to the beginnings of colonialism and, through allegory, suggesting the underlying, recurrent patterns of Caribbean history. Each of his novels is both complete in itself and part of a continually developing vision linked to the changing political scene in the Caribbean, with its urgent problems of political and psychological decolonisation, and to Lamming's evolving understanding of the human condition.

His earliest writing, the poetry and short prose he wrote before emigrating to England in 1950, expresses primarily a rejection of West Indian society and politics. From 1946 to 1950, while living in Trinidad, he devoted himself to the creation of an 'artistic personality' through poetry. Romantic and ethereal in the earliest poems, the persona soon came into conflict with West Indian colonial society. In 1948, Lamming describes a Trinidadian 'Dutch party', with the poet on one side, brooding on the 'permanent disease of society', and the 'glittering chatter' of the party on the other.[1] The West Indies in Lamming's poetry is a spiritually sterile prison for the creative spirit: 'islands cramped with disease no economy can cure'. In the short story 'Birds of a Feather', his young protagonist dreams of a 'way of escape'.[2] The colonial politics of the time are seen as an exercise in futility:

> Contestant and onlooker,
> The leading and the led fusing danger and delight
> In an original pattern, an automatic violence.[3]

In a later poem, Lamming speaks of retreating from 'the multitude's monotonous cry/For freedom and politics at the price of blood', to an aesthetic world where the spirit can 'Live every moment in the soul's devouring flame.'[4]

Emigration to England marked a turning point in his attitude towards the West Indies. A black West Indian in an unfriendly city, he discovered not creative freedom, but alienation. His feelings are best expressed in his poem 'Song for Marian', about a concert given in London by the black American Marian Anderson. Her songs awaken him to their common experience as blacks confronting white civilisation:

> Now I venturing from scattered islands
> To rediscover my roots
> Have found an impersonal city
> Where your tales are incredibly true.[5]

His experience in England showed Lamming the need to define himself not only as an artist but as a West Indian. The poems he wrote before beginning work on *In the Castle of My Skin* return to the society he had earlier rejected. 'The Boy and the Sea' celebrates the freedom of boyhood, and 'The Illumined Graves' introduces a central motif of his later work: the living seeking communion and reconciliation with the dead on All Souls' Day:

> To renew the contagion of living,
> So these by similar assertion of love
> Promote their faith in flame,
> Remembering the ceremony of undying souls

With a meek congregation of candles.[6]

In the Castle of My Skin is the best-known of his works and is perhaps the most widely read West Indian novel. It is Lamming's most autobiographical work, covering nine years in the life of G., the novel's artist-hero, from his ninth birthday to his departure for Trinidad. Interwoven with G.'s story is that of his village, which also undergoes dramatic changes during the course of the novel. From the outset, G.'s sensibility is distinct from that of the other villagers. His birthday coincides with a flood which threatens to wash Creighton's village into the sea. The villagers' resistance to the flood is signified by a song taken up from house to house until 'the whole village shook with song on its foundation of water'.[7] But the song has a second purpose: it is started by G.'s mother to suppress the boy's inquiry into his past—this 'always happened when I tried to remember'. His attempt to find out who he is by probing into his family's history poses another threat to the village, since the past, with its story of slavery and oppression, has been buried. Even teachers at the village school know nothing of it and Barbados, the villagers believe, has always been a junior partner of England, 'Little England'—not a subservient colony.

It is not only curiosity which separates G. from the village, but his mother's ambition. Education gradually separates him from his friends like Bob and 'the gang at the corner'. The long poetic chapter describing G.'s day at the beach with his friends opens with a quarrel between G. and Bob, and the chapter is concerned mainly with change, as the boys perceive it through games, stories and symbols. 'You never know as you yourself say,' says Boy Blue, 'when something go off pop in yuh head an' you ain't the same man you think you wus.'

G.'s transition to manhood coincides with fundamental changes in village life. In the opening chapters of *In the Castle of My Skin* the village is united by common values, a deep attachment to the land and faith in the landlord, the 'Great'. Lamming shows, in his ironic handling of the school inspection scene, that their faith is based on illusions about England and ignorance of the slave past; yet he also shows, through the periodic appearances of Ma and Pa, the quiet stability and continuity of peasant consciousness.

Chapter 5 is pivotal. It contrasts the timeless patterns of their lives, as the villagers gather around the pastry cart to gossip and quarrel, with a group of working men watching the clock, waiting to hear from Mr Slime whether they are to go on strike against a shipping firm owned by the landlord. The strike meshes with others going on throughout the West Indies, and begins a chain reaction of events culminating in the village's invasion by a band of city workers intent on killing the landlord. A new political power, represented by the trade union leader Mr Slime, threatens to assume the landlord's position.

When G. reappears in the novel he is on the verge of leaving for Trinidad. In an act of cleansing for a new life ahead, he wades into the sea. His imagination focuses on a pebble he had hidden earlier; its disappearance embodies for him the qualities of village life from which he has become irrevocably separated by his high school education. Though a part of his sensibility remains in the village, 'It was as though my roots had been snapped from the centre of what I knew best.' The uprooting of the village itself begins, as the land is sold to outsiders, middle-class men with legal deeds laying claim to the estate that Mr Creighton had sold them through Slime's company. Like Slime himself, they are rootless men, 'intransit passengers', who want to own property. For the villagers, whose life is ruled by almost feudal customs, the law is irrelevant, but in the new capitalist economic and social system which Slime and his colleagues are introducing into the island, land has become a commodity. Change has accumulated throughout the novel, but the dispossession of the villagers happens in the novel's penultimate chapter when the three central village characters are uprooted: first, the shoemaker, who had earlier defended change but believed himself uninvolved in the outcome; next, Mr Foster, who at the opening of the novel had refused to leave his home during the flood; and finally Pa. G. and the village undergo a similar experience of displacement and breaking with the past, though for different reasons. Both events, G.'s departure and the destruction of the semi-feudal system of

Creighton's village, are inevitable, but G., as a writer forced to leave the source of his creativity, is divided in his attitude toward them.

In the Castle of My Skin ends the evening before G.'s departure. His new maturity is suggested by his use of a diary to record his thoughts and by an ironic, affectionate distance from his formerly dominating mother. Yet he is still far from discovering the identity he had sought nine years earlier, and the ideas of his boyhood friend Trumper about black pride and political struggle are almost incomprehensible to him. He departs for Trinidad as bewildered and rootless as the society he leaves behind. Although the artist–hero plays a less important role in Lamming's subsequent novels, his quest for his roots remains a recurrent and significant part of the struggle of West Indian society for freedom.

Lamming's second novel, *The Emigrants* (1954), begins where the earlier book leaves off. 'Those four years in Trinidad', recalls the novel's first-person narrator, 'seemed nothing more than an extension of what had gone before, but for this important difference. I had known a greater personal freedom.'[8] As Lamming's poetry suggests, personal freedom soon became less important than the spiritual limitations of a colonial society, and on his birthday the narrator becomes aware of the need for something more: 'to get out . . . go elsewhere . . . start all over again'. Educated to believe in England's cultural superiority, he chooses the Mother Country as his natural destination.

But the artist–narrator plays a minor role in the novel; he soon merges into Collis, a young poet whose experience cannot easily be separated from that of the other emigrants. 'We're all in flight,' he thinks, 'and yet as Tornado says we haven't killed. We haven't stolen.' Lamming's concern in the novel is less with personal experience than with the powerful myth of colonialism that draws West Indians to emigrate to England. 'This *myth*,' Lamming writes in his book of essays *The Pleasures of Exile* (1960), 'begins in the West Indian from the earliest stages of his education. . . . It begins with the fact of England's supremacy in taste and judgement: a fact which can only have meaning and weight by a calculated cutting down to size of all non-England. The first to be cut down is the colonial himself.'[9]

During the long first section of the novel, the emigrants discuss their reasons for emigrating; each shares Collis's desire to begin again. As England—which Tornado calls 'the land of the enemy'—nears, the emigrants draw closer together and seek a basis for West Indian unity. But their tenuous shipboard nationalism is never stronger than the myth of England, for colonials 'whose only certain knowledge said that to be in England was all that mattered'. Once they land, the emigrants disperse and the leisurely movement of the voyage gives way to a series of episodes.

Despite their fragmentary effect, the episodes are carefully plotted to show the inevitable disintegration of the emigrants' unity and their faith in England. At first they maintain a degree of contact in barber and hairdressing shops and their hostel, although the subterranean, shabby nature of these gathering places emphasises exclusion from English life. Their windows look out from basement level rooms through bars onto walls which proclaim the compulsive privacy of English life. Of the twenty-one scenes which follow their arrival in England, only two occur outside, in contrast to *In the Castle of My Skin*, where most of the action takes place in backyards, on street corners or beaches, where the villagers are free to move about. Later, the emigrants are found in even smaller rooms and flats, 'alone, circumscribed by the night and the neutral staring walls'. Even the middle-class emigrants, though enjoying a more comfortable existence, live amidst fear and intrigue. Their dilemma is typified by Dickson, a respectable schoolteacher from Barbados, who forms a liaison with an Englishwoman, and then discovers that she is curious about him only as a stereotyped sexual object, the black male. The episode shatters his concept of himself as a 'black Englishman'. In various ways, each of the emigrants undergoes a similar experience of disillusionment and loss of identity, including Collis, whose ambitions for a writing career are reduced to doing liner notes for record albums. He makes his living as a factory worker, at which he is unlucky and incompetent. His alienation from people is expressed in a tendency to see them as objects.

A similar division from community affects the Governor, who plays the role of the political leader, a recurrent figure in Lamming's fiction. His main quality is a determination to control events, but after arrival in England his control of situations slips away and he loses all sense of responsibility to his people. By the end of *The Emigrants*, both the Governor and Collis have lost all relation to the society in which they should have functioned. 'I have no people,' Collis says; and indeed his fellow emigrants no longer exist as a community after emigration has exposed the colonial illusions about the Mother Country upon which their identity had been based. For Lamming, emigration is a phase of discovery that leads back to the West Indies and the rejuvenation of the spiritually moribund society the emigrants fled. In his next two novels, his characters struggle to create what Tornado—in exile in London—could only dream of: 'some new land where we can find peace . . . a place where they can be without making up false pictures 'bout other places'.

In the four years before the publication of his third novel, *Of Age and Innocence* (1958), Lamming travelled widely in Europe, the United States and the Caribbean. His travels broadened his artistic concerns. In his address to the First Congress of Negro Writers and Artists in Paris in 1956, he argued that the black colonial experience of being partly defined in terms of racial and cultural stereotypes, confronting the white 'Other' in conditions that make understanding impossible, is an example of a contemporary human condition. 'It is . . . the universal sense of separation and abandonment, frustration and loss, and, above [all] else, of some direct inner experience of something missing.'[10] Nationalism is one form of the human effort to overcome the separation between men; another is the desire to participate in a close fraternity with other individuals. In Lamming's earlier novels, his English characters had been mostly unsympathetic; in *Of Age and Innocence* his four English visitors to San Cristobal play an important role in extending the novel's themes.

The novel is set on Lamming's fictional island of San Cristobal. With its multiracial population, and place names and geographic features drawn from throughout the Caribbean,

San Cristobal is a Caribbean microcosm. *Of Age and Innocence* was published in the year the short-lived West Indies Federation came into existence, and is prophetic in its treatment of the failure of Isaac Shephard's multiracial People's Communal Movement. While it affirms the yearning of West Indians for unity and freedom, it is also a critique of independence movements and their leaders.

Despite their ideals of harmony, Shephard and his allies Singh and Lee turn toward violence against colonialism, without realising the extent to which their actions are dictated by the historical circumstances against which they are struggling. The drift towards violence begins after a conference in which the three leaders discuss meeting with the English Governor about a threatened strike. The response of each man is shaped by his racial experience and upbringing. Shephard, the descendant of slaves and most 'colonised' psychologically of the three, is indecisive. As Lamming has pointed out in a separate discussion of Shephard, he never overcomes the division within himself between his commitment to nationalism and his need to 'achieve the approval and ultimate embrace of a spiritual authority which is dedicated to his perpetual self-imprisonment'.[11] Through Shephard, Lamming offers a brilliant comment on the nature of West Indian political leadership, with its roots in religious demagogy. His analysis of Shephard's character reaches back to reveal a lifetime of struggle for recognition against petty humiliations, and an obsession with absolute power beginning from his competition with his aggressive father, a preacher. Neither Singh's nor Lee's ancestors had been victims of slavery, and Singh's uncompromising stance reflects the attitude of one who has no doubts about his identity: 'The point is,' he says, 'that we must never trust them. That is like a golden rule in this movement.'

The issue of the meeting is still in balance when it is interrupted by the arrival of Bill Butterfield. The leaders' fatal weakness is revealed by their hostility towards Bill, 'a perfect example of teamwork in ill-will'. Unable to trust any Englishman—though in fact Bill has come to warn of a plot against Shephard's life—they find themselves distrustful of one another. Challenged to prove their unity, they give way to

Singh's extreme position. But their distrust remains: 'From now on I must be careful with Singh', thinks Shephard, while Singh wonders if Shephard has been collaborating with 'the enemy'.

Shephard, Singh and Lee have in common a failure to escape from the conditions history has imposed upon them. The future ideal of community is represented instead by the four boys of the Secret Society, who are inspired by a legend of the island's primordial harmony and spirit of resistance, the Tribe Boys. Like the Guyanese novelist Wilson Harris, Lamming reaches back to the aboriginal past for a model of community in which West Indian consciousness has its roots. *Of Age and Innocence* is a clear statement of Lamming's conviction that political change must be accompanied by a profound change in outlook: 'In order to change [his] way of seeing,' he writes in *The Pleasures of Exile*, 'the West Indian must change the very structure, the very basis of his values.'[12] Failure to do so leads to the sort of violence and murder in which the novel ends, initiated by the madhouse fire. The fire's 'red wall . . . transparent and impenetrable' parallels the vengeful wall of hostility the leaders create.

Interwoven with the public political drama is a private one, the story of four English visitors to San Cristobal who have only a tangential involvement in the political struggle. They too have an ideal of community, a 'little world, made by four people' in the tranquillity of the Balearic Islands. But in the turbulent milieu of San Cristobal, each undergoes a crisis of identity which divides him from the others. England, for the quartet, is the Old World of established self-concepts and relationships; San Cristobal is a New World, an abrupt break with the settled past and a confrontation with the realities of existence. Penelope Butterfield's concept of herself is jeopardised when she discovers her lesbian desire for Marcia and is afraid of revealing it to the others. She becomes isolated from them by her awareness of the stigma she bears. 'The Negro, the homosexual, the Jew, the worker', she realises, suffer a similar stigma, and the realisation enables her to understand the motives behind Shephard's rebellion.

Mark Kennedy's cold distance from his girlfriend

Marcia—leading to her insanity and death in the madhouse fire—is part of a similar existential detachment from the world. Mark is an exile and drifter, like G. and Collis; he has lived away from San Cristobal for twenty years. He returns there with a vague sense of searching for his origins. After drifting apart from his friends he briefly joins Shephard's movement and gives a speech at a party rally expressing his deep yearning for identification with the land. But he remains unable to escape his alienation or, as a biographer, to make a pattern out of the fragments of West Indian history.

While Mark's failure is in part a comment on the continued inability of the colonised West Indian intellectual to return to his roots, the story of the four English visitors illustrates the contemporary problem of human isolation and lack of communication that Lamming had explored in his 1956 address. *Of Age and Innocence* continues Lamming's concern with the private search for identity—focused on the problem of understanding between men and women—but expands it into a universal quest.

The novel ends with San Cristobal's occupation by British troops. When *Season of Adventure* (1960) opens, the island has become independent, but power is in the hands of a new indigenous ruling elite, shaped by colonialism and divorced from the working and peasant masses. As *Of Age and Innocence* proved prophetic of the failure of the West Indies Federation, *Season of Adventure* anticipates the fall of the 'First Republic', a society controlled by an elite with alien values.

The focus of contention between the elite and the masses in the novel is the Ceremony of the Souls, an African retention. In the vodun ceremonies he witnessed in Haiti in 1956, Lamming found a suitable metaphor for communication between the present and a buried past. The ceremonies were also a reminder of an African and slave past that middle-class West Indians would prefer to forget. In San Cristobal, the Ceremony is practised only by those living in wretched areas like Forest Reserve, who are also the guardians of the steel bands, symbols of the survival and continuity of West Indian peasant consciousness. The Ceremony of the Souls at the *tonelle*, the canopied space where vodun ceremonies take place, is the route which Fola, the novel's middle-class mulatto heroine, follows back to her roots. Her quest leads not back to Africa but to the common folk of the West Indies in whom the society's essential values survive. During the Ceremony of the Souls that she witnesses at the beginning of the novel, Fola is shocked into an awareness of a part of herself, 'her forgotten self',[13] that her upbringing has concealed. Her subsequent quest for her father forms the narrative thread of *Season of Adventure*. It overlaps with conflict between the inhabitants of Forest Reserve and the elite, who attempt to suppress the steel bands and the *tonelle*.

A mediator between the two levels of society appears in the painter, Chiki, who had been separated from his origins in Forest Reserve by his education, but who has returned to live there. Like the other artist figures in Lamming's novels he is plagued by a loss of creativity, but nevertheless plays an important role as teacher in relation to several characters. Chiki persuades his friend Powell to see the 'gift' of independence as another form of enslavement, he inspires the drummer Gort, and leads Fola through her 'backward glance' into an understanding of her past, painting a portrait of her father—who could be either African or European in origin—as they imagine him.

The portrait becomes in turn the link between Fola's private quest for her father and the political conflicts in San Cristobal. Fola's personality undergoes a split between the Fola who had been formed and imprisoned by alien middle-class values and another self, Fola 'and other than, outside and other than', whose reality must be discovered through a re-examination of her personal past and the secret of her parentage. When Vice-President Raymond is assassinated, Fola chooses to side with Forest Reserve against her own class. Wading through water, like a dead soul in the Ceremony seeking release from its imprisonment, Fola steps into the Reserve and declares it was her father—represented by the portrait—who had murdered him. Her announcement throws the Republic into disarray, as people are forced to see in the appearance of this mythical ancestor the mirror of their own abandoned past. As Fola's stepfather and the rest of the San Cristobal elite prepare to use the assassination as an excuse for wiping out the steel bands and *tonelle*, steelbandsmen from throughout the island gather under Gort's leadership to play the forbidden drums. The First Republic falls, to be replaced by the Second, led by Kofi James-Williams Baako.

Baako's name suggests a synthesis of European and African, but he speaks only vaguely of possibilities for the future. If the novel concludes on a more hopeful note than Lamming's earlier fiction, it is clear that the process of renewal initiated by Fola's quest has only begun. *Season of Adventure* takes the historical and political development of the West Indies up to the present stage—the stage of the 'First Republic' dominated by a Europeanised elite without a clear vision of a truly West Indian future—and suggests the potential source of renewal in the experience of the common man, 'the very soil from which our consciousness springs'.[14] The danger of failure is suggested by the fact that Powell, the Vice-President's murderer whose lessons from Chiki had been corrupted into fanaticism, remains at large.

Thus Lamming's first four novels trace the evolution of West Indian society from the disintegration of a tradition-bound colonial society through the dispersal of the displaced West Indians by emigration to the struggle for a still-unrealised form of community. At that time, Lamming later commented, there was 'no further point for me to go without in a sense going beyond what had actually happened in the society'.[15] Over a decade separated the publication of *Season of Adventure* from that of *Natives of My Person* (1972), in many ways the culmination of Lamming's work. Lamming has described the novel as 'a way of going forward by making a complete return to the beginnings; it's actually the whole etiology of *In the Castle of My Skin*, *The Emigrants* and *Season of Adventure*. I think it might be possible to find in *Natives of My Person* elements, parallels and so forth in each of the preceding volumes.'[16]

The novel returns to the roots of Caribbean colonialism, gathering four centuries of history into a span of six months, the time it takes the *Reconnaissance* to complete two legs of the triangular route from Europe to the Guinea Coast and thence to the West Indies. Moving freely forward and backward in time, Lamming establishes the essential pattern of West Indian history, from the subjugation and looting of its Indian civilisations to the terrifying monstrosities of slavery, to the exploitation of the islands under various forms of European colonialism.

Europeans believe that non-Europeans lack humanity and use this belief to justify their exploitation. To the ship's carpenter, Pierre, and his fellows, Africans are less than human: they go 'naked everywhere like beasts' and are possessed of unusual sexual powers.[17] Pierre's view, and indeed much of the section of the novel describing the Guinea Coast, is adapted from Hakluyt's *Voyages*. As early as 1960, when he was writing *The Pleasures of Exile*, Lamming's imagination had been fired by Hakluyt's narratives, as a record of the period when England's experiment in colonisation was beginning. In the attitude of Hakluyt's adventurers toward Carib Indian and African slave he discovered the roots of an outlook which continues to affect coloniser and colonised alike. 'The slave whose skin suggests the savaged deformity of his nature becomes identical with the Carib Indian who feeds on human flesh . . . both seen as the wild fruits of Nature, share equally that spirit of revolt which Prospero by sword or Language is determined to conquer.'[18] Like Hakluyt's Englishmen, both the Commandant in his persecution of the Tribes and the crew in their treatment of African slaves are morally blind and cannot comprehend the stubborn 'spirit of revolt' of the oppressed.

Lamming's Lime Stone represents England and Europe, as its House of Trade and Justice combines in a single entity the whole spirit and thrust of colonialism over several centuries. The slave trade has brought both wealth and moral corruption to the Kingdom, symbolised by the Severn asylum, the hell-like repository of the nation's ills. The Commandant, a philosopher-adventurer like Shakespeare's Prospero, envisages a new society in San Cristobal, cleansed of the Kingdom's corruption. But he is himself a veteran of the extermination of the Tribes, and his vision of a New World society is based on the tainted model of the Old.

The origin of the Commandant's obsession lies in his relation to his lover, the Lady of the House, who had abandoned him after he had repeatedly broken his promise not to go to sea again in pursuit of imperial goals. The expedition is intended to establish a new society where he and the Lady can be reunited. The officers of the *Reconnaissance* have different reasons for joining the illegal expedition, but share in a sense of the insecurity of their power and fear of the 'men below'. Each—with the exception of Priest and Pinteados—has in his background a woman he has wronged in pursuing his private obsessions. The officers' failure to show humanity and compassion towards their women—who have seen beyond their 'purity of intention' into their innermost anxieties and weaknesses—is the ultimate cause of the expedition's failure. When Surgeon and Steward learn of the Commandant's intention to reunite them with their wives in San Cristobal, they murder the Commandant and are themselves murdered by the cabin boy Sasha.

The officers' inhumanity towards the women is, Lamming has said elsewhere, symptomatic of the 'pervasive corruption of the society in which they lived',[19] a society built on the exploitation and dehumanisation of others. But their failure is given a wider significance by Pinteados, the pilot and architect of the expedition. 'To feel authority over the women! That was enough for them. But to commit themselves fully to what they felt authority over. That they could never do. Such power they were afraid of.' Pinteados's remark intersects with the underlying allegorical themes of the novel, in which the Commandant is a type of the early independence leaders in the West Indies, men like Cipriani, Manley and Bustamante, whose goal of independence was tempered by their admiration for England and commitment to her economic system. The Commandant and his group of officers representing the middle-class inheritors of power in ex-colonial territories fail to escape from the colonial legacy of conquest, command and exploitation, as their relation to the women testifies.

The determination of the men, under Baptiste, in alliance with the painter Ivan, to continue the expedition without the officers may be seen as a statement of the role of the common man in shaping a future West Indian society. Like Lamming's other novels, *Natives of My Person* ends, however, without a conclusive resolution. The women wait alone and isolated in a cave on San Cristobal, the 'future they must learn', as the Lady of the House observes. *Natives of My Person* draws together the complex themes of Lamming's previous work: his concern with the quest for identity and the enduring myth of colonialism, and with the problem of human misunderstanding as a reflection of the distortions in relationships created by colonialism.

The novel also marks Lamming's most significant stylistic achievement. For Lamming, style is more than a manner of writing: it is an expression of artistic identity. 'Nothing matters more than a man's discovery of his *style*,' he writes in a tribute to the late Edgar Mittelholzer, 'a discovery which is also part of his own creation, and style—not a style—but *style* as the aura and essence, the recognised example of being in which and out of which a man's life assumes its shape.'[20] In his first two novels, his style is often imitative of other writers, notably James Joyce, though strongly influenced by the rhythms and idioms of West Indian speech. Lamming's style, his creation of characters, events and even landscapes, is characteristically concerned with underlying meanings, expressed through highly symbolic descriptions. An allegorical level is present in all his fiction, in characters like Ma and Pa in *In the Castle of My Skin*, for example, who embody the historical will of their community, or in the symbolic descriptions of the boys' day at the beach.

Lamming's use of language as a means of symbolic exploration and interpretation is perhaps the most distinctive stylistic feature of his work, but in *Of Age and Innocence* and *Season of Adventure* it too often overwhelms the narrative. Descriptions of the weather or the landscape are invariably used to reinforce the mood of an episode or as a comment on events, and while the results are often successful and striking, the technique is so insistent that it becomes difficult to read such dense passages with real attention.

Lamming's concept of the artist as teacher has led him toward the adoption of an entirely allegorical mode in his most recent novels, *Natives of My Person* and *Water With Berries*. In

Natives of My Person, the metaphor of the journey imparts a new structural control to Lamming's work. The novel's structure enables him to put to work the whole range of his stylistic abilities as a novelist, combining concrete and abstract, realistic and fabulous, since allegory allows a separation of the two levels and suggests at the same time a synthesis between them. An advantage of allegory, for a writer with Lamming's political ideals and concept of the artist as teacher, is that once the allegorical meaning has been established it does not have to be repeatedly returned to and insisted upon in every scene and event.

Water With Berries (1971) was written after *Natives of My Person*, though published almost simultaneously.[21] In the broad line of development of Lamming's work from realism towards an allegorical form based on West Indian history, the novel appears a digression, returning to the life of West Indian exiles in London dealt with in *The Emigrants*. The novel's main concern, however, is with creative sterility and the artist's relation to English society, a problem which may have been especially urgent for Lamming during the long process of writing *Natives of My Person*.

On a 'realistic' level, *Water With Berries* is the story of three impoverished artists from San Cristobal living in London. During the two weeks the narrative covers, the West Indian past they had rejected encroaches on their private, routine worlds. Roger, a musician of East Indian descent, repudiates his pregnant wife Nicole, out of an unconscious fear of racial mixing, arising from his childhood horror at the creolised 'impurity' of West Indian society. The actor Derek is driven by his Christian upbringing to reveal Roger's accusations of infidelity to Nicole; his idealism ends in her suicide. And Teeton, a painter, learns that his wife has committed suicide in San Cristobal. He had abandoned her after she became the wife of the American ambassador in order to secure Teeton's release from prison after an uprising.

The suicides of Randa and Nicole mark the end of the isolated, aesthetic lives the three had created for themselves. In their quest for artistic freedom they had betrayed the love of women for whom self-sacrifice was the only virtue. The

suicides assume a wider significance, however, on an allegori-
cal level, with the introduction of motifs from Shakespeare's
The Tempest, which Lamming treats in his non-fiction work,
The Pleasures of Exile, as an allegory of colonialism.

In *Water With Berries*, Shakespeare's Prospero is dead, but
his widow is represented by the Old Dowager, who as a
survivor of the spirit of colonialism exerts a subtle, mothering
control over her colonial tenant, Teeton. Shakespeare's Miranda is resurrected both as Randa, Teeton's wife, and as Myra, a
prostitute he meets on the heath. Myra had been brutally
ravaged by her father's servants in San Cristobal, but makes no
connection between her fate and her father's demonic treatment of his servants. Like the Old Dowager, who was deserted
by him, Myra still admires her philosopher-father: 'Never
showed any interest in personal fortunes,' she recalls. 'No taste
at all for possession. Must have been a saint.'[22] Ironically, the
three artists share a similar indifference to the materialism of
the 'social herd' and a commitment to the purity of art as a style
of life. Myra's fate is thus linked to Randa's and Nicole's, as
Caliban's is to Prospero's, by a common relation to what
Fernando calls the 'curse' of colonialism. Fernando, the Old
Dowager's lover and Myra's true father, alone realises that
Myra's rape had been the result of Prospero's 'experiment in
ruling over your kind', as he tells Teeton. But the knowledge
has driven him mad; he is convinced that the curse will last
until 'one of us dies'. The novel indeed ends with murder,
arson and rape as the artificial harmony between the English
and the West Indian immigrants disintegrates.

Lamming's use of *The Tempest* provides a framework for his
argument that the experiences of slavery and colonialism have
left a lasting mark on coloniser and colonised alike which can
only be exorcised through some collective Ceremony of the
Souls of the sort Teeton envisages on the heath before events
overtake him. 'Sometimes they argue all through the night,' he
tells Myra. 'For hours. The living and the dead. It will go on
until they reach a point of reconciliation. Then you know it's
the end. The end of all complaint from the dead, the end of all
retribution for the living.'

If Teeton's, Roger's and Derek's final acts of violence proceed from a will to freedom and a desire to escape from the false 'safety' of their refuge in London, they also renew the pattern of violence begun by Prospero's conquest and enslavement of Caliban. Derek's assault on the actress on stage duplicates Caliban's attack on Miranda, as Roger's arson parallels Caliban's firing of Prospero's home. It is a blind and tragic striking out in reaction to brutalisation, without the re-examination of the past and the collective Ceremony of the Souls that Lamming believes is necessary if the spirit of Prospero's imperial enterprise is to be finally exorcised. Not surprisingly, for Lamming the Ceremony of the Souls is an imaginative rather than political quest.

Lamming's concern with the function of the imaginative contact with, and purgation of, the past goes back to his poem 'The Illumined Graves', published twenty years earlier, and forward through his methodical treatment of the struggle for independence and decolonisation in his first four novels to his realisation, in *Natives of My Person*, of the process Teeton envisages. *Natives of My Person* is a journey into the souls of both coloniser and colonised by a writer who feels himself part of both worlds, in search of a new, imaginative vision of human community. For Lamming, political change in the Caribbean must be accompanied by a profound psychic transformation which it is the artist's responsibility to articulate 'at the deepest levels of our reflective self-consciousness'. The imaginative journey into the psyche, 'the symbolic drama, the drama of redemption, the drama of cleansing for a commitment towards the future',[23] is as vital to Lamming's creative purpose as the drama of political struggle and change. Lamming's fiction has been a means of exploration into the self, and an important argument for the necessity of art and the imagination in shaping a new vision of human freedom and Caribbean unity.

10 Derek Walcott *by Mervyn Morris*

While often concerned to define his identification with a specific region or a particular historical condition, Derek Walcott has always, in theory and in practice, been willing to draw on the total heritage available to him as an alert and enquiring human being. He was born in Castries, St Lucia, on 23 January 1930, and he is racially mixed: 'Mongrel as I am,' he has written, 'something prickles in me when I see the word Ashanti as with the word Warwickshire, both separately intimating my grandfathers' roots, both baptising this neither proud nor ashamed bastard, this hybrid, this West Indian.'[1] But as a writer he has a wider ancestry than that; the whole world is his family, and he has argued that 'maturity is the assimilation of the features of every ancestor.'[2]

Walcott has described his background as 'a genteel, self-denying Methodist poverty'.[3] His father died when Derek and his twin brother Roderick were only one. Their mother, who was headmistress of a Methodist infant school, worked hard to keep them at college, by taking in sewing. As is frequently revealed in 'Leaving School', 'What the Twilight Says: An Overture', 'Meanings' and *Another Life* (1973),[4] Walcott had a thorough grounding in European history, art and literature, and was also in contact with the black Africa-based culture of the St Lucian majority. He was not European; and circumstances kept him somewhat apart from the majority of St Lucians: they were black, he was part-white; they were overwhelmingly Catholic, he was Methodist; and he was a lover of English on an island where the mass of the people speak a

144

French patois.

'Years ago, watching them, and suffering as you watched, you preferred silently the charity of a language which they could not speak, until your suffering, like the language, felt superior, estranged.'[5] Walcott often returns to the search for a language, a form, that will seem entirely appropriate. 'The West Indian poet', he wrote in 1965, 'suspects the raw spontaneity of dialect as being richer in expression, but is not willing to sacrifice the syntactical power of English. Naturally enough, where the conflict is realized the poetry is strongest. That dramatic ambivalence is part of what it means to be a West Indian now.'[6]

For most of his career Walcott has written both in dialect and in standard English. Sometimes a fusion of the two serves to suggest 'that dramatic ambivalence', as in these lines from *Another Life*:

> But I tired of your whining, grandfather,
> in the whispers of marsh grass,
> I tired of your groans, grandfather,
> in the deep ground bass of the combers.

Here the standard English past preterite 'I tired' is also a dialect present indicative for 'I am tired': as the persona is addressing a white grandfather (whose ancestral language is English) and a black grandfather (whose descendants speak dialect, mostly) the tension is particularly appropriate.

As in the poetry, so too in the plays. Walcott will draw on anything, and in discussion of his own work is often conscious of his attempt to fuse elements drawn from differing sources. 'I am a kind of split writer: I have one tradition inside me going one way, and another tradition going another. The mimetic, the narrative, and dance element is strong on one side, and the literary, the classical tradition is strong on the other.' With the Trinidad Theatre Workshop which he formed in 1959 (and left in 1976) he tried to create 'a theatre where someone can do Shakespeare or sing Calypso with equal conviction'.[7]

Walcott has been consistently hostile to any force which seeks to limit his creativity or restrict access to anything which might feed it. 'Most black writers', he has said, 'cripple themselves by their separatism. You can't be a poet and believe in the division of man.'[8] Although so much of his own writing explores and dramatises divisions within himself, the thrust is usually towards reconciliation, acceptance, compassion. Aware of history and the manifold cruelties it records, he has in recent years sought ways to avoid its uncreative traps. He has argued that 'The truly tough aesthetic of the New World neither explains nor forgives history. It refuses to recognize it as a creative or culpable force.' He finds in poets such as Neruda, Césaire and Perse an 'awe of the numinous', the 'elemental privilege of naming the new world which annihilates history . . . They reject ethnic ancestry for faith in elemental man.'[9]

In a Green Night (London, 1962), subtitled 'Poems 1948–1960', includes versions of six poems from Walcott's first book, *25 Poems* (Bridgetown, 1949), and one from *Poems* (Kingston, 1952), two volumes which, like *Epitaph for the Young* (Bridgetown, 1949), were privately published. *In a Green Night* was followed by *Selected Poems* (New York, 1964) which has a selection from *In a Green Night* and a number of new poems. Except for 'Origins' which does not reappear, revised versions of these new poems are included in *The Castaway* (London, 1965). *The Gulf* (New York, 1970) offers corrected texts of *The Gulf* (London, 1969) and those poems from *The Castaway* not already published in *Selected Poems*. *Another Life* (1973) and *Sea Grapes* (1976) have also appeared.[10]

25 Poems and *Epitaph for the Young* are impressive work from a young man of nineteen, though the anguish sometimes seems over-earnest, the wit facetious. Like his radio play, *Harry Dernier* (Bridgetown, 1951), these books display not only Walcott's talent but also his reading. Eliot, Pound, Dylan Thomas, Auden are among the overwhelming influences.

'Of course you will soon shed your influences.'[11] Walcott tends not to; he absorbs them instead. In 'The Muse of History' he has written: 'Fear of imitation obsesses minor poets. . . . We know that the great poets have no wish to be different, no time to be original, that their originality emerges only when they have absorbed all the poetry which they have read, entire, that their first work appears to be the accumulation of other people's trash but that they become bonfires.'[12] In the later Walcott, from *The Castaway* on, it is difficult to make a distinction between influence and allusion. Not so in the earlier books, where the poet is less confident in voice, trying on the manner of others. 'Other men's voices,/other men's lives and lines.'[13]

Even in *In a Green Night* there are assured achievements—'A Letter from Brooklyn', for example, which seems almost casually unaware of itself.

> 'I am Mable Rawlins,' she writes, 'and know
> both your parents;'
> He is dead, Miss Rawlins, but God bless your tense:
> 'Your father was a dutiful, honest,
> Faithful and useful person.'
> For such plain praise what fame is recompense?

Some of the early poems are in dialect or have notable dialect elements. But, dedicated to 'purifying the language of the tribe', Walcott seems at this stage not yet to trust the dialect; he does not merely select, he tends conspicuously to modify. Poems such as 'Parang' and 'Pocomania' are fruitful experiments, moving the dialect noticeably towards standard English. 'Chapter V' and 'Chapter VI' of 'Tales of the Islands' are the outstanding achievements, more fully recognised when compared with earlier versions published in *Bim* 26. But we are a long way yet from the confidence that will allow Walcott to publish in *Sea Grapes*:

> O so you is Walcott?
> You is Roddy brother?
> Teacher Alix son?

It is many years before 'The Schooner, Flight' where dialect moves with ease and seriousness:

> My first friend was the sea. Now, is my last.
> I stop talking now.[14]

In *The Castaway* Walcott begins to try on a series of related masks: Crusoe, Friday, Adam, in particular. The dominant concerns are isolation, estrangement from society, hunger for human contact; separation from other persons, from other races, from history, from God. The title suggests William Cowper's poem of that name; there the castaway 'Of friends, of hope, of all bereft ... wag'd with death a lasting strife,/Supported by despair of life.' The epigraph to 'Crusoe's Journal' might well have been applied to the volume as a whole; taken from *Robinson Crusoe*, it begins: 'I looked now upon the world as a thing remote, which I had nothing to do with, no expectation from, and indeed no desires about.'

In isolation there may be greater imaginative activity and increased awareness of the natural world. 'If I listen I can hear the polyp build,/The silence thwanged by two waves of the sea./Cracking a sea-louse, I make thunder split.' The castaway may make something out of 'nothing'; like the old poet imagined in *Another Life*, 'facing the wind/and nothing, which is,/the loud world in his mind'.

A number of poems in *The Castaway* and *The Gulf* are concerned with the poet's vocation and craft. The concern is apparent in, for example: 'The Flock', 'A Tropical Bestiary', 'Crusoe's Journal', 'Crusoe's Island', 'Codicil' (*The Castaway*); 'Ebb', 'Metamorphoses', 'Mass Man', 'Homage to Edward Thomas', 'Guyana', 'The River', 'Star', 'Nearing Forty', 'Hic Jacet' (*Gulf*). Sometimes the effort is to establish a tension between surface plainness and actual complexity: in 'A Tropical Bestiary' the sea crab is envied, 'obliquity burrowing to surface/from hot plain sand'; and the tarpon provokes the question:

> Can such complexity of shape,
> such bulk, terror and fury fit
> in a design so innocent?

Sometimes the movement is towards 'the style past metaphor' ('Nearing Forty'), 'the passion of/plain day' ('Star'), towards acceptance of the ordinary for itself: 'Everything IS' ('A Map of Europe'); 'there's terror enough in the habitual,/miracle enough in the familiar' ('Ebb'); 'All styles yearn to be plain/as life' ('The Gulf'). Sometimes the emphasis is on the transforming power of the imagination, of an extraordinary receptivity which may approach transcendence, as in 'Metamorphoses' and 'Guyana': 'He was a flower,/weightless. He would float down' ('Guyana IV: The Falls').

Another recurring concern is with the relationship between black people and white, colonisers and the colonised. As in 'Ruins of a Great House' and 'A Far Cry from Africa', Walcott sometimes identifies with both sides—in 'Crusoe's Journal', for example. Of Crusoe/Defoe we are told:

> like Christofer he bears
> in speech mnemonic as a missionary's
>   the Word to savages,
> its shape an earthen, water-bearing vessel's
>   whose sprinkling alters us
> into good Fridays who recite His praise,
>   parroting our master's
> style and voice, we make his language ours,
>   converted cannibals
> we learn with him to eat the flesh of Christ.

The colonial ambivalences are skilfully focused. The spelling 'Christofer' (instead of Christopher) suggests literally 'bearer of Christ' and hints at a connection with the (evil) bearer of light, Lucifer. The 'Word' suggests both the *logos* of St John's Gospel chapter 1 and the beginnings of a literature. 'Savages' is nicely ironic, especially as it leads into 'us' and 'we' (altared/altered); so, of course, is 'good Fridays' which suggests not only 'Good Friday', a significant day of suffering, but also 'good niggers'; so too is the notion of 'converted cannibals' who 'learn . . . to eat the flesh'. In 'His praise' and 'his language' it is quietly suggested that God and the Englishman similarly require reverence, a suggestion reinforced in 'our master's' which primarily applies to Crusoe but also suggests the Master, Christ.

Later in the poem the persona identifies with Crusoe:

> So from this house
> that faces nothing but the sea, his journals
>   assume a household use;
> we learn to shape from them, where nothing was
>   the language of a race.

In a number of poems with subtexts of black–white tension
or conflict, Walcott focuses almost entirely on the blacks. This
is so, for example, in 'The Glory Trumpeter', 'Goats and
Monkeys', 'Laventille', 'God Rest Ye Merry Gentlemen',
'Lines in New England', 'A Change of Skin', 'Elegy', 'Blues'.
Whatever the racial emphases, however, the poems usually
invite compassion, as at the end of 'The Gulf':

> The Gulf shines, dull as lead. The coast of Texas
> glints like a metal rim. I have no home
> as long as summer bubbling to its head
>
> boils for that day when in the Lord God's name
> the coals of fire are heaped upon the head
> of all whose gospel is the whip and flame,
>
> age after age, the uninstructing dead.

The 'coals of fire' are from Romans 12:19–21 which recom-
mends that vengeance be left to the Lord and advises kindness
to the enemy, 'for in so doing thou shalt heap coals of fire on his
head'. The whip and flame suggest both white hatred and
black: the slave-master's whip, the flame for the branding iron,
and the slave's preoccupation with remembered suffering, as
well as the fires lit by slaves in rebellion or by 1960s black
militants in American cities. The weary movement of the final
line reminds us that violence has a long history; so many have
died, and yet we have not learnt: 'age after age, the uninstruct-
ing dead'.

Another Life began in notebooks as a work of prose, and a
section broke into verse.[15] As we have it now, *Another Life* is an
autobiographical long poem of considerable range and flexibility, efficient in carrying a burden of narrative and factual
information, yet able to soar into lyrical celebration or passion-

ate contumely. Like 'What the Twilight Says' it is alternately self-critical and combative. Our interest is steadily maintained by the progress of the narrative and the many variations in pattern and rhythm; scene and commentary of varying form and significance are cunningly juxtaposed. As is appropriate in a poem preoccupied with visual art and memory, many recurrent images are drawn from painting, photography, cinema.

The book, of twenty-three chapters, is divided into four main parts, each preceded by a strictly relevant epigraph. (The epigraph for Part Two, incompletely printed in the English edition, is from Alejo Carpentier's *The Lost Steps*.) Part One, 'The Divided Child', introduces us to the young artist and his island environment: the landscape, his mother, some village characters presented like figures from classical mythology, impressions of the religious and commercial life, and the colonial education imbuing the values of a whiter world; 'he fell in love with art,/and life began'. In Part Two, 'Homage to Gregorias', art and life are pursued mainly in the company of the towering Gregorias (Dunstan St Omer), painting, drinking, arguing. Guided by a senior painter, Harry Simmons— 'that astigmatic saint'—they vow never to leave the island until they have recorded it in art: 'For no one had yet written of this landscape/that it was possible.' The poet discovers that, unlike Gregorias, his talent is not for painting; 'I lived in a different gift, its element metaphor.' Part Three, 'A Simple Flame', deals mainly with the 1948 fire which burnt down most of the capital, Castries, and with the poet's love and loss of Anna (Andreuille), the schoolgirl introduced at the end of Part One: 'her golden plaits a simple coronet/out of Angelico'. Their love is undermined by the poet's love of art:

> every step increased that subtlety
> which hoped that their two bodies could be made
> one body of immortal metaphor.
> The hand she held already had betrayed
> them by its longing for describing her.

He finds 'life within some novel's leaves/more real' than Anna, 'already chosen/as his doomed heroine'. The lyrical flow contains a disturbing combination of fulfilment, rejection, guilt.

At the end of Part Three, when the poet is leaving St Lucia (to attend university in Jamaica), there is a passage which underlines the basic structure of the poem and redirects our attention to one of its most central concerns, the inter-relation between art and life:

> three lives dissolve in the imagination,
> three loves, art, love and death,
> fade from a mirror clouding with this breath,
> not one is real, they cannot live or die,
> they all exist, they never have existed:
>
> Harry, Dunstan, Andreuille.

'Three lives', three persons whom Walcott has loved; 'three loves', three subjects of which he loves to write: art, love, death, variously associated with the three persons. He is looking into a mirror from close enough to cause it to cloud, and 'breath' suggests the breath of creation. Looking into the clouded mirror the poet sees himself in and through three of the important figures in his life. The technique is cinematic: softened, blurred, 'clouded'; the others 'dissolve' in the imagination, to reveal the poet. In 'reality' they all exist, live, die; yet what Walcott has created are figures of art which 'never have existed', which 'cannot live or die'. Like everything else in the poem, they exist in 'another life'.

In Part Four, 'The Estranging Sea', Harry's death is reported. While the poem partly in celebration of him is being written, the painter has killed himself. 'When I began this work, you were alive,/and with one stroke, you have completed it!' For the bereaved poet, Harry comes to represent 'the fervour and intelligence/of a whole country'. Grief for a dead mentor shades into a poet's passionate denunciation of a society which neglects its artists. As in 'What the Twilight Says' and 'The Muse of History', Walcott attacks some of the black power postures fashionable in the late 1960s and early 1970s. 'Sick of black angst', contemptuous of 'the literature of the factory', he insists on his right to sidestep history, to 'begin again,/from what we have always known, nothing'. The poem comes reverently to rest, asserting the holiness of creation. The last lines of the poem, recalling recurrent imagery of fire and light, address Gregorias, companion in art and drunkenness:

> Gregorias listen, lit
> we were the light of the world!
> We were blest with a virginal, unpainted world
> with Adam's task of giving things their names.

Analysing his failure as a painter, Walcott recognises the importance to him of metaphor:

> in every surface I sought
> the paradoxical flash of an instant
> in which every facet is caught
> in a crystal of ambiguities.

Characteristically, 'a crystal of ambiguities' functions as an example of its meaning: it is ambiguous, and it is lucid: 'crystal' simultaneously suggesting 'many-faceted' and 'transparent'.

In *Sea Grapes* Walcott seems less concerned with ambiguity than in earlier volumes. He seeks, however, so to arrange his words in time and space as to create an aura around them. A line in 'Names' refers to 'the right of every thing to be a noun'. In 'Sainte Lucie' the persona seeks to repossess the nouns of his French patois:

> Come back to me
> my language.
> Come back,
> cacao,
> grigri,
> solitaire,
> ciseau.

At the heart of the collection, the sequence called 'Saint Lucie' includes a poem entirely in French patois, a 'St Lucian *conte* or narrative song, heard on the back of an open truck travelling to Vieuxfort, some years ago', followed by Walcott's version in English. It is as though Walcott is rediscovering his language. He is also, in *Sea Grapes*, searching for simplicities, a word that recurs in the volume.

Many of the poems are reticent; they 'wish to hide'; they move towards silence, another word that recurs. The prevailing mood of the volume is resignation, middle-aged acceptance:

> Now, I require nothing
>
> from poetry, but true feeling,
> no pity, no fame, no healing. Silent wife,
> we can sit watching grey water,
>
> and in a life awash
> with mediocrity and trash
> live rock-like.

The colour grey is invested with new value: 'grey has grown strong to me,/it's no longer neutral.' Elation tends to be muted: 'One could abandon writing/ . . . /and be the greatest reader in the world./At least it requires awe,/which has been lost to our time.'

The most energetic poems tend to be largely curses, such as 'Party Night at the Hilton' and 'The Lost Federation' which abuse politicians, or 'At Last', addressed 'to the exiled novelists'.

Adam in 'The Cloud' has an advantage over God and the serpent: 'Neither could curse or bless.' *Sea Grapes*, like *Another Life*, does both. It blesses, *inter alia*, Jean Miles who had the courage to speak out, Dunstan St Omer and a whole sheaf of writers. Two of the strongest poems which bless are among the best things Walcott has written: 'For the Altar Piece of the Roseau Valley Church, Saint Lucia' (a section from 'Sainte Lucie') and 'Oddjob, a Bull Terrier' which ends:

> in the drizzle that comes to our eyes
> not uttering the loved thing's name,

the silence of the dead,
the silence of the deepest buried love is
the one silence,
and whether we bear it for beast,
for child, for woman, or friend,
it is the one love, it is the same,
and it is blest
deepest by loss
it is blest, it is blest.

In 'The Muse of History' Walcott remarks: 'The great poetry of the New World does not pretend to . . . innocence, its vision is not naive. Rather, like its fruits, its savour is a mixture of the acid and the sweet, the apples of its second Eden have the tartness of experience.' Like *Sea Grapes*.

It is possible to list the names of twenty-eight plays by Derek Walcott, but such a list would include juvenilia, fragments and texts available only in personal collections. Some of the plays which can be read in libraries are of interest mainly for what they tell us of Walcott's developing skills, as he becomes more and more adept at blending varied material and influences. Some, such as *Franklin* (*c* 1960 and 1973), *In a Fine Castle* (1970) and *The Joker of Seville* (1974 and 1975) are of permanent interest in themselves.[16] With limited space, we shall look briefly only at the four plays put together in *Dream on Monkey Mountain and Other Plays*.

In *The Sea at Dauphin* (first performed in 1954) the obvious and acknowledged model is J. M. Synge's *Riders to the Sea*. But Walcott's naturalistic play is grounded in the life and language of St Lucian fishermen and has its own authentic force. Its angry fisherman, Afa, vividly attacks God and the Church: 'Dirt and prayers is Dauphin life, in Dauphin, in Canaries, Micoud. Where they have priest is poverty.' By the end of the play we recognise that Afa does possess kindness, love, compassion; his anger expresses his determination to survive. The sea is both positive and negative. For the fishermen it provides the possibility of daily bread; it offers a life—young Jules, growing to manhood, is determined to go to sea. The sea is a destroyer indeed, but it may also be a comfort. Having lost his wife—her name, Rama, suggesting God—old Hounakin seeks to return to the womb of the sea: 'I did feel to die in Dauphin sea, so I could born.' The godless Afa will fight it, but to him too it may be the final mother: 'The land is hard, this Dauphin land have stone/Where it should have heart. The sea/It have compassion in the end.'

Walcott invests heavily in compassion. Even the Devil in *Ti-Jean and His Brothers* (first performed in 1958) has his moment of human feeling. But the Devil is not permanently humanised, not permanently defeated; and the fight between good and evil will continue. The Devil sends a challenge to a poor mother and her three sons who live in a forest. Anyone human who can make the Devil feel anger, rage and human weakness will be rewarded by the Devil; anyone who fails will be eaten. Gros Jean's brute force and Mi-Jean's book learning are easily outwitted by the Devil's cunning. Ti-Jean's humility and common sense carry him through. Unlike his brothers, he pays attention to his mother's advice; courteous to the animals of the forest, he is assisted by them, and he refuses to play the game by the Devil's rules. He castrates the Devil's goat that will not remain tied; instead of counting cane leaves, he has the Devil's property burnt down. Unlike Gros Jean he uses force intelligently; unlike Mi-Jean he puts his mind to practical use. Their penalty was death (though they live in the memory of others); Ti-Jean's reward is life, not only for himself but also for the Bolom, the unborn. Ti-Jean asks the Bolom: 'Is life you want, child?/You don't see what it bring?' and, like Jules in *The Sea at Dauphin*, the Bolom chooses to enter life:

> I am born, I shall die! I am born, I shall die!
> O the wonder, and pride of it! I shall be man!
> Ti-Jean, my brother!

Is it God or the Devil who grants the Bolom life? Walcott seems to be suggesting a necessary inter-relation between good and evil, between God and the Devil, eternal absolutes. The Bolom, referring to the Devil, says, 'Ask him for my life!' But, with careful ambiguity, the speech continues: 'O God . . .'. Mi-Jean argues: 'I believe in the Devil, yes,/Or so my mother

make me,/And is either that, papa,/Or not believe in God.'
When he has goaded the Devil into revealing his true face,
Ti-Jean finds 'this is like looking/At the blinding gaze of
God.' The Devil, replacing the mask, concedes: 'It is hard to
distinguish us.'

It is important to Walcott's meaning that in folklore Papa
Bois is beneficient: it is not easy to distinguish good from evil,
and evil may disguise itself as good. Gros Jean assumes the
goodness of the Old Man whose cloven hoof has been revealed
to the audience; Mi-Jean, observing the cloven hoof, looks up
'cow foot' in a book and discounts the possibility that he has
already met the Devil: 'he would never expose/His identity so
early.' Mi-Jean, recognising that 'To know evil early, life will
be simpler', does not take it for granted that the Old Man is
what he seems to be; he examines him thoroughly.

Centrally, *Ti-Jean* is an allegory of the contest between good
and evil. It has other levels of meaning.[17] It is, for example, also
a political-historical allegory: the black man contends with the
white oppressor (the Devil disguised as a white planter);
Caribbean black man is seen in three stages of response to
white power, from slave (and other) violent rebellions (Gros
Jean), through the attempt to master the white man's book
learning (Mi-Jean), to the ultimate triumph of the small man
(*petites gens*—little people) combining force and native intelligence. Ti-Jean frees the Bolom of the black or Caribbean
future from thraldom to the white oppressor.

Ti-Jean makes considerable use of St Lucian folklore. Traditionally Papa Bois is an old man who protects the animals of
the forest from hunters. The Bolom, which works for the
Devil, is the foetus of what would have been a first-born child,
stolen just before birth. The refrain '*Bai Diable-là manger un 'ti
mamaille*' ('Give the Devil a child for dinner') occurs in a
traditional masquerade performed in St Lucia at Christmas and
New Year; the devils ('*jabs*', '*diables*') threaten the crowd,
receive small gifts of money and put on short performances in
the street.

In an article Walcott tells of having wanted 'without really
knowing it, to write a softly measured metre whose breathing
was formally articulated yet held the lyrical stresses of dialect

speech.'[18] He explains how he achieved the particular effect of
Ti-Jean's verse and how it is linked in his mind with the
conditions of storytelling in his St Lucian childhood and,
ultimately, with the African art of the storyteller. Typically,
however, he acknowledges a variety of influences—'tradition
and the sweat of others before us, of whatever culture, in the
brotherhood of folk poetry'. He mentions specifically Lorca,
Brecht and the Japanese Noh theatre.

The extraordinary pleasure *Ti-Jean* can give in performance
owes more than a little to the exhilarating music of André
Tanker, 'a composer disciplined enough to be simple'.[19] In the
theatre the success of *Malcochon* (first performed in 1959)
depends as much on music, dance and mime as on the social
concern and philosophical probing of Walcott's text. It is
modelled on the Japanese film *Rashomon*. Walcott has told of
having wanted to reduce the play 'almost to an inarticulateness
of language'. He would have liked to have had the play 'made
up of grunts and sounds which you don't understand, like you
hear at a Japanese film. The words would be reduced to very
primal sounds.' But he found that 'in writing the play another
more literary tradition took over' and he 'made the figures
voluble'.[20]

The main focus of attention in *Malcochon* is a powerful figure
from St Lucian life and legend. The conteur warns the audience
initially: 'Don't believe all you heard or read/Chantal the tiger
cannot dead.' Chantal is a derelict, 'the wood demon' used to
frighten children into behaving properly. Ironically, this is
precisely what Chantal does for adults in the play.

The six who take shelter from the rain are an old man and his
nephew (quarrelling), a young husband and his wife (quarrelling), a deaf mute called Moumou, and Chantal 'the madman,
the tiger out of prison!' It transpires that a white planter, Regis,
has been murdered (but by whom?). The play contrives to
have Chantal, the criminal, turn judge and confessor, forcing
others to stop behaving 'like beasts'. With the help of a
waterfall said to have 'strange powers', he compels them to
know truth, forgiveness, reconciliation. Believing Chantal is
about to kill others, the deaf mute murders him. 'You see', says
Chantal, 'how a man can have a good meaning and do the

wrong thing?'

Chantal prefigures Makak, the hero of *Dream on Monkey Mountain* (first performed in 1967). Through the dream Makak discovers himself, neither God nor beast, only a man, an old black man who knows his name. But in and through the dream Makak has become something far larger; he has grown into a representative figure of myth, a prophet, one of those 'heraldic men'.[21]

A 'Note on Production' echoes Strindberg's Preface to *The Dream Play*: 'The play is a dream, one that exists as much in the minds of its principal characters as in that of its writer, and as such, it is illogical, derivative, contradictory.' Yet *Dream* is by no means incoherent, either in the theatre or when read.

Central to any interpretation of the play is the Apparition. Why does Makak behead her? What is the meaning of that act? In the list of characters she is described as 'the moon, the muse, the white Goddess, a dancer'. What matters most is that the Apparition, 'Lady of Heaven', inspires Makak to a belief in his own dignity. By association with the moon, which emerges at the critical moment, she appears to be the source of Makak's healing power. Yet, at the end of the play, Makak, enthroned, is enquiring of her: 'Who are you? Who are you?' and is persuaded to behead the Apparition. That the main persuaders are Basil, the figure of death, and Corporal Lestrade, who has newly discovered blackness, should make us wonder whether the play is inviting us to approve.

There is an element of ambivalence in the way the Apparition is presented: her song, for example, makes her sound like a siren and therefore dangerous though attractive; as described by Robert Graves, the White Goddess may transform herself into something loathsome or dangerous;[22] in the list of characters in *Dream* the Apparition is called not White Goddess but 'white Goddess', which gives greater emphasis to her colour. Moustique wonders whether what Makak described is really a white woman or a *diablesse*. After the death of Moustique at the end of Part One, 'the figure of a woman with a white face and long black hair of the mask' is seen dancing with assorted symbols of evil. When at the end the Apparition is on trial, Corporal Lestrade proclaims her 'the wife of the devil, the white witch'. But the Corporal can largely be discounted at this point as an anti-white racist, and Moustique by this time has begun to understand Makak's vision—having died once in betraying it—and here, in the trial scene, he is a more trustworthy voice: 'Once you loved the moon,' he tells Makak, 'now a night will come when, because it is white, from your deep hatred you will want it destroyed.' Makak has loved the Apparition because, at one level of meaning, she is part of him, his deeper self, his Jungian *anima*. She has always known his name. That he must now behead her, exclaiming 'Now, O God, now I am free'—and whom is he addressing?—is more of a nightmare than an act of liberation, though in a sense it is both.

Makak and his vision have been corrupted and betrayed, first by Moustique (for money), then by Tigre (for money and power), finally by Lestrade (for black power); and Makak himself (*macaque*—monkey, imitator) has been inveigled into complicity in each betrayal. In the trial scene it is significant that the two victims are Moustique and the Apparition, the two figures closest to the earlier, uncorrupted, Makak. Moustique is very much to the point when he advises Makak: 'Look around you, old man, and see who betray what . . . Who are all these new friends?'

'Getting rid of his overwhelming awe of everything white is the first step every colonial must take,'[23] Walcott has said. In so far as she represents whiteness, the vision has to be beheaded if Makak is to be free. He wakes up in prison. But, after the dream and the nightmare, he knows his name. With his friend Moustique, the practical complement to Makak the visionary, 'this old hermit is going back home, back to the beginning, to the green beginning of this world.' The vision is Adamic, hopeful. He walks away from history and from race; 'he becomes a working hermit—with a raceless god.'[24] But 'the world is a circle': *Dream* implies that Makak (the Christ figure, the Don Quixote) will descend again. 'He has to face reality, too. He has to go down to the market every Saturday to make a living.'[25] *Dream* explores the comprehensive ambivalence at the heart of Walcott's work.

11   V. S. Naipaul *by Bruce King*

V. S. Naipaul's father, Seepersad Naipaul (1906–53), came from an impoverished, rural, Hindu-speaking, immigrant family. A well-known reporter for the Trinidad *Guardian*, he published *Gurudeva and Other Indian Tales* (1943), among the earliest Trinidadian fiction that treated of the local East Indian community from within. While published locally during a time of Indian cultural assertion (in response to Indian nationalism), their record of individuals within a community includes an ironic awareness that Indian civilisation is dying in Trinidad from ossification and sterility as a result of exile. They are objective, satiric, anti-romantic, yet non-western in point of view. It is now apparent that they influenced the writing of his elder son, Vidiadhar Surajprasad Naipaul. His younger son, Shiva Naipaul (born 1945), also became a novelist, best known for *The Fireflies* (1970) and *The Chip-Chip Gatherers* (1973).

V. S. Naipaul was born in Trinidad in 1932, attended Queens Royal College and then received a scholarship to University College, Oxford. After taking his degree in English he became an editor for the B.B.C. *Caribbean Voices* and a reviewer for the *New Statesman*. Although he has returned to Trinidad for short periods, he mostly has lived in England. His early novels draw upon actual persons and events, especially among the East Indians, in recent Trinidadian history. His best-known novel, *A House for Mr Biswas*, is based upon family history.[1] The later fiction might be said to reflect the problems resulting from his own expatriation. His feelings of displacement in the West Indies and subsequent exile are the sources of his analysis of the effects of colonialism on the modern world.

Naipaul was early concerned with how to write of the West Indies where there had been no major literary tradition and where an insufficient audience existed for a novelist. If he allowed himself occasional broad comic touches for the benefit of foreign readers, the essential problem was how to create a fictional world which seemed real and densely textured, with a feeling of community, when the society involved was chaotic and rapidly changing. To record such a society and its significance, he blended the art of the reporter with that of the satirist. Numerous details of clothing, housing, manners and speech are precisely noted and usually set within an exact historical chronology. But the satirist also notes, through caricature, irony and juxtaposition, the aspirations, energy, vulgarities, inconsistencies and corruption of characters who belong to a rapidly changing society in which there are few stable values. The later, less satirical novels develop upon these techniques to show individuals and nations that because of their history and lack of resources are threatened by disorder.

While his novels often seem conservative in manner and attitude, it is more likely that they mask a personality so radical in its scepticism, insight and yearnings that it will never be in tune with the political rhetoric of either emerging or developed nations. It is this essential distrust of slogans and gestures that makes Naipaul appear a critic of the Third World. He fled from colonial Trinidad, but soon learned that neither India nor England were ideal societies; after some years of confused disillusionment with his role as an exile, he has become increasingly concerned with the problems of the newly independent nations. His style in recent novels, however, paradoxically appears even more detached; his sympathies conflict with observed actualities. Thus the now recurring character in his later novels of the deluded foreign liberal. Nor is Naipaul involved with the racial drama between whites and blacks where guilt and accusation have become favourite themes. His point of view is that of an East Indian. His early novels record an East Indian society to which those of African descent were as foreign as whites; his later novels often remind us that the Third World is also guilty of racism. He has said that for an Indian 'the race issue is too complicated' to be treated on a simple black-and-white level.

Although *Miguel Street* (1959) was Naipaul's third published book, it was probably the first in order of composition.[2] The narrator of the short stories, a young boy, begins in open-eyed innocence accepting the values of the street. Its ways are, however, the desperate gestures of those on the fringes of a colonial society who can only attract momentary notoriety through eccentricity, petty violence and lies. Man–Man pretends to be a new messiah who will undergo a crucifixion, but when the first big stone hits him he begins shouting, 'Cut this stupidness out!' In the final stories the boy sees that the street consists of illusionary triumphs and achievements; it is a community of failure: 'I no longer wanted to be like Eddoes. He was so weak and thin, and I hadn't realized that he was so small. Titus Hoyt was stupid and boring, and not funny at all. Everything had changed.'

The stories reveal Naipaul as a social historian. We see the influence of American films on Trinidadian youth—Bogart, for example, gets his nickname and takes his attitudes from the film *Casablanca*. Such mimicry occurs because colonial society has no viable models of its own and therefore the young falsify reality. The West Indian emphasis on manliness is a common theme in these stories and Naipaul's later novels. His characters act as if the assertion of masculinity through toughness, violence and mistreating women is the only way to earn respect. Naipaul gives his characters their due. They are interesting, lively, and have created a sense of self within an environment which otherwise would provide little satisfaction. But the limitations are clear. The carpenters, writers, mechanics create nothing; there is no dignity, no hope in such a community. The stories are entertaining but disturbing portraits of an impoverished colonial society that lacks resources and opportunities.

The Mystic Masseur (1957) is the humorous history of a hero of the people on the eve of independence when older racial and class lines were breaking down but before new cultural loyalties and standards had been formed. Although he is a poor student, far behind others of his age, Pundit Ganesh becomes a school teacher. He is inept, soon quits, and is saved from starvation by oil royalties inherited after his father's opportune death. Such coincidences occur throughout the novel and are interpreted by Ganesh as examples of Hindu destiny. Part of the comedy results from the contrast between Ganesh's rapid changes of career and his claim that his fate was preordained. He writes an absurd pamphlet entitled *101 Questions and Answers on the Hindu Religion*, which he publishes at his own expense and which no one buys. Again a failure he advertises himself as a mystic masseur and dresses in traditional Indian clothes. After another period of failure he manages by a combination of common sense and fakery to cure a black child of obsessive guilt. His reputation spreads throughout the island. His success is an example of the creolisation of the various ethnic groups. He becomes rich and is elected to the new Legislative Council at the first election with universal adult franchise. An opportunist, he soon changes from being a rebel to a government supporter, is awarded an M.B.E. and sent abroad by the British government to defend colonial policy. Earlier unable to use a knife and fork in a European fashion, his manners change with social advancement. Self-government and the appearance of self-rule have brought mimicry of European ways. His mimicry of colonial values is shown at the end of the novel when he changes his name to G. Ramsay Muir, Esq., M.B.E. The similarities to some West Indian politicians of the period are recognisable.

Naipaul has taken a changing society and by slight caricature given it shape and significance. If traditional Indian culture has decayed, leaving a lack of sensitivity, or ethicality, there is a New World ability to shift gears and make use of chance opportunities to create a new personality and rise socially. Where the novel lets us down is in the disproportionate weight given Ganesh's early life, in contrast to the rapidity with which he becomes a politician and earns his M.B.E.

The Suffrage of Elvira (1958) shows an expansion of technique from the episodic structure of the previous novel, organised around one main character and an observer, to the presentation of a large cast of characters involved in a situation, the second election to be held in Elvira, the most 'backward' area of the island. The contrast between the ideal of democratic elections and its reality in such a community is treated as satiric comedy. The corruption, in its crudeness and transparency, is representative of a chaotic society where older East Indian values no longer have any power. Religious traditions have broken down: 'Things were crazily mixed up in Elvira. Everybody, Hindus, Muslims and Christians, owned a Bible; the Hindus and Muslims looking on it, if anything with greater awe.' Religion is now the equivalent of ethnic group and party, not a matter of spirit. Money is the main value of society, and those who obtain money by cunning or cleverness are applauded regardless of the means they have used.

Naipaul is extremely sensitive to language and makes excellent use of local speech expressions: 'You drawing photo?'; 'He go make you dead like a cockroach'; 'It look as if your brains drop to your bottom'; 'Your eyes always longer than your tongue'. The earthiness of the dialogue is humorous: 'You is a big man. Your pee making froth'; '"Old Edaglo really pee on you, Goldsmith." "Not only pee," Chittaranjan said. "He shake it."' Other good touches include Foam's overenthusiastic slogan 'VOTE HARBANS OR DIE!'; the noting of the use of the expression 'tea' to cover many beverages in 'What sort of tea you want, eh, Mr Harbans? Chocolate, coffee or green tea?'; and the confused morals of 'Is my top. I thief it from a boy at school.'

Naipaul's masterpiece, *A House for Mr Biswas* (1961), has a reputation as a New World epic celebrating the struggles of an immigrant towards acculturisation and success. Certainly passages in the prologue give such an impression. Biswas's house is 'a welcoming world, a new, ready-made world. He could not quite believe that he had made that world.' Property ownership has also created a new sense of respect between Mr Biswas and his wife. 'He had grown to accept her judgement and to respect her optimism. He trusted her. Since they had moved to the house Shama had learned a new loyalty, to him and to their children; away from her mother and sisters, she was able to express this without shame, and to Mr Biswas this

was a triumph almost as big as the acquiring of his own house.'
In contrast to his own home is the large Tulsi household, ruled
tyrannically by his wife's mother, a place of humiliation for Mr
Biswas, but formerly a necessary refuge for someone without
money, training or useful family of his own:

> How terrible it would have been . . . to have died among the
> Tulsis, amid the squalor of that large, disintegrating and
> indifferent family; to have left Shama and the children
> among them, in one room; worse, to have lived without
> even attempting to lay claim to one's portion of the earth; to
> have lived and died as one had been born, unnecessary and
> unaccommodated.

While Naipaul's prologue implies that Mr Biswas's history
is to be seen as celebration, the actual emphasis of the novel is
on those born 'unnecessary and unaccommodated' in the New
World. Naipaul tells two interrelated stories, that of Mr Biswas and his family and that of the Tulsis into which he marries.
Both histories range over three generations of East Indians in
their struggle to survive and find a place in Trinidad. The
narrative is told in such a way as to express the gradual Indian
accommodation to what was originally a foreign land.[3] The
opening sections of Part One tell of Mr Biswas's birth and
childhood from an essentially limited, Indian peasant point of
view. His mother's father is an indentured immigrant: 'Fate
had brought him from India to the sugar-estate, aged him
quickly and left him to die in a crumbling mud hut in the
swamplands.'

The psychology of the East Indians is respected, although
sometimes humorously, by the narrative; the pundit's warning
to keep Mr Biswas away from water and that he has an
'unlucky sneeze' is validated when the father's death by
drowning is announced after the son has sneezed. As Mr
Biswas's vision expands outside his own family we are made
aware of an essentially enclosed East Indian world centred
upon families, villages and land, trying to live by custom but
forced to make adjustments to the circumstances of the New
World. For all the Tulsis' attempts to preserve traditional

Indian culture, Hanuman House represents its decay; religious observances are carried on without knowledge of their meaning, the new Indian intellectual movements are ignored, and, most significant, the husbands of the Tulsi daughters live there since they are too impoverished to build homes of their own. Life in Trinidad, especially its estate system, has resulted in a new protective form of family organisation unlike that of Indian tradition. The decay of the Hindu spirit in the New World is further shown by the marriage of the Tulsi sons to Presbyterian Indians. As the dispossessed begin to assimilate, their contacts with other races increase. Mr Biswas discusses in 'a Chinese restaurant' the purchase of his long desired home from a 'tall, thin coloured man'. The move, by Mr Biswas and the Tulsis, from the countryside to Port of Spain is representative of the East Indian incorporation into the national society; it is accompanied by learning new professions, such as journalism and social work, and by the increased importance of western education, which becomes the main means of advancement.

If the novel traces the progress of a transitional generation of East Indians from isolated rural poverty to the first stages of assimilation within a westernised urban society, its celebration is strongly tempered by an awareness of the hardness of the struggle and of its lasting effect. Trinidad offered Mr Biswas no opportunities for a quick, American rags-to-riches success. It is only with the coming of the American bases during the war that the island offers chances for wealth and social mobility. The house that he finally owns is 'jerry-built' and disillusioning. That he dies unemployed and unable to pay off the mortgage shows how little he has progressed towards security despite his sufferings. The irony of 'the *Trinidad Sentinel* had no choice' but to fire Mr Biswas, giving him no pension, after his 'doctor advised him to take a complete rest' shows the continuing harshness of the society. Significantly his children need to go abroad to obtain a further education and qualifications. Years of poverty and chaos appear to have had a lasting effect on his son, Anand. While it is difficult to summarise briefly such a fully achieved, richly detailed novel, its power results from having given a tragic fulness to what could in other hands

have been sentimentalised or seen beneath the dignity of
serious literature. It is this realism that makes *A House for Mr
Biswas* a more profound work of art than the usual fictional
celebrations of national achievement and history.

Naipaul, who had lived in England since 1952, travelled in
1960 through Trinidad, Jamaica, Guyana, Surinam and Martinique. There are no doubt those who will never forgive his
oft-quoted claim in *The Middle Passage* (1962): 'History is built
around achievement and creation; and nothing was created in
the West Indies.' It is often forgotten that the remarks are part
of a radical criticism of colonial myths: 'In the West Indian
islands slavery and the latifundia created only grossness, men
who ate "like cormorants" and drank "like porpoises"; a
society without standards, without noble aspirations,
nourished by greed and cruelty; a society of whose illiteracy
metropolitan administrators continued to complain right until
the middle of the last century.' The middle-class West Indian,
Naipaul claims, has rejected his race and mimics white English
and American behaviour; the poor black fantasises a romantic
African history that never existed. Because of poverty and
appeals to race the region is in danger of 'protest' leaders who,
lacking vision, stir up hatred and ignore the real problems of
new nations. *The Middle Passage* reveals the disillusioned
analysis of the islands that went into Naipaul's early stories and
novels:

> Nationalism was impossible in Trinidad. In the colonial
> society every man had to be for himself; every man had to
> grasp whatever dignity and power he was allowed; he owed
> no loyalty to the island and scarcely any to his group. To
> understand this is to understand the squalor of the politics
> that came to Trinidad in 1946 when, after no popular
> agitation, universal adult suffrage was declared. . . . The
> new politics were reserved for the enterprising, who had
> seen the prodigious commercial possibilities. There were no
> parties, only individuals. Corruption, not unexpected,
> aroused only amusement and even mild approval.

If Naipaul has become one of the best travel writers of our

century, it is because his reporting is part of his own quest for identity in the world left by colonialism. Naipaul thought of himself as an exiled Indian and was soon disenchanted with England. *An Area of Darkness* (1964) records the failure of his attempt to settle in India. During his stay in India he learned that racial similarities have no meaning and that he had been shaped by his Trinidadian upbringing and western education; he is a colonial without a country, an international man, a product of an empire that has withdrawn. To be western is to believe in the importance of the individual life in the present world; but Indian values are shaped by the negation of the present and of selfhood. Thus the apparent irrationality Naipaul finds in India, where Indians see their problems through western eyes but leave the solutions to fate. East and West never really met; the British were unwilling to assimilate. India was left stranded between a heritage to which it could not return and a world it was not permitted to enter. The nationalist movement symbolises the problem. The claim to nationhood was based upon the assertion of traditional spiritual values, but such values have become traps preventing economic and cultural growth; rituals have replaced experience. In *India: A Wounded Civilisation* (1977) Naipaul claims that Gandhi's traditionalism encourages Indian quietism and passivity, leaving the nation unable to cope with its contemporary problems.

The year Naipaul spent in India appears to have been a turning point in his life. The earlier writing was primarily about the Hindu community in Trinidad. The attitude was satiric, as Naipaul noticed how an immigrant culture simplified, decayed and became chaotic during creolisation. The attitude was also of brahmin superiority. Life in the West Indies lacked dignity, purpose, value; for life to have significance, it must be based upon the traditions and achievements of a large, stable culture. India, however, proved the opposite of what he expected. By contrast Trinidad, with its energy, individuality and mobility, now seemed lively, vital, hopeful. If the East Indians of Trinidad lost their traditional culture, they had become part of the New World with its sense of adventure and possibilities.

While he was living in India, Naipaul wrote *Mr Stone and the Knight's Companion* (1964), a curiously dry, flat novel about a self-satisfied, unimportant, ageing Englishman who unexpectedly marries late in life. Afraid that retirement will imprison him at home with his wife, he conceives a scheme to aid his company's pensioners. The success of the plan further destroys the security of his carefully routine life, bringing excitement, anger, hope and disillusionment. Ideas when turned into practice attract human greed and vanities. Having experienced a period of despair, Mr Stone appears at the end of the novel to be on the verge of another burst of renewed energy. Stone's grey routine might be said to represent the solid, unchanging tradition that Naipaul sought in England and India. Once challenged by innovation such comforting habits cannot be regained, and the resulting freedom disturbs by offering vistas of achievement which are complicated by all the messiness of human emotions. The slight hope at the end of the novel is not convincing, and it is implied that the idea of creative activity is superior to its practice.

There is in Naipaul's work of this period a puzzled inability to find satisfaction in either the excitement of activity or the calm of passively accepting tradition. Neither seems real. One might speculate that the decision to leave the West Indies for the seemingly more impressive societies of England and India had resulted in disillusionment. The ideal of a more vital culture remained, but the reality of exile had fallen far below the ideal. If Naipaul has not flattered the West Indian, he has also been critical of the Indian and English.

His renewed involvement with the West Indies can be seen in *The Loss of El Dorado* (1965), a selective but detailed examination of two moments of early Trinidadian history which left a national legacy of confusion and anger. Naipaul's focus has changed from his early satiric reports of Trinidad into an exploration of the historical and psychological causes of the region's problems. The book might be considered a study in the greed and mistaken idealism which produced colonial empires. Outside settled society every dream is doomed, every achievement is soon destroyed; pettiness, corruption and chaos destroy equally the unscrupulous and the good. Without the traditions, restraints and competition of the metropolis, settler society becomes ignorant, feeding upon envy and racial distinctions. The introduction of slaves and the extermination of the Amerindians left a legacy of brutality. The worst tyrants recorded in the book begin with high ideals and good intentions; forced to use power to uphold ideals in chaotic circumstances, men are soon corrupted.

The Mimic Men (1967) is probably Naipaul's second most important novel. Here is, however, life observed, reported on, seen through spectacles. And that is part of the novel's significance. Ralph Kripal Singh, the main character, is representative of a generation which gains power at independence and can only mimic the authenticity of selfhood. His many unsatisfactory sexual encounters are similar to his house and politics; they show someone more concerned with the thought of possession than the actual experience. His failures are indicative of a larger failure—the very lack of purpose, will, energy and creativity of which he accuses the political leaders of his island.

The island in the novel is symbolic of former colonies after independence. Since nationalist politics aim at destroying an older order, and since there are few materials available to build a new order, only chaos can follow. But chaos does not bring freedom, since real power is elsewhere; the economy necessary for social improvement still depends upon foreign investment and aid. Even government is a problem since society is made up of various nationalities and races with radically conflicting interests. 'The career of the colonial politician is short and ends brutally. We lack order. Above all, we lack power, and we do not understand that we lack power. We mistake words and the acclamation of words for power.' Singh feels that history has left him shipwrecked. What is he, an Indian, doing on a 'slave island'? In contrast he admires England with its folk tales, long history, and comforting nursery rhymes. An ex-colonial, he is still a child who wishes to be mothered. But the comforting, orderly England of his imagination does not exist; London is a place of 'private cells' for those who seek 'the idea of the city'.

The Mimic Men is perhaps the clearest expression of the themes that shape Naipaul's novels. Poverty-stricken and feeling isolated on the fringes of power, the Third World escapes into fantasy. The new middle and professional classes become rich but are isolated from the populace. Appeals to race and colour begin to dominate politics. Various political and religious movements spring up which, if ineffective, offer a sense of drama and excitement. Fantasy, the need for drama, leads to disorder. Drama and violence will not change the essence of a situation where there is a lack of power, shared myths, competence and resources.

The structure of *The Mimic Men* is an advance on Naipaul's previous novels. It is told in the form of memories by the main character, who is implicitly criticised by what he reveals about himself. It starts and ends in the present, but the narrative shifts back and forward in time, between Singh's childhood, life as a student in London, return to the island, political career and exile in England. Naipaul's instinct has been rather to string tightly compressed incidents into a sequence of contrasting events than build a single unified plot around a limited consecutive action. The fragmented structure of *The Mimic Men* looks forward to the mixture of stories and autobiography in *In a Free State* and the mosaic organisation of *Guerrillas*. There is an increasing mastery of striking phrases: 'I no longer seek to find beauty in the lives of the mean and the oppressed. Hate oppression; fear the oppressed.' 'With his nose he made the sign of the cross over the baby.' 'I will be honest with you. I stole this.' The distillation of a scene to epigram, a striking image or a fragment of conversation allows freedom from filling in narrative details and chronology. In the later novels there is an open texture in which more is *felt* to be happening between sentences than is stated.

While *The Mimic Men* is a more serious treatment of the kind of material found in *The Mystic Masseur*, it is also Naipaul's attempt to understand how his own personal and colonial past has shaped his character, vision and approach to writing. The unchronological narration, which shifts attention from social causes and effects to the mood and psychology of the memorialist, creates an imaginative kind of order, an order suggestive of a novelist's attempt to understand the sources of his own feelings of unease rather than the failures of others.

This is not to imply that Kripal Singh, the narrator, is Naipaul. He is not. His rotund, somewhat inflated, pompous, rhetorical style, with its many parallel sentences, is the opposite of Naipaul's own sharp, economical, understated prose. But through him Naipaul examines his own relationship to the Caribbean and to his life in England. The richness of the novel is a wealth of mood, of generalisation, of insight, the power that comes from an involvement beyond what is actually said or shown. This creates complexities that do not lend themselves to simple interpretations. When the narrator uses phrases that echo, allude to, or parody such writers as John Donne, Thomas Hobbes and T. S. Eliot, we recognise and appreciate Singh's sophisticated irony but his self-conscious display subverts our acceptance of his wisdom. Towards the end of the book, Singh remembers weeping with gratitude at the hotel Christmas party when he is toasted as the overseas guest; he feels the lord and lady who run the hotel have accepted him into their ordered English lives. The passage is understated but clear irony by Naipaul and recalls the conclusion of *Gulliver's Travels*. It mocks Singh's sentimentality, his attraction to England, his confusion of such a gentility for order, and it implicitly questions Naipaul's own often expressed dreams of order and nobility.

The stories in *A Flag on the Island* (1967), the earliest of which, *The Mourners*, is dated 1950, range from portraits of Trinidad street life to early attempts at recording English social behaviour. As usual there is good writing, including such similes as 'She carried herself into the churchyard, awed by her own temerity, feeling like an explorer in a land of cannibals.' The main interest is the long title story, written in a crude American style appropriate to the narrator, which shows a West Indian island in a period of transition. The poor, backward British colony has become independent and an American tourist resort. History which left it stranded on the fringe of world importance has now converted it to the mimicry of the Third World behaviour expected by Americans. The shift in mimicry, from British to American expectations, is shown by the novelist, Mr Blackwhite. He formerly tried to write romantically about lords and ladies. After independence, sup-

ported by American foundations, he writes stories of interracial marriage with such titles as *I Hate You* (subtitled *One Man's
Search for Identity*). The main irony is the artificial 'nationalist'
culture which has replaced the authentic if chaotic society of
the past. Instead of the vitality of the street, a national theatre is
being built in which the audience can walk across the stage and
put on 'happenings'.

The prologue and epilogue of *In a Free State* (1971) relate
incidents that occurred during Naipaul's travels in Egypt. In
the former Naipaul observes foreign businessmen humiliate an
elderly English vagabond. The epilogue tells of an incident
when the author surprisingly tries to prevent an Egyptian from
humiliating some impoverished beggars. The two situations
imply that freedom is a delusion when there are no communal
traditions of human dignity. *One out of Many*, the first of the
three thematically related short stories in the book, alludes to
the usual slogan of multiracial Third World nations: 'Out of
many, one nation'. Santosh, a servant from Bombay, is taken
by an Indian diplomat to America. He leaves his employer,
becomes an illegal immigrant worried about deportation, and
marries a black woman to obtain citizenship. His escape from
Indian servitude is, paradoxically, a fall from innocence. In
Washington his manners and customs are all wrong. There is
no one to whom he can speak; the blacks who accept him as a
'soul brother' violate his Hindu sense of racial purity. Freedom
brings confusion, worries and a loss of self-respect. Once
freedom is acquired, however, it is not given up willingly.
Santosh is both a hero and a victim of the modern world. Has
his new awareness of himself, symbolised by watching his face
in the mirror, really been a blessing, or has it stripped him of
his communal comforts and given him in return only the
illusion of experience and freedom?

In the longest story, *In a Free State*, the experiences of two
white expatriates in East Africa during a civil war, the problems of personal freedom and modern exile are set in the
turbulence which has resulted from decolonisation. The title
thus applies both to the conditions of modern individual lives
and to the African country. As usual in Naipaul's work, sexual
behaviour is symbolic of cultural and political matters. Linda's

sexual life, like her other conduct, is casual, without scruples. Her circle of expatriate friends is rootless, without loyalties, preoccupied with sending money to more secure countries and with finding new jobs. Bobby tries to assimilate but, as a homosexual who wishes he were born black, he can no more be a member of the nation than Linda. Indeed he is the more deceived in his liberal slogans. He is humiliated at a bar by a young African, his car windows are ruined at a petrol station, he is brutally beaten by some soldiers, and his servant laughs at his condition. Bobby becomes, like Linda, one of the many rootless foreigners who will flee to other places of exile.

The African country, an amalgam of various East African states, is radically unstable. It is not really a nation but several large tribes thrown together, lacking any basis for unity beyond the boundaries imposed by the British. Its capital was built by the English and Indians. Most of the participants at a conference on community development are English; those Africans who attend have nothing to contribute. Foreigners man the helicopters which are used to hunt for the secessionist king, and foreigners in helicopters were previously used by the president to impose order when the government was on the verge of being toppled by disturbances. If the capital city is symbolic, so is the station where Bobby's windscreen is damaged. To give the illusion of Africanisation, the Indian manager is not present; there is no one responsible. The politics of independence have made tribal animosities worse. Bobby claims that Africans must be left 'to sort these things out themselves', but independence in such a situation is mimicry, the adoption of foreign political forms without the social structures upon which such order is based. The dilemma of Santosh is pertinent here; his confusion and helplessness is in small that of the African nation. The problem of freedom in the modern world has become Naipaul's main theme. As Bobby's fate shows, liberal or compassionate involvement is no solution. Naipaul's attempt described in the epilogue to stop the Egyptian beggars from being beaten receives no approval from bystanders, Egyptian or foreign.

Naipaul has said that he wants his non-fiction to be seen as integral to his fictional work. Indeed they have the same themes and reflect the same sensibility; even the style is similar. His novels are often an assemblage of real events that have happened during his travels, although not usually in the place and sequence presented in the novels. *The Overcrowded Barracoon* (1972) is a selection of essays and reporting from 1958 to 1972. Although Naipaul's sympathies are with the poor of the Third World, he sees that revolutionary rhetoric often is the play-acting of those who have not been able to control their destinies: 'The enemy is the past, of slavery and colonial neglect and a society uneducated from top to bottom; the enemy is the smallness of the islands and the absence of resources.' The title essay concerns Mauritius, a small, over-populated, newly independent island in the Indian Ocean. Once uninhabited, it was colonised by the French who imported Indians and Africans to grow sugar cane. With the eradication of malaria in 1945 the population increased and wide-scale unemployment followed. The island has no resources beyond its sugar crop and tourism, and depends on South Africa for its survival. Unable to cope with the economic situation, unable to convince an uneducated society to accept family planning, the government uses politics as 'the opium of the people'. Black Power slogans are a means of playing down failure and enable those in power to portray themselves as the party of protest; the government is trying to recapture the role it had in pre-independence days. Given the situation, however, any political programme is likely to fail:

> at the end of the day, they will be left with what they started with: an agricultural colony, created by empire in an empty island and always meant to be part of something larger, now given a thing called independence and set adrift, an abandoned imperial barracoon, incapable of economic or cultural autonomy.

The lasting effect of colonialism on the modern world is illustrated by the relationships between Jane, Peter and Jimmy in *Guerrillas* (1975). Jane belongs to a class once enriched by the empire but now of diminished status in post-colonial England. As her upper-class breeding turns into nihilistic rage at the pettiness of life, she seeks drama and meaning through vicarious involvement with the Third World. She follows Peter, whom she mistakes for a political activist who will upset the existing social order, to a West Indian island where she is soon disillusioned. The island seems the end of the universe, totally different from the dynamic Third World imagined from London. Peter works as a public relations officer for a company which, ironically, had its origins in the slave trade, from which he obtains land, food and secondhand equipment for Jimmy's hopeless, unproductive commune. Jimmy, of mixed Chinese and African descent, had a reputation in England as a radical black leader. Deported to the West Indies, he preaches his fashionable London slogans of Black Power, revolution and a return to the land, although he has no local following. From boredom, seeking more excitement, Jane turns her interest towards him. She represents the white British culture which Jimmy both hates and envies. He furnishes his house in English style, imagines himself still admired in England, and feels superior to local blacks. At other times he identifies with Bryant, an angry, deformed black youth. Bryant and Jimmy both have fantasies of being accepted by whites as sophisticated, handsome heroes. Jimmy's ambivalence is expressed in a recurring fantasy of raping, then chivalrously helping, a white woman.

Jimmy's confusion is a product of colonialism. Independence has left him with a past against which he rebels, but which nothing has replaced. His posters proclaim that he is not a slave or stallion, but he calls Peter 'Massa' and he beds two English women. The political chaos on the island reflects the cultural breakdown. There is no sense of community; each character is isolated and alone. Jimmy says, 'When everybody wants to fight his own little war, everybody is a guerrilla.' Peter, knowing that Jimmy is responsible for Jane's murder, flees from involvement by destroying the remaining official evidence of her stay on the island.

With the post-colonial world so chaotic, it is fitting that the narrative should be expressed in fragments, with shifts of perspective, and with an emphasis rather on feelings than actions. The texture of the novel is both open, with spaces between scenes, and yet detailed in its descriptions of impoverished landscapes and disagreeable emotional excitement. Close focus on the disagreeable contrasts with the fragmentary narrative and dialogue, creating an impression of tension, alienation, cross purposes, and irrationality.

If Naipaul's early novels use as their subject the cultural confusions and comedy that paralleled the emergence of the East Indian community into the wider society of Trinidad, the later novels can be said to reflect Naipaul's own attempt to define his identity within the post-colonial world. The novels and non-fiction seem significant to new and developed nations because the mixing of cultures, the collapse of older traditions, and rapid political changes have left most people confused, sceptical and uncertain. His achievement results from a profoundly analytical vision. His characters and their society are seen both from inside and outside, without excesses of criticism or sympathy. There is an understanding of what makes people and nations what they are. While economically emphasising selected details, the novels offer a sense of life observed and meditated upon in depth. There are, however, no fixed positions that are identifiably Naipaul's. The sympathies and perspectives change; each novel has a life and form of its own.

12 Wilson Harris *by Hena Maes-Jelinek*

He refused to impose a false coherency upon material one had to digest—perhaps all one's life—to begin to find . . . a true groping equation in art or language to the fundaments of existence *through* history or the void which was native to history.

Ascent to Omai

The Guyanese novelist, poet and critic, Wilson Harris was born in 1921 of mixed European, African and Amerindian ancestry. While working as a land surveyor in the Guyanese interior he contributed poems, stories and essays to *Kyk-over-al*, a literary magazine edited in Georgetown, then published two collections of poems in Guyana in the early fifties and emigrated to England at the end of the decade. His first novel, *Palace of the Peacock*, came out in 1960. Since then he has published thirteen novels, two volumes of novellas and a large number of critical essays.

Its constantly evolving character notwithstanding, a remarkable unity of thought informs this considerable opus. Two major elements seem to have shaped Harris's approach to art and his philosophy of existence: the impressive contrasts of the Guyanese landscapes, with which his survey expeditions made him familiar, and the successive waves of conquest which gave Guyana its heterogeneous population polarised for centuries into oppressors and their victims. The two, land-scape and history, merge in his work into single metaphors symbolising man's inner space saturated with the effects of historical—that is, temporal—experiences. The jungle, for example, is for Harris both outer and inner unreclaimed territory, the actual 'landscape of history' for those who only survived by disappearing into it and a metaphor for that inner psychological recess to which his characters relegate both their forgotten ancestors and the living whom they dominate. It contrasts with the savannahs and is itself full of contrasts. Though teeming with life, much of it is invisible to the ordinary 'material' eye, just as those who, willingly or not, lead an underground existence remain unseen save to the 'spiritual' (imaginative) eye. The jungle's extra-human dimensions suggest timelessness and offer a glimpse of eternity, while the constant renewal of the vegetation confirms its existence within a cyclical time pattern. In Harris's words the jungle 'travels eternity to season'; and the Amerindians, who move to and fro between that secret primeval world and the modern areas where they can find work, subsist, as he writes in *Tumatumari* (1968), 'on a dislocated scale of time'. They are an essential link between the modern Guyanese and the lost world of their undigested past, and must be retrieved from their buried existence in both real and symbolical *terra incognita* if Guyana (and the individual soul) is to absorb all its components into a harmonious community.

Already in his poetry Harris had dealt jointly with the contrasts and polarisations in nature and history, and presented spiritual freedom as a capacity to move between opposites: 'The tremendous voyage between two worlds/is contained in every hollow shell, in every name that echoes/a nameless bell' ('Bering Straits'). The very form of his verse reflects the reconciliation of opposites by freely mixing concrete with symbolical or outer with inner planes of existence: 'but earth-bound living cheeks/are too solemn to be punctured/by splinters of the wind . . . until translucent curiosity contrives upon the mood of still death/a frail entrance and exit for the spirit' ('Fetish'). His more substantial volume of poetry, *Eternity to Season* (1954)—significantly subtitled 'Poems of separation and reunion'—is an epic in which the characters, called after Greek mythological heroes, turn out to be humble Guyanese labourers. Their mythological stature indicates perhaps where the Guyanese should look for their archetypes. Harris gives his own idiosyncratic interpretation of Homeric adventures just as he was later to fill Christian and Amerindian myths with new content. His free borrowing from various cultures is one of many ways in which he attempts to break down barriers between men and between civilisations. He does not deny the specific character and experience of each people, and his poems are meant to awaken the sensibility and imagination of the Guyanese to the real nature of their environment. But he rejects all static ways of being. Man cannot help being imprisoned within time and history; he can, however, achieve partial liberation and distance from even necessary orders by tending towards an 'other', provided this 'other' is not allowed to become another absolute. This dualistic and dynamic view of existence accounts for Harris's many-layered and paradoxical language, particularly his juxtaposition of contradictory terms which challenge our modes of perception and thought (as in 'blossoming coals of immortal imperfection'). Many of the basic metaphors Harris was to use in his fiction are already found with a potentially double meaning in his poetry. But while the vision is as boldly original in the one as in the other, it has achieved a greater impact by being embodied in the more concrete setting and highly individualised characters of his fiction. Harris is primarily a novelist even though his fictional language has the concentrated richness of poetry and, as has often been pointed out, demands the same minute reading and explication. True, the poet has always had greater licence than the novelist to deal with the transcendental, but Harris's way of dealing with it has introduced a new dimension into the novel.

Harris's fiction began to appear at a crucial time for both the nascent West Indian fiction and the novel in English since, in the fifties and early sixties, the trends in English and American fiction indicated that many inheritors of established traditions had ceased to believe in them. The dissolution of values and forms due to the combined action of history and science had left artists in a void similar in kind to that experienced with more tragic intensity by West Indians throughout their history. With a few notable exceptions, English and American novelists reacted to this loss of certainty by either seeking refuge and renewing their faith in realism, or turning experimental fiction into an art of the absurd, technically brilliant and innovatory but often undermining the very purpose of art. Wilson Harris is among the few West Indian writers who pointed out the irrelevance of both trends to a 'native' art of fiction. While insisting that the disorientation of the 'diminished man' in formerly strong societies had been experienced for centuries by the conquered populations in the Caribbean and the Americas, he warned particularly against the influence on West Indian writers of the post-war European art of despair. His own 'art of compassion' does not involve, as has sometimes been suggested, a withdrawal from history in order to transcend it. It is, on the contrary, intensely concerned with the impact of history on the ordinary 'obscure human person' and expresses a passionate denial of what has been termed the 'historylessness' of the Caribbean: it shows that people exist by virtue of their silent suffering as much as by celebrated deeds or a materially recognisable civilisation, of which incidentally obscure men are the unacknowledged executors. My main purpose is to show how Harris's view of Caribbean history has shaped his art of the novel.

The major historical facts endured by the Caribbean peoples were dismemberment, exile, eclipse and, for many, slavery, with the result that for several centuries they lived destitute and inarticulate in a political, social and cultural void. In much of Harris's fiction these catastrophic experiences are recreated both as facts and as inner states to be digested by the individual consciousness. Most of his novels present an outer-world and an inner confrontation between a conqueror or oppressor and his victim, as well as the traumas that result from the violation of a people or of an individual soul. They all explore possibilities of rebirth and of genuine community between polarised people(s) and between antithetical ways of being. This basic and recurrent theme determines Harris's conception of character, the structure of his novels and their narrative texture as well as his style. Harris equates dominant and fixed forms in art with dominant and static social structures, local, national or international. Hence his attempt to find a fluid mode of expression to render the duality of life, the necessary movement between its opposite poles, and above all the mobility of consciousness.

Harris's fictional work to date can be divided into three major phases. In the first of these the *Guiana Quartet*[1] creates a composite picture of the many facets of Guyanese life: the paradoxes and unpredictable manifestations of a nature that is not easily mastered, the historical vestiges, visible and invisible, that give each area a specific 'spirit of the place', and the activities of a multiracial population often self-divided and alienated from its 'lost' or unintegrated groups such as the Amerindians or the descendants of runaway slaves. There is a sense in which the first novel, *Palace of the Peacock*, contains in embryo all further developments. It recreates the main fact of Caribbean history, the endlessly renewed exploitation of land and people, from time immemorial through the Renaissance to the present day, by waves of invaders intent on winning the country's riches for themselves. 'Rule the land . . . and you rule the world,' says the skipper Donne, who pursues an invisible Amerindian tribe on a nameless river through the jungle, and shows the mixture of idealism and brutality that has characterised many an ambitious enterprise in modern times. Donne's acknowledged purpose is to find cheap labour for his plantation, though in the course of the expedition his initial intention of building an empire turns into a quest for spiritual salvation. The novel opens with the death of Donne, shot by the vengeful Mariella, the Amerindian woman he has beaten and exploited, an occurrence which dramatises the end of the relationship between conqueror and colonised. This end, however, marks the beginning of an exploration through which the foundations of community are discovered. The shot that killed Donne has awakened his brother or spiritual alter ego, who starts reconstructing their original journey into the interior. His reconstruction renders with striking immediacy the obstacles met on the rapids and the corresponding obstructions in their souls, for the recreated expedition is both actual and metaphorical. Donne's multiracial crew are very real men—moved now by murderous instincts, now by a deceptive idealism—but they are also 'the crew every man mans and lives in his inmost ship and theatre and mind'.

The opening of the novel on the frontier between life and death establishes at the outset Harris's dual view of existence and his conception of death as eclipse rather than annihilation. The dead in his fiction are an essential part of a community of being and must be retrieved from oblivion by imagination. In *Palace* the narrator's reconstruction of the past is both an 'act of memory' and a 'dream', Harris's word to describe an intuitive, imaginative apprehension of reality, one that frees man from the limitations of exclusively rational and/or sensory perceptions and makes possible the reconciliation of apparently incompatible opposites. The double perspective due to the juxtaposition of material perception and spiritual vision in Donne and the Narrator is paralleled by a similar duality in the phenomenal world itself, which offers an insight into its immaterial counterpart. There is the 'skeleton footfall' on the river bank disclosing an invisible presence, or the tree that suddenly sheds all its leaves, revealing the simple inner structure that underlies its external profusion.

Donne and the crew must recognise their exploitation of both land and people (united by a similar 'namelessness'). As they travel upriver and re-enact their possessive or murderous deeds, the dangers they meet gradually decimate their ranks and turn them into pursued men longing for redemption through the muse they have all abused in one way or another. They never actually catch up with Mariella and the fleeing tribe but 'come home . . . to the compassion of the nameless . . . folk', though not until they achieve self-knowledge and die. The main effect of the trials they have gone through has been to shake them out of their fixed sense of identity, and although they are not aware of it until they come together in the manifold symbol of the peacock's tail at the very end, their dying to themselves (their 'Second Death') is a momentary surrender to 'otherness', the lifeblood of community. The final conversion, however, occurs in Donne and offers the first example in Harris's fiction of the necessary interdependence between the imaginative artist (for Donne is also that) and the ordinary folk.

A further illustration of duality is to be found in the shift from the concrete to the purely symbolical as the narrative draws to an end, suggesting that spiritual rebirth is a feat of the imagination, which is itself regenerated. Donne and two remaining members of the crew have reached a waterfall; leaving behind the 'repetitive boat and prison of life', they begin to ascend the cliff on its side. In the veil of the waterfall Donne sees 'images' of an Arawak Christ, Virgin and child (presented in the naked poverty of the people and not as the glorified Virgin of the Christian Church), native figures of sacrifice and beauty that seem to have been retrieved from his own consciousness, although the life they represent used to stand for nothing in his eyes. The situation he has always known is now reversed; as he hangs in the void on the cliff, the certainty of his own void and nothingness penetrates him slowly and he feels excluded from the warmth and love in the pictures he envisages. Donne's fall into the void is a symbolical re-enactment of the fate of the victims of conquest. Whether in *Palace*, *Tumatumari* (in which the severing of Roi's head in a collision with a rock in the waterfall symbolises the dismemberment of the Amerindians and the loss of their leadership) or in *Companions of the Day and Night* (1975), the fall down a natural escarpment in Guyana or from a Mexican pyramid stands for the collapse of a people and recreates the terrifying sense of void they experienced.

The fall in *Palace of the Peacock* is followed by a rebirth from what Harris sees as both the 'grave' and the 'womb' of history. It is Donne's spiritual self that is resurrected to apprehend the evanescent moment in which the members of his heterogeneous crew or community come together as stars and eyes in the peacock's tail, fragments of the splintered sun, which in the first part of the novel was a symbol of Donne's implacable tyranny. The metamorphosis of images corresponds to a similar transformation and displacement of formerly fixed attitudes within the characters. That is why the vision of the crew's reunion at the end is so brief. It actualises the Narrator's moments of intuitive perception of wholeness which have alternated with the crew's actions and physical progress throughout the narrative. Owing to this alternation the structure of the novel is informed by the ebb and flow movement that Harris sees in all forms of outer life and deems essential within man's consciousness.

The other novels of the *Quartet* also illustrate the frightening but necessary disorientation this regained fluidity of being entails in men confronted by violence and murder, the residues of slavery and the desire of former victims to become exploiters in their turn, 'as though the oppressed convention nurses identical expectations of achieving power',[2] and the continuing exploitation of minority or eclipsed groups. *The Far Journey of Oudin* focuses on the master-servant relationship on the East Indian rice plantations between the savannahs and the coast. *The Whole Armour* takes place on the Pomeroon river and the precarious strip of land between bush and sea. Cristo, a young man wrongly accused of murder, agrees to sacrifice himself to redeem the community. In *The Secret Ladder* the land surveyor Fenwick and his crew stationed in the jungle gauge the river Canje prior to the building of a dam that would flood the territory from which the descendants of slaves refuse to move. None of these novels has the linear simplicity of *Palace of the Peacock*; the more commonplace experiences of the earthbound characters and the more complex plots give them a density and an immediacy further enhanced by a more extensive use of dialect. But the issues raised do not find a worldly resolution. The emphasis is on spiritual freedom, responsibility and a genuine authority which, like the sense of unity in *Palace*, are envisaged through the recognition of the alien and weak element in the community as its true roots and therefore springhead of change. The crux of each novel lies in the possibility of unlocking a fixed order of things and eroding the certainties and imperatives that imprison the protagonists within a one-sided and rigid sense of self. Hence the crumbling rather than 'consolidation' of personality, the disturbing resemblances between dead and living characters, or sometimes even the reappearance of the dead among the living, and the frequency of 'doubles' or twins to 'break through from patterns of implacable identities'. In keeping with Harris's concentration on process rather than achievement, the end of the *Quartet* is inconclusive. A central motif running through its four movements is the need for the Guyanese (as for Donne) 'to understand and transform [their] beginnings'. That is why each novel raises the question of who the characters' true parents are. What Harris calls 'the mystery of origins' can only be penetrated, though never completely, by 'dismantling a prison of appearance'. This course of action, initiated by Fenwick in *The Secret Ladder*, is the major theme and shaping factor of his next cycle of novels.

Harris's fifth novel, *Heartland* (1964), is an essential link between the *Guiana Quartet* and his next works. Its protagonist, Stevenson, comes to the heartland as a watchman and meets three characters who had vanished from ordinary life in the *Quartet* and who make him aware in their various ways of the significance of the jungle. At the end of the novel Stevenson himself disappears into the heartland, leaving in his half-burnt resthouse fragments of letters and poems. The uncertainty of his fate in the intermediate life-and-death world of the jungle suggests that, like characters in the following novels, he has lost himself in the third nameless dimension Harris has now started to explore. This is the void once inherent in the Caribbean psyche, seen as a possible vessel of rebirth for all men and as a state to be experienced by the artist who shuns the tyranny of one dominant world-view and allows contradictory voices to speak through him. The novel tends towards the interiorisation of action that is wholly characteristic of Harris's second phase. At the same time the pattern of pursuit and flight specific to the *Quartet* gives way momentarily, through Stevenson's relationship with the Amerindian woman, Petra, to reciprocity between the exploring consciousness and the eclipsed 'other'. Petra runs away all the same after he has helped her give birth to her child, and as he tries to overcome his sense of frustration Stevenson realises that she has seen through him and eluded his possessiveness. He is last seen, in *Heartland*, following.

the crumbling black road . . . [which] was but an endless wary flood broken into retiring trenches or advancing columns, all moving still towards fashioning a genuine medium of conquest . . . vicarious hollow and original substance.

'Crumbling', 'retiring' and 'advancing' outline the course henceforth taken by Harris's characters, first an erosion of biased assumptions followed by a double movement of advance and retreat (for the self as for the other) which precludes total identification with another and therefore total loss or gain for one or the other. The 'vicarious hollow and original substance' towards which Stevenson moves, but is not known to have reached, sums up the simultaneous condition of nothingness and starting point of creation that Harris sees as the essence of Caribbean experience and art.

Without unduly schematising, one can discern in Harris's next four novels some common features which throw light on his purpose as a novelist. They all recreate the past of an individual Guyanese family, whose trials and present circumstances reflect the 'burden of history' that still weighs on the society they live in. The condition explored in each novel is one of void or loss. The Narrator in *The Eye of the Scarecrow* (1965), which evokes the economic depression of the twenties and the Guiana strike in 1948, suffers 'a void in conventional memory' as a result of an accident. In *The Waiting Room* (1967) Susan Forrestal, deserted by her lover and blind after four eye operations, finds herself in a physical and a psychological void. She and her husband have died in an explosion, and the substance of the novel is drawn from their half-obliterated log-book and 'edited' by the author. Prudence, the protagonist of *Tumatumari*, has a nervous breakdown after the death of her husband and her delivery of a stillborn child. In *Ascent to Omai* (1970) Victor, who feels 'on the threshold of breakdown or collapse', explores the heartland in search of his lost father, who disappeared after serving a sentence for setting fire to the factory in which he was working.

There is a double preoccupation in these novels, with the state of loss incurred in the past and the kind of fiction that the artist, his narrator or protagonist attempts to conceive. The two are closely linked together and it will be seen that these works are as much about the art of fiction as about the revival or 'art' of community. The Narrator in *The Eye* who re-lives his past again and again, Susan and her lover re-living their affair through the author's editorship, Prudence re-creating twentieth-century Guyanese history from her own memories and her father's papers, and Victor writing a novel about his father's trial, all are creators or characters in search of a 'primordial species of fiction'.[3] The phrase implies that the stuff of fiction is to be found in what is both fundamental and primeval (in themselves and in the outer world) which the protagonists have long neglected, ignored or misrepresented to themselves. The primordial is shown to be a dynamic relationship between all forms of life but first and foremost between human beings. We saw that in *Palace of the Peacock* the essential part of himself to which Donne had been blind appeared to him as an Arawak Christ and Virgin. In the novels now under scrutiny the sacred is always a suppressed 'other': in *The Eye* the Narrator's closest friend, his relatives and a prostitute in the interior whom he unwittingly made use of, but also those he calls the 'uninitiate' or the 'unborn', that is, the consenting eclipsed victims of conscious or unconscious exploiters; in *The Waiting Room* each lover in his relation with the other; in *Tumatumari* the Amerindians and Prudence's black brother as well as her misunderstood husband and father; and in *Ascent to Omai* Victor's father, the faceless destitute miner who fades into the jungle, giving Victor the impression that he is a *tabula rasa*. As each explorer of the past discovers, however, the nothingness, deadness, stagnation or even inflexibility of those whom the Narrator in *The Eye* seeks beyond 'a dead masked frontier' is only an illusion. Their essential livingness and even capacity to reverse given situations and become tyrannical in turn is one of the protagonists' main discoveries. The basic rapport the protagonist achieves with the object of his exploration is one in which each moves towards the other without ever finally succumbing or identifying with that other. This is the bare outline of a process that must be traced through the complex structure and the rich metaphorical texture of the narrative; these vary greatly from one novel to another as Harris extends the limits of the reality he explores and approaches his material from different angles.

Nature and society (even when the latter is refined and abstracted, as in *The Waiting Room*) are the starting point of the characters' exploration, for in Harris's fiction it is always a keen sensitivity to the material world which leads to the perception of an immaterial perspective (or of those that are judged immaterial: 'the nameless sleeping living and the nameless forgotten dead'). The emphasis is no longer as in the early novels on the breakdown of the protagonists' personality: this is now their condition when the novels open. Their breakdown, however, turns out to be an asset: in their initial state of weakness or emptiness they no longer try to imprison within a given or final view the experience they re-live or the people they knew. Each becomes a medium ('vicarious hollow') in which the past re-enacts itself. In both *The Eye* and *The Waiting Room* the narrator's declared purpose is to allow a free and living 'construction of events' to emerge from the evocation of the past. What happens is that the 'broken' memory or the unsettled state of the characters yields a fragmented version of events; these gradually reveal possibilities of interpretation different from their original one. In other words, the past, which is now the main substance of the novel, is subject to the same process of crumbling and reshaping as the character who re-lives it. Time and space (inner and outer) are not seen as rigid and divisive frames of existence; these barriers come apart too, disclosing, for example, the disregarded or unsuspected feelings of individuals and peoples whose behaviour had been represented in one light only. There is thus a dislocation of surface reality in all its forms—and therefore a fragmentation of the narrative structure—which makes the protagonists aware of 'the stranger animation one sees within the cycle of time'[4]—in nature, that is; in the seemingly frozen past; in the retrenched and silent existence of the uninitiate and in the protagonists' own unconscious. This fragmentation alone opens the way into what is apparently dead within and beyond the perceptible world but is in fact alien, mysterious, 'opposite' life, sometimes fierce destructive force, sometimes frail, indistinct spirit. The protagonist himself is healed, his own memory and imagination regenerated, to the extent that he can *feel* that life by incurring its 'burden of authenticity, obscurity or difficulty'.[5] It is what Harris means by 'revising contrasting spaces' in order to allow a 'new dimension of feeling' to emerge. It is brilliantly illustrated in *Tumatumari* in the symbolic vision of harmony between Prudence and her husband's despised Amerindian mistress, Rakka, revolving together and changing places in a whirlpool of death and rebirth.

The characters' transformation ('gestation of the soul') is rendered symbolically through serial metamorphoses of metaphors, which is wholly consistent with Harris's belief that the individual consciousness is saturated with 'given' images of the past, and with the fact that metaphors alone can convey the unity underlying the apparently disparate shapes of life. A good example of this is the scarecrow in the first novel of this cycle, a metaphor for the diminished state of man, for the disruptions that can be observed in nature, for disintegrating tenements in Georgetown and for the dying British Empire. This accumulation of various scarecrow images (like the many versions of the severed head perceived by Prudence in *Tumatumari*) renders the underlying unity or 'unfathomable wholeness' that belies the void or *tabula rasa*. Wholeness is also expressed in single metaphors as, for example, in the symbolic union of Prudence and Rakka mentioned above or (in *The Waiting Room*) in an image inspired by the myth of Ulysses; his dependence on an insensitive mast and deaf crew is used to convey the union between the lovers, each being for the other the deaf mast or crew which allows his or her companion to hear the otherworldly muse. Some single key metaphors, like the sun and the whirlpool, develop fresh contrasting meanings from one novel to another. Single words also frequently express one thing and its opposite. So the word 'silence' in the same novel is both Susan's injunction to her lover, which denies him, and the expression of her longing for the silence and potential fulfilment allied to the nameless dimension.

Although I have already suggested as much, it is necessary to insist that while wholeness is tentatively reconstructed or approached in the narrative through an accumulation of images, and perceived by the protagonist in visionary moments, it is never actually attained. The narratives trace the characters' oscillations between the finite world and their vision of the 'infinite' as they grope towards a metaphysical reality which both fascinates and terrifies them. They make some progress towards it as they move towards the nameless in probing into

human history, into the mystery of eclipsed lives and of
injustice. When they have shed their own identity, have become *in imagination* and temporarily 'Idiot Nameless' (the
trickster without identity of Caribbean history), the metamorphosis of their vision, and therefore of themselves, takes place.
Self-negation achieved, their consciousness becomes a vehicle
for the transmutation of static images and is itself transformed
metaphorically: the scarecrow, an image of unconsciousness
when the novel opens, is released, like the Narrator, from the
blindness of self-sufficiency and becomes the medium of an
interplay of opposites, the foundation of true vision; the
waiting room, at first a place where Susan broods over the past
and suffers, becomes a 'womb' of rebirth (reconciliation and
vision); the severed head in *Tumatumari* turns into a smiling and
flowering Gorgon's head; in *Ascent to Omai* the stone in the
pool, which sends out concentric rings or horizons of memory
delimiting frustrating periods of Victor's life, initiates a dance
(a series of harmonious movements) between these formerly
blocked slices of life.

Namelessness, moreover, is not wholeness (the coincidence
of opposites) but only the contrary and negative pole of a
clearly defined identity. In *Black Marsden* (1972), which initiates the third cycle of his fiction, Harris warns against the
danger of erecting former victims into the powerful instru-
ment of a new tyranny in the name of a misconceived revolution. During his trip to Namless [sic]—at once his country of
origin and an imaginary wasteland, modern man's ruined
consciousness—Goodrich, the main character, realises that
formerly exploited workers have been trapped into a spiral of
self-destructive strikes by their employers and by obscure
forces. The *tabula rasa* state of Victor's father in *Ascent to Omai*
has developed into the *tabula rasa* theatre directed by Black
Marsden, who stimulates Goodrich's generosity and spiritual
liberation but threatens to engulf and 'deplete' him like all
Marsden's other agents when they yield to him. Through
Goodrich's association with Marsden it becomes clear that the
material generosity of individuals (or nations) will not redeem
them from their sense of guilt towards the poor. Goodrich
possesses 'the eye of the scarecrow' which eventually helps him

resist the hypnotic spell Marsden had cast over him. At the end of the novel he stands 'utterly alone', free from imposed thought yet still moved by 'the strange inner fire' that had first sent him on an expedition into 'infinity'.

This state of aloneness and the passion for infinity that Goodrich cannot wholly assuage if he wants to stay alive are further explored in *Companions of the Day and Night*, a sequel to *Black Marsden*, in which he becomes more deeply involved in the smouldering existence of the dead by editing Idiot Nameless's paintings and sculptures, the 'equation' of his exploration of Mexico. Through Nameless's 'descent' into Mexican historical vestiges, Harris brings together the theme of the enforced eclipse of civilisations and his belief in a possible 'treaty of sensibility between alien cultures'. Essentially, the novel is about the fall of man and his terror of extinction; it gives the experience of the void a universal and even a cosmic scale. Goodrich compares the pre-Columbians' dread that their world might come to an end unless they offered the sun human sacrifices with modern man's fear that his world might fall into a 'black hole of gravity'.[6] The pre-Columbians fell under Cortez and the conquering, not humble and life-giving, Christ that followed in his wake; the Christian Church, however, was itself driven underground by a revolution early in the twentieth century that led to further repression. Nameless too suffers from a 'falling sickness' (a psychological equivalent to the possibility of cosmic fall) which nevertheless enables him to confront and unravel the self-destructive models of pre-Columbian and Christian institutions, to retrieve also the original 'spark' or element of conscience, inherent in each civilisation, which was buried with these institutions when each in turn was sacrificed. Nameless lives at once through the days of the Mexican calendar and the pre-Easter period as the predicaments of the interchangeable conquerors and victims merge in his consciousness. It is indeed the contradictory aspects of his own condition as both victor and victim that Nameless explores and reconciles in himself. At the same time his transformation into a spark after his fall from the pyramid of the sun together with the impression he gives at the end that he is a frail Christ who is once more denied physical life suggest the possible emergence of a new centre of illumination from within the very deadlock of history.

A fundamental aspect of *Companions* is the way in which old forms (such as institutions or myths[7]) prove susceptible of new content through the mediation of the individual consciousness. Together with Nameless's 'painting' this leads to yet another development in Harris's presentation of characters. The aspect of namelessness explored in *Black Marsden* is still there, symbolised by the coat of uniformity worn by post-revolutionary workers and by the destitute madonna in the next novel, *Da Silva da Silva's Cultivated Wilderness* (1977). But more importance is given to Nameless's own freedom from codified ways of thinking and the capacity it gives him to play many roles in life and suffer the predicament of different people. Already in *Ascent to Omai* the judge, not knowing what became of Victor, shuffles blank cards while recreating the trial, thus envisaging for him alternative existences, for this blankness is like 'a consciousness without content which nevertheless permitted all alien contents to exist'.[8] While in *The Eye* Harris presented language as an equation of the arousal of vision from that blankness, in his latest novels he has added a term to the equation: painting as an art of grasping the 'inimitable'. The main character is now a painter whose works are so many partial versions of, yet also 'doorways' into, an inner reality or light that can be neither wholly unearthed nor trapped. The narrative itself is like a large canvas which corresponds to the painter's field of vision. The existences on this canvas reveal unpredictable resources that modify the relation between the two faces of tradition, the conqueror's and the victim's or, in a different form, the 'dying' tradition of perceptible achievements and its immortal counterpart growing out of unacknowledged sacrifice. The need for an imaginative, necessarily precarious balance between the two underlies the painter's ceaseless effort to create a 'middle ground' between the contrasting figures he 'paints' into existence, people whom he sees as resurrected selves moving in and out of his consciousness.

Since *Black Marsden* these 'painted' resurrected lives (resurrection leading to community is the major theme of the third cycle of novels) are evoked with increased sensuousness. Because the main concern in Harris's novels lies in the impact of the outside world (the apparently trivial as much as the more dramatic incidents of everyday life) on the individual's inner self, the recreated 'drama of consciousness' involves flesh-and-blood people. In the novels of Harris's second phase the possibility of reconciliation between the protagonist and those he revives is largely expressed metaphorically. Although the metaphors are borrowed from *living* nature, the reconstructed experience has a more abstract or structural character than in the earlier or later fiction. In the third phase, however, the revived figures are always solidly there; in the Da Silva novels[9] they are significantly conceived, brought to life, through the tender physical relations between the creative artist and his earthly muse or madonna. A contrast suggests itself between the metaphorical climax of *Palace of the Peacock* and the end of *Da Silva da Silva* when the painter's wife announces that she is pregnant:

> And then he caught her to him with the joy by which he had been first consumed; he felt her gloves against the back of his head; he felt the handle of the shopping bag against his fingers as his arms encircled her fleecy coat; he felt his masked feet touch her masked feet.
>
> He was almost tempted to laugh or cry at the paraphernalia of winter costume, thick gloves, furred coat, high suede boots, until his lips touched hers with a naked instantaneous delight.
>
> He encircled the globe then, a global light whose circulation lay through and beyond fear into unfathomable security.

13   Jean Rhys *by Cheryl M. L. Dash*

Jean Rhys, like many other West Indian writers, has spent the greater portion of her life abroad. She was born in Dominica of a creole mother and an English father. At sixteen she left the West Indies for Britain and shortly thereafter moved to Paris where she wrote five books by 1939.[1] After that, little was heard of her until the publication of *Wide Sargasso Sea* (1966) which was acclaimed as her best work. Primarily because of the success of *Wide Sargasso Sea* her earlier works have been reprinted and in 1976 she brought out a new collection of short stories, *Sleep it off Lady*.

There are certain themes that recur in her novels and short stories, making each work seem a continuation of the previous ones. The early books give the impression of an overwhelming and cohesive statement on the situation of the woman in regard to society in general and men in particular. Although *Wide Sargasso Sea* is widely considered Jean Rhys's most important work, the extent to which it differs from her other books is not always appreciated. *Wide Sargasso Sea* is Rhys's 'West Indian novel', her one major work in which her experiences, memories and knowledge of the West Indies are inextricably and fundamentally part of the story and not there to evoke sympathy for a heroine or to serve as a brief comparison with the coldness and loneliness of the metropolis. It is indisputably her most complete and fulfilling work; in it she gathers all the themes which preoccupy her and incorporates them into a wider and more comprehensive statement on the intricacy of human relationships that does not focus on the plight of the woman alone, although the springboard of the novel is still a female figure, Antoinette. It is therefore useful to analyse the main themes in Rhys's earlier work before focusing on *Wide Sargasso Sea*.

Rhys's heroines are overwhelmingly vulnerable. The women are so sensitive to the whims of their male acquaintances and so at the mercy of their society and environment that they seem to have no will. One heroine after the other succumbs and becomes ultimately self-destructive. They move through life not knowing how to make use of their experiences and live eternally in the present. Their major tragedy is the gap between their awareness of their condition and their ability to formulate a *modus vivendi*. Their lucidity is no protection against the inevitable tragedy of their existence.

Women are victims. This is the image which remains and which overrides any consideration of them as individuals. In fact, the heroines are basically interchangeable: Julia (in *After Leaving Mr Mackenzie*), Anna (in *Voyage in the Dark*), Sasha (in *Good Morning Midnight*) and Marya (in *Quartet*) are all one and the same person at various ages and in slightly differing situations. This is not to deny the sensitivity with which Rhys evokes the plight of these women. We are involved in their suffering and debasement, but in these novels it is the condition of the women themselves and not the external, varying details of their situation which interests the reader—and there are certain qualities and characteristics common to them all.

Their immediate physical surroundings, whether in Paris or England, are always seedy and sordid. Anna Morgan goes from one dilapidated rooming house to another; Sasha Jensen exchanges a Bloomsbury bedsitter for a third-rate Parisian hotel; Marya Zelli is rescued from her Parisian hotel room which was 'large and low-ceilinged, the striped wall-paper faded to inoffensiveness'[2] and Julia Martin lives in a hotel where 'the staircase smelt of the landlady's cats, but the rooms were cleaner than you would have expected'.[3] It is as if the depressing nature of their physical environment imposes itself on their personalities; the heroines all become apathetic and oppressed:

But I stopped going out; I stopped wanting to go out. That happens very easily. It's as if you had always done that—lived in a few rooms and gone from one to the other.[4]

The inability to cope with the difficulties of their existence and the subsequent withdrawal, here expressed by Anna Morgan, is reflected physically on the women in Rhys's work. They lose their spontaneity and youthful vigour and become haunted, afraid to face life: 'It was strange how many of the older women looked drab and hopeless, with timid, hunted expressions. They looked ashamed of themselves, as if they were begging the world in general not to notice that they were women or to hold it against them.'[5] The women are vulnerable, their happiness is in direct proportion to their success with men. They see themselves not as individuals but as extensions of their male counterparts; a rejection, however slight or imagined, leads them to question their worth as human beings.

The justification of their existence lies in their relationships with men, or more precisely, in their ability physically to attract men. This reliance on physical attraction and the consequent trauma which follows its loss are seen in *Wide Sargasso Sea* in both Antoinette and her mother, but they are even more poignantly and vividly expressed in the short story 'Rapunzel, Rapunzel' in *Sleep it off Lady*.[6] Mrs Peterson, in hospital, agrees to have a barber trim her long hair. Instead of just trimming it, he cuts off most of it and leaves with her hair in a plastic bag. Mrs Peterson, shaken, remarks, 'Nobody will want me now' and goes into a decline. Some mornings later, her bed is empty and we are not sure whether she died or had a nervous breakdown. This is not important. What matters here is that the barber, the man, has been responsible for what she considers her loss of femininity and this has brought with it a form of emotional or spiritual death which is more important than her actual demise.

The heroines have no well defined sense of self. Not fully accepting their importance as individuals, they make no plans. Their actions depend on fate and not on an effort of will. They live on what they can get from their lovers and are seldom convinced that they are fully functional human beings; they seem to be without any moral centre and will go whichever way the wind blows or do whatever seems easiest at the moment. The effort needed to harness and control their lives is lacking. Julia, in *After Leaving Mr Mackenzie*, realises that she has to make a decision about her life. She is too tired and defeated to take responsibility, however, so she allows fate to decide: 'If a taxi hoots before I count three, I'll go to London. If not, I won't.'

Rhys's heroines live for the present and have no sense of future, or they fear the passing of time so that the present becomes all-important. Mrs Peterson's reply to the other patients who told her that her hair would grow back is, 'No, there isn't time.' Living as they do, going from man to man, the externals exclude all else and when those fail, Mrs Peterson declines, Anna withdraws, Julia remains in her room so that her landlady is forced to remark: 'But it's the life of a dog.'[7]

The mention of the dog conjures up images of a whipped cur, defeated, with its tail between its legs, the image of an animal caught in a trap. It is an image which occurs numerous times in the novels and expresses the plight of these women. In *Quartet*, Marya is filled with fright—'Fright of a child shut up in a dark room. Fright of an animal caught in a trap.' These are obvious statements and the allusions leap to the eye. However, in *Mr Mackenzie* there are several occasions where Rhys's use of imagery is more subtle. After meeting Mr James in London and being disappointed at his obvious lack of genuine interest in her loneliness, Julia notices a vase of flowers in the hall of her hotel:

There was a vase of flame-coloured tulips in the hall—surely the most graceful of flowers. Some thrust their heads forward like snakes, and some were very erect, stiff, virginal, rather prim. Some were dying, with curved grace in their death.

Further in the novel, in an interlude which seems addressed to the reader, Julia thinks of the last time she was happy. She remembers walking along and catching butterflies which were put in a tin—butterflies which had been flying around happily in the sun. Inevitably, they fluttered so much in the tin that some were horribly battered and you lost all interest in them. And occasionally they were then unable to fly properly again. But you didn't feel guilty because:

> you knew that what you had hoped had been to keep the butterfly in a comfortable cardboard-box and to give it the things it liked to eat. And if the idiot broke its own wings, that wasn't your fault, and the only thing to do was to chuck it away and try again.

These two descriptions, one of flowers, one of butterflies, are metaphors of the female condition as described in Rhys's novels. The flowers in the vase reflect three types of reaction to existence—the last, that of the dying flowers, referring to the female in Rhys's *oeuvre*. The image of the butterflies is even more apt. The butterflies symbolise women who are made comfortable in boxes, gilded cages where their desires are not important; they are fed and cared for and their will is not taken into account. They are vulnerable. As time passes and they are no longer desirable, no longer decorative, they are eventually discarded and the cycle begins again.

We are not sure whether these women never had a strong sense of self or whether their various love affairs have undermined it, but essentially they lack identity and they wonder who or what they are: 'But who am I then? Will you tell me that? Who am I, and how did I get here?'[8] This crisis of identity and of the self is a strong theme in *Wide Sargasso Sea* and one of the evident links between that novel and Rhys's earlier works. It is the final, most important and tragic aspect of her heroines—the complete loss of their identity and the subsequent total abandonment of the self. The last novel before *Wide Sargasso Sea*, *Good Morning Midnight* (1939), has a terrifying and dramatic ending which not only underlines the humiliations which Sasha has endured, but epitomises the utter self-abandonment of Rhys's heroines, which is the reflection of their complete despair. Sasha has given in to a young gigolo she has met in Paris. He offers her money which she refuses and he leaves. She lies there, alone, hoping he will return. Her door opens. Without looking, she realises it is the commercial traveller who lives across the corridor and at whom she has often laughed. Yet, in her despair, she finds it difficult to refuse him—not only will he temporarily ease her loneliness but she recognises in him another lost, lonely human being and at this point she has nothing left to lose:

> He doesn't say anything. Thank God, he doesn't say any-thing. I look straight into his eyes and despise another poor devil of a human being for the last time. For the last time . . .
>   Then I put my arms round him and pull him down on to the bed, saying: 'Yes—yes—yes . . .'⁹

There is a certain arbitrariness about the setting in the four earlier novels. The heroines' plight would be essentially the same wherever they were and the external, physical details of their surroundings are not important. Rhys's formative years in the West Indies also do not have an influence on her early novels in terms of subject-matter, although in *Voyage in the Dark* there is constant reference to the warmth and spontaneity of the West Indies in contrast to the grim, cold calculation of Britain. In her short stories, especially in her recent collection, *Sleep it off Lady*, half the narratives deal with the West Indies. But in *Wide Sargasso Sea* the setting is of primary importance; the characters react to it and are what they are largely because of it. Setting here refers not only to physical but to historical setting. The historical events are the story at times and explain much of the motivation and situation of the characters. *Wide Sargasso Sea* is completely West Indian, not only because of the setting but primarily because of Rhys's way of seeing the events, resulting from a knowledge of the West Indies which comes from having lived there and having absorbed the es-sence of the place. There is an authenticity and a sense of felt reality.

The novel is situated in the West Indies immediately after the total Emancipation of slavery in 1838 (Emancipation actually began in 1834 but the final agreements did not come into being until 1838). The novel depicts a society in a state of decay financially and socially and Antoinette's family epitomises this decay. There were various historical factors which contributed to this condition.

In 1783 the American colonies became independent. The West Indies came into being as a plantation economy which depended for its survival on the exportation of sugar. After 1783 direct trade was cut off with the American colonies and there was competition on the market from Cuba, the East Indies and Brazil. During the Napoleonic wars, beet sugar produced in Europe was further competition. This seriously eroded the financial situation of the West Indian islands, still based on a slave and plantation economy.

Perhaps the greatest single economic problem was that of labour. After 1838 the plantations lost their right to free labour, and with less money—because of the fluctuations in the market—had now to pay the labourers whose services had formerly been free. But the problem was further aggravated by the reluctance of the blacks to stay on the estates which to them, understandably enough, represented bondage and enslavement. This led to the further deterioration of the once flourishing estates. Trinidad and Guyana attempted to fill the labour gap by importing labour from China and India but Jamaica did not do this on as large a scale. The final economic blow came in 1846 when the British government withdrew their protection of the market for sugar. This left the islands—which were primarily sugar economies—with a financial dilemma.

It is to this situation that the novel belongs and as it opens one immediately sees Coulibri—the once imposing and economically viable estate—in a condition of physical decay and deterioration. But these historical facts do not explain the ambivalent attitude towards the creolised whites which is so much a part of the novel and is reflected in their treatment by British whites and local blacks. The creolised whites in the West Indies were a minority group. Most of the plantation owners were absentee landlords and preferred to live in Britain where their children and families could enjoy untainted British culture and receive a British education. Very few whites chose to remain and live on the estates and those who did were consequently ostracised and felt to be not quite as good as the 'real British' were. By remaining in the West Indies, a generation grew up for which Britain was only a name, almost a mythical place; in reality they had nowhere to go back to as their West Indian plantations were the only homes they knew.

It is also a little-known fact that even during slavery there were some whites who were regarded as being totally despicable socially. These were a few very poor white people who actually took in washing and occasionally did the laundry even for the blacks. The attitudes of the blacks to poor whites were, therefore, deeply entrenched even before Emancipation, and the creoles were despised by the expatriate whites. The closer the economic plight of Antoinette and her family approximated the financial situation of the 'poor whites', the more their social situation was affected in the eyes of both the black and white population.

The superiority of the white population was maintained but was now being challenged because their economic power was no longer evident. This challenge of the existing circumstances in post-Emancipation Jamaica finally resulted in the Morant Bay rebellion—the first major organised black rebellion in Jamaica, which took place in 1865.

In the novel society is not romantically portrayed. It remains unfathomable, dark and savage. The two main characters—Antoinette and Rochester—both seem overpowered by it. They play out their roles as if fated, as if they are being manipulated by the power of history, of nature and of the dark forces around them. Yet, it is a mark of Rhys's artistic strength that the characters are both representative and individuals.

One is conscious in the novel of physical deterioration, not only that of the characters—for example, Antoinette's mother and brother—but that of the estate. The depiction of the dilapidated garden at Coulibri Estate is a symbol of decaying life:

Our garden was large and beautiful. . . . But it had gone wild. The paths were overgrown and a smell of dead flowers mixed with the fresh living smell.[10]

The physical deterioration mirrors the economic and social decay which resulted from the end of slavery. By depicting a society in decay Rhys shows her understanding of the complexity of the situation. Antoinette's double alienation comes out of this situation in which her position in relation to the blacks and the British whites is no longer clearly defined.

Antoinette in a way is inextricably part of the black society. She shares their lives—at least superficially—as for instance in her experiences with Tia:

> We boiled green bananas in an old iron pot and ate them with our fingers out of a calabash.

She also shares their superstition, believing, for example, that it is unlucky to kill a parrot and wanting to have Christophine work obeah. When she realises that Rochester no longer loves her, Antoinette's first reaction is to seek Christophine's help in the form of a potion which will regain Rochester's affections. If to an extent Antoinette is part of the society which formed her, an irony lies in the tenuous nature of these links—tenuous in that she herself feels a difference and the blacks are always aware of it.

The novel depicts the confrontation of two alien worlds, or rather of people from those two incompatible worlds. Antoinette's relationship with Tia emphasises this point. In the midst of their seemingly harmonious relationship, they have a disagreement and both revert to old reflexes. Antionette calls Tia 'a cheating nigger' and Tia tells Antoinette that she is not 'real white people' but a 'white nigger'. One of the scenes which underline the complexity of the relationship between the creolised whites and the ex-slaves is that which occurs on the night Antoinette leaves Coulibri for good. She sees Tia and her mother standing by the side of the road. Her first impulse is to run to Tia and stay with her since they had eaten the same food and shared similar experiences. Tia represents a part of her life which she did not want to end. She runs towards Tia:

> When I was close I saw the jagged stone in her hand but I did not see her throw it. I did not feel it either, only something

wet, running down my face. I looked at her and I saw her
face crumple up as she began to cry. We stared at each other,
blood on my face, tears on hers. It was as if I saw myself.
Like in a looking-glass.

All the tragedy of the white creole is embodied in this scene.
Tia is also affected because her tears reflect the knowledge of
something lost. But the image of the mirror matters. They are
reflections of each other, similar but somehow, as in a mirror
image, not real, not quite the same. The element of illusion is
always present.

Antoinette's involvement is an emotional one, but in reality
she is basically as much an outsider as Rochester. Christophine
embodies the ultimate incomprehensibility and complexity of
the society for both Rochester and Antoinette. Her attachment
to Antoinette is based on the emotion engendered by shared
experience, but experiences shared, as it were, from different
sides of a mirror; in the final analysis Christophine is as far
from Antoinette in sensibility as she is from Rochester.

Antoinette's alienation is manifested in various crises. Her
sense of identity has already been shaken after her experience
with Tia. Rochester further undermines her confidence by
calling her Bertha instead of Antoinette, using her mother's
name and in so doing reduces her own idea of herself.
Antoinette therefore wavers in a state of uncertainty; she is
rejected by the blacks, not fully accepted by Rochester, and is
caught between two opposing worlds. One evening Rochester
and Antoinette overhear Amelie singing. Only Antoinette can
understand the words. This is ironical as it suggests some
affinity with the singer which Rochester does not have. But,
she tells Rochester,

> It was a song about a white cockroach. That's me. That's
> what they call all of us who were here before their own
> people in Africa sold them to the slave traders. And I've
> heard English women call us white niggers. So between you
> I often wonder who I am and where is my country and
> where do I belong and why was I ever born at all.

This crisis of identity is a further development in

Antoinette's deep-rooted crisis of self. Her passivity and inability to cope link her irrevocably with Rhys's other heroines. Early in her life at Coulibri she comments that the family would have died had Christophine left them and the thought to her is not one of horror. On the contrary, it is a good thing, 'To die and be forgotten and at peace. Not to know that one is abandoned, lied about, helpless.' Her inability to cope forces her into total emotional and economic dependence on Rochester and into a final alienation of the psyche, a total entrapment in limbo. Like her mother, unable to control her environment, she withdraws.

The double alienation culminates in Antoinette's 'losing her way' to England. For Antoinette, England has always been a place of myth, somehow not real. Her lack of actual knowledge of the home of her ancestors is the result of her creolisation and one of the problems between herself and Rochester. Here, in this the last section of the novel, when the marriage has already totally collapsed, Rochester takes Antoinette to England. But Antoinette, like her mother before her, has retreated into her own universe and is considered insane. She is forever unable to save herself or to realise that she has reached England. The feeling of England's not being real is perhaps not so much the result of Antoinette's 'madness' as it is a statement by Rhys that for the creolised white England can never be real, never be as alive and as vibrant as the West Indies which has formed their psyche. This is evident in *Voyage in the Dark* where Anna frequently refers to the sense of alienation she feels in the cold detachment of British society and, through a series of flashbacks, keeps longing for and revelling in the experiences and warmth of 'home', that is, the West Indies. This inability to perceive England gives emphasis to the difference between Antoinette and Rochester. Her inability to save herself, her ultimate self-destruction, as revealed in the last section of the novel, does not come as a surprise. One remembers Antoinette's early dream while at the convent. One is struck by the sense of doom, of fate, and passivity:

I make no effort to save myself; if anyone were to try to save me I would refuse. This must happen.

It is significant that this dream occurs when Antoinette knows she has to leave the convent, her refuge, her place of safety, and the dream is a premonition of her life after leaving Coulibri and the safety of the past.

Her final dream represents, like the first, an inability to face reality and an underlying desire to recapture the past. It is Rhys's master stroke. Antoinette's end comes in a dream which is itself not real but foreshadows the reality. It emphasises her complete withdrawal. When she leaps, she leaps backwards in time, into the arms of history and, most important, to safety. Ironically, she leaps to her death, the final illusion, the final annihilation.

Antoinette makes a last desperate attempt to salvage her past. But Rhys, in a short story, 'Heat', in *Sleep it off Lady* suggests that the past cannot be salvaged. Mont Pelée erupts and there is extensive damage; the father of the child in the story brings back a pair of candlesticks as a souvenir —candlesticks which obviously come from a church:

> The heat had twisted them into an extraordinary shape. He hung them on the wall of the diningroom and I stared at them all through meals, trying to make sense of the shape.

The past cannot be recaptured. One has to try to make sense of it, to mould and use one's experiences to help one cope with the present. This Rhys's characters are unable to do. Antoinette embodies this inability. Christophine makes a comment which reinforces Rhys's theme. She tells Antoinette, 'Get up, girl, and dress yourself. Woman must have spunks to live in this wicked world.' Antoinette encompasses the apathy and crisis of identity in Rhys's conception of the female as victim. But beyond that Antoinette is the symbol of a group hitherto virtually ignored in West Indian fiction: the creolised white, a group caught in the middle, the flotsam of a system that exploited and corrupted both black and white.

In several ways, the novel marks a development in Jean Rhys's work. The story is told from two points of view. Quite often in the earlier novels, Rhys's desire to state the case of exploited women led her into sentimentality and melodrama.

In *Wide Sargasso Sea* there is more control and objectivity, which is largely due to the form of the novel—that is, the fact that events are seen through the eyes not only of Antoinette but of Rochester as well. The men in Rhys's works, until *Wide Sargasso Sea*, are shadowy figures, important only in so far as they represent the destructive forces which crush the heroines. Their characters are never developed and it is perhaps only J. H. Heidler in *Quartet* who is given any motivation for his actions or appears to have any independent existence apart from his role as man, the agent of destruction. Throughout *Wide Sargasso Sea*, however, one's sympathy for Antoinette is evoked but is counterbalanced by a corresponding sympathy and understanding for Rochester, himself a victim, an out-sider, brought into a society he is unable to comprehend. The novel in this way shows the alienation not only of Antoinette but of Rochester.

At the start of their honeymoon Rochester rides along behind Antoinette:

> Everything is too much, I felt as I rode wearily after her. Too much blue, too much purple, too much green. The flowers too red, the mountains too high, the hills too near.

He is overwhelmed by what seems to him the extremity of nature, a lushness that is overdone and to which he cannot react positively. Nature is so overpowering that that night the scent of the river flowers coming into the room makes him feel giddy. His fear of the strangeness of his new life is transmitted into a fear of his physical surroundings as depicted in the flora and fauna of the small West Indian island. Nowhere is this more vividly portrayed than when he becomes lost in the bushes. 'It is hostile', he thinks. And after he fully realises he is lost he thinks, 'I was lost and afraid among these enemy trees, so certain of danger.'

It is not, however, only the physical aspects of the setting which scare Rochester and make him feel ill at ease. His reaction to Christophine symbolises his reaction to the blacks around him whom he finds inscrutable and consequently threatening. His inability to relate to them is only an extension, however extreme, of his inability to relate to Antoinette who he says is 'a stranger who did not think or feel as I did'. Consequently, Rochester's sense of alienation is both physical and cultural. Both these aspects are fused towards the end of the novel. Rochester has just slept with Amelie, a servant girl, and Antoinette in her grief has attacked him with a bottle. Christophine arrives and soothes Antoinette; Rochester is completely rejected and ignored. In the repetition of the creole endearments he feels something threatening. The violence of the culture and society is expressed by Christophine's gory tales, one of which tells of holding on to a woman's nose—a nose that her husband had just chopped off. The hostility of Rochester's surroundings, physical, social and cultural is now complete:

> It seemed to me that everything round me was hostile. The telescope drew away and said don't touch me. The trees were threatening and the shadows of the trees moving slowly over the floor menaced me. . . . There was nothing I knew, nothing to comfort me.

There is a dearth of literature written about white West Indians or by white West Indians in the years following Emancipation. It is interesting that, within the same era as Rhys's novel, we have three others by white West Indians. *The Orchid House* (1953) by P. Shand Allfrey has, interestingly, a negro narrator—the old nurse of a white colonial family who reminisces over the various generations of the family she has served. *Christopher* (1959) by Geoffrey Drayton is a novel of childhood, seen through the boy's consciousness, and a precursor to *The Year in San Fernando* by Michael Anthony (1965). *Brown Sugar* (1966) by J. B. Emtage is an attempt at satire on present-day West Indian politics. Traditionally in West Indian fiction it is the problems of the black West Indian which have been the subject of novels, plays and poems. In *Wide Sargasso Sea* we have portrayed in fiction the ravages wrought on the white West Indian.

14   Edward Brathwaite *by J. Michael Dash*

Probably the best introduction to the poetry of Edward Brathwaite is his largely autobiographical essay entitled 'Timehri'. In this account of his own experiences and how they combined to form an awareness of certain literary and cultural problems, the poet attempts to situate himself in terms of the evolution of West Indian writing. In tracing various tendencies among his fellow writers, Brathwaite isolates two important phases in a gradual movement from an initial sense of dispossession and fragmentation towards a more recent attempt to go beyond this sense of disintegration and to envisage the positive forces of creolisation in the Caribbean context:

> The problem of and for West Indian artists and intellectuals is that having been born and educated within this fragmented culture, they start out in the world without a sense of 'wholeness' . . . The achievement of these writers was to make the society conscious of the cultural problem. The second phase of West Indian and Caribbean artistic and intellectual life, on which we are now entering, having become conscious of the problem, is seeking to transcend and heal it.[1]

There is no attempt by Brathwaite to disown any of the writers who preceded him and whose preoccupations he sees as different from his. What he is taking care to outline is a crucial shift in sensibility within recent West Indian writing. The evolution is away from that obsessive sense of loss, that once fed the violent

210

protest or inveterate cynicism of the earlier phase, towards a newer more speculative vision of 'wholeness' in the Caribbean situation. He not only identifies closely with the second phase but sees it as a way of resolving the problems posed in the work of his literary forebears.

Indeed this notion of estrangement from one's community and landscape becomes in Brathwaite's various critical articles or surveys of West Indian writing the main criterion for judging individual Caribbean writers. For instance, Claude McKay's ability to visualise Bita Plant's reintegration into Banana Bottom makes him a precursor of the second phase. In contrast to the vision of V. S. Naipaul, McKay presents a positive world from which one was not tempted to escape. In this progression Wilson Harris emerges as the artist whose work represents a conscious investigation of the previously overlooked creolising forces or 'native consciousness' in the Caribbean experience.[2]

An insight into Brathwaite's formative literary experiences can be had from the early poems published in the literary journal *Bim* in the 1950s. In what must be one of the first poems published by Brathwaite, 'Shadow Suite', we have a private, contemplative mood which has obviously drawn on the abstract metaphysical brooding of T. S. Eliot for inspiration:

> You who expect the impossible
> Know that here you will see
> Only what you have already seen
> What you hear
> 　　　is only what you have already heard
> For life is an eternal pattern.[3]

This sombre, meditative verse does not indicate the poet's alienation from reality; it illustrates the introspective quality present in his early period of literary apprenticeship which also directly informs his later vision of the New World.

A pattern emerges from this poetic contemplation of the human condition. What the poet seems to be doing is linking a fundamentally religious notion with the process of artistic creativity. Brathwaite seems to consider reality in general in

terms of a world fallen from grace; the poet's special role
revolves around his awareness of this fall and his capacity to
recapture the lost state through his vision. For instance, the
poem 'South' which first appears in *Bim* in 1959[4] (and is later
included in an edited form in *Rites of Passage*) concerns the
poet's ability to transform this fallen world through his creative imagination. The poem's very first line indicates the
difference between the vision and the ordinary world: 'But
today I recapture the islands.' This poetic fantasy comes to a
climax with: 'And gulls, white sails slanted seawards,/fly into
the limitless morning before us.' The restoration of a state of
grace is seen as fragile and tentative in the 1959 version. The
ending, which he later removed, suggests a world which easily
relapses into its former state as the vision fades:

> Night falls and the vision is ended.
> The drone of the groaners is ended.

The same is true of the poem 'The Leopard' which when it later
appears in *Islands* can be made to suggest the Black Panther
organisation and certainly a more militant context. The caged
animal in the first version of 'The Leopard' becomes a
metaphor of betrayal with obvious religious overtones. It
connects with the poet's concern for a world heedless of
spiritual values and vainly attempting to tame or shut out a
deeper dimension to human existence:

> We breed our haggard rages
> And lock Christ up, a leopard
> in cold unheeded cages.[5]

A final illustration of this quality in Brathwaite's early work
is seen in the short poem 'The Vision'. This might be considered a poetic manifesto as it stresses the need for restoring
that lost hallowed quality to the world, what he would later
term 'wholeness'. The poet's role in this process of recreating a
sense of wonder before reality is made explicit here:

> Without fear or faces. There
> should be places where the roots

can grow, where green shoots
Sing, where the gold blown pollen
Blossoms. But feet that walk
the rootless walk, find no way here
No water. And so the blind eyes, wells,
Lack tears, lack pity, lack their proper use.[6]

The poem is a prototype for the world of Brathwaite's trilogy. The very images of roots, pollen, green shoots are to recur in the later work as symbols of a world restored. The blind eyes that 'lack their proper use' relate to the inhibited and insensitive world that has lost its sense of the fantastic which can only be regained through a poetic consciousness.

The recent appearance of *Other Exiles*[7] completes the pattern we have been examining. This collection of miscellaneous poems has no dominant theme. Many of the poems are largely personal poems of his early period, and their inclusion seems to be based on their success in evoking certain impressions or moods. For instance, a love poem such as 'Schooner' reveals Brathwaite's ability to use sustained imagery to suggest, in this case, a relationship between two individuals. The collection is given some coherence by being enclosed by two poems that allude to the theme of re-creation and that awesome moment of wonder in which communion is made with the spiritual. The first poem, 'Ragged Point', refers to the east coast of Barbados where the landscape is untamed and is easily linked with the idea of freshness associated with the dawn light, and the new year:

We watched what there was to watch
saw the cold rocks come clearer
sky rise.

The vision cannot be sustained:

Next morning the weather was clear
we'd forgotten our notions.

The final poem, 'New Year Letter', symbolises the same moment of intense revelation:

So softly now this moment fills
the darkness with its difference.
Earth waits, trees touch
the dawn.

Brathwaite's work can be seen as a slow progression towards
this moment when the vision of 'wholeness' is established.

In his early work Brathwaite conceives of the poetic imagination as a superior way of perceiving the world. The poetic
reconstruction of the world could redeem reality from its fallen
state. In another early poem in *Other Exiles* Brathwaite expresses the need for 'words to refashion futures like a healer's
hand'. The same line recurs in the trilogy as the poet is
attempting to liberate the region from its sterile fallen state.
The poet's public voice has its roots in this early recognition of
the role of art as a means of discovering unconscious figurative
meanings behind the concrete and the visible. What was
essentially a private literary quest for the young Brathwaite
later becomes the point of departure for an aesthetic exploration of the Caribbean that transcends the historical stereotype
of pluralism and fragmentation.

Even though Brathwaite situates himself in a new vanguard
of West Indian writing, his actual career and experiences are
not unlike those of the generation of the 'first phase'. Born in
Barbados in 1930 he follows the familiar pattern of metropolitan exile and an eventual return to the West Indies. He receives
his higher education in Cambridge in the early fifties and
becomes in his own words 'a roofless man of the world' before
returning to the Caribbean. As is the case with most artists
who underwent this sequence of experiences, the odyssey
served to heighten the poet's sensitivity to the dilemma of
alienation which plagued West Indian intellectuals in exile.

During this period of exile Brathwaite's work reflects his
various experiences. For instance, 'The day the first snow fell'
(1953) is basically about the poet's disappointment at discovering his estrangement in Britain from a world which he thought
he could possess. The frustration normally expected at this
point in the career of the exiled artist, when all worlds appear
strange to him, never really emerges in Brathwaite's work. We

have an important departure from the sense of dispossession that comes with exile, in the poet's eight-year stay in Ghana (1955–62). It is here that he discovers that sense of the sacred so crucial to the poetic imagination. He discovers a world which he cannot adopt but one which seems to retain a communion with the mysterious and numinous which is absent in the historically disadvantaged New World. His awareness of the customs and language of the Ghanaian people is seen in his adaptation of *Antigone* to a Ghanaian context in *Odale's Choice* (1962). This does not represent an original project since the adaptation of classical drama to local situations was not unknown, but it does show a closeness to the environment in which he found himself, which is central to his dramatisation of this experience in his trilogy.

Brathwaite returned to the Caribbean in 1962 and began work on the trilogy, *The Arrivants*,[8] which meant a coming to terms with his European and African experiences. The earlier, more introspective mode would now yield to an epic reconstruction of the cultural and historical situation of the Caribbean. The first section of this long work, *Rites of Passage* (1967), evokes the sterility and dispossession inspired by his own experiences growing up in Barbados and his awareness of Caribbean history. *Masks* (1968) draws heavily on the world observed during his stay in Ghana and is a marked contrast to the fragmented and desecrated world of the previous section. The final part, *Islands* (1969), treats the poet's physical and spiritual return to the Caribbean and attempts to restore that vision of grace that was absent in his first negative picture of waste and sterility.

When one considers the epic and dialectical structure of Brathwaite's trilogy, a comparison is inevitable with Aimé Césaire's *Cahier d'un retour au pays natal*. Essentially the same pattern emerges in both these poets—from an initial evocation of devastation in the Caribbean, the poem moves to a concluding vision of renascence. This progression can be shown by the following examples.

The *Cahier* first presents the islands 'shipwrecked in the mud of this bay' and later returns to the islands as 'scars upon the water . . . waste paper torn and strewn upon the water'. The movement is from the static and pathetic to an image which, while retaining the sense of absurdity and tragedy, suggests new possibilities. Brathwaite in his long poem locates the progression in his work in the same way. The cabin presents Old Tom as a casualty of history, his suffering forgotten by his descendants. The later section, *Islands*, contains the poem 'Anvil' which evokes a less resigned Tom: 'But from the edge/of dark, defeated silence,/what watchful patience glitters.' Césaire's poem could easily have had some influence on Brathwaite. The *Cahier* is an unprecedented attempt to deal with the Caribbean region on such a scale and with such insight. Indeed, solely on the evidence of the literary activity in *Bim* in the 1950s, there was obviously an awareness of the literary renascence in the French-speaking Caribbean. Translations of Haitian and French West Indian poets are present as early as 1953, and in a review of Harris's poetry in 1960 Brathwaite mentions 'the influence of Césaire and French West Indian poets on modern French writing'.[9] Yet it would be a simplification to present *The Arrivants* as an English version of the *Cahier*. The *Cahier* may have presented identical issues a few decades earlier than Brathwaite's poem and was in general a shaping force on the younger poet, but the latter work can be more usefully interpreted in terms of a response to certain issues raised within Anglophone West Indian writing.

These issues touch on two important areas—the history of the New World and the problems of the literary imagination in such a context. V. S. Naipaul, because of his outspoken views, can easily illustrate what these ideas meant. The tension between Naipaul and Brathwaite has been overworked but it is important to see the distance between these writers in order to state the point of departure of *The Arrivants*. The two stereotypes that emerge in Naipaul's essays hinge upon a particular attitude to the absurdity of the New World situation. In *The Middle Passage* the Caribbean is presented as uncreative and philistine:

> The history of the islands can never be satisfactorily told. Brutality is not the only difficulty. History is built around achievement and creation; and nothing was created in the West Indies.[10]

Brathwaite's trilogy can be conceived as a demonstration of how the writer can emerge from such a despairing attitude to the Caribbean. The second notion which follows on this one concerns the enormous difficulty faced by the writer who attempts to use such an environment as a source for literary creation. Naipaul is perceptive on the question of the problems faced by such a writer attempting to repossess this experience and landscape:

> Fiction or any work of the imagination, whatever its quality, hallows its subject. To attempt . . . to give a quality of myth to what was agreed to be petty and ridiculous . . . required courage.[11]

Brathwaite as a writer of the second phase saw it as his duty to resolve this question. For him George Lamming started this process with *In the Castle of My Skin* (1953) in his attempts to 'hallow' the commonplace and the petty. *The Arrivants* can be read as a metaphor of the literary process, namely an attempt to redeem through literary means a world thought to be trivial and debased. This latter preoccupation neatly ties in with the attempts to retrieve a communion with the spiritual values present in Brathwaite's earlier work. The poet's own literary development is now tied in with our ideological debate and is the prime motivation for the literary and psychic journey traced in his trilogy.

The poems of *Rites of Passage* are clustered around the theme of spiritual dispossession. They are an attempt to remove the amnesia about historical events in the West Indian psyche and create an awareness of the historical injustice perpetrated in the region and the blind materialism of the present. In this instance, the actual historical events in the New World are symbolically related to the Fall of Man; one of the most effective fantasies describes the arrival of Columbus in the West Indies. This arrival is an important hieroglyph for the poet as it marks the transition from a state of grace to a desecrated and profane reality. It is one of the few instances when images of decay and waste are not used to describe the Caribbean. Columbus first sees an untainted world:

> Columbus from his after-
> deck watched stars, absorbed in water,
> melt in liquid amber drifting.

'Liquid amber' suggests a state of sustained harmony existing before Columbus's intrusion. The latter is portrayed as an innocent, not fully aware of the horrors this encounter would precipitate:

> What did this journey mean, this
> new world mean: dis-
> covery? Or a return to terrors
> he had sailed from, known before?

Brathwaite's reconstruction of this moment is not done as a strident protest against the European conquest, but rather he imagines it in terms of a process of desecration that makes the Spaniard no different from self-seeking politicians, from Mammon.

This section is devoted to a recall of the violations that are part of the New World heritage. In the same way that Césaire shattered the picture of an exotic, fun-loving Caribbean, Brathwaite undermines such superficiality with a sustained tableau of absurdity and frustration. This is interestingly done in 'Calypso' as the tragic consequences of the Imperialist Adventure emerge. The contrast lies between the glorification of the adventure and the awesome truth of what took place. The light-hearted jingle of the following lines emphasises the irony of what is suggested:

> O it was a wonderful time
> an elegant benevolent redolent time
> and young Mrs P.'s quick irrelevant crime
> at four o'clock in the morning.

This picture of 'the hurt of history' is continued in the numerous references to the historical suffering of the black race. This is a repeated theme of the negritude writers and the Harlem Renaissance; Brathwaite adds his voice to tracing the journeys of 'the wretched of the earth' or in his words, 'Columbus' coursing Kaffirs'. Poems such as 'Didn't he ramble', 'The Journeys', 'The Emigrants', all suggest the sufferings and humiliations of the black diaspora.

The images that dominate *Rites of Passage* convey the atmosphere of desolation the poet sees around him. In 'Prelude' these images are introduced as engraved in the landscape:

Dust glass grit
the pebbles of the desert:
Sands shift
across the scorched
world water ceases
to flow.

These lines recur in 'Epilogue' with the same suggestion of a sordid, barren world: 'desert/sands still shift'.

The religious associations of this sterile world become clear in a poem such as 'Mammon'. The title is significant in itself and the poem deals with a profane world trapped in a blind materialism. The Caribbean of the present makes no attempt to retrieve the spiritual, or to establish traditions, but forges 'brilliant concrete crosses'. This ties in with the general picture of a paralysing materialism in the Western world not unlike the dry, sterile Europe of Senghor and Césaire. New York epitomises this tendency, 'soilless, stainless, nameless'.

The following sequence, *Masks*, is a contrast to the first in that it is an evocation of serenity and reverence totally absent in the violated New World. It is tempting to locate Brathwaite's vision of Africa as part of the mythical, nostalgic picture evident in such poets as Senghor, to cast Brathwaite in the role of the prodigal son returning to his roots. However, it is significant to note the section is entitled *Masks* and not 'Africa' and to see the extent to which we witness something more complex than blind romanticising of the ancestral past.

What Brathwaite does is situate his quest for a hallowed world in the Ghanaian experience. There he makes contact with a world where there is still communion with the spiritual. So *Masks*, as the word implies, represents a borrowed way of interpreting the world, of making contact with the numinous:

> So for my hacked
> heart, veins' mem-
> ories, I wear this
> past I borrowed.

Three hundred years have made him a stranger and the agony of this recognition is felt in a poem such as 'The New Ships'. *Masks* is not a reintegration into the African past. It is a significant stop on the way back to the New World.

Masks is also used to provide a corrective to the traditional myth of savagery and primitivism in African societies. It describes the kingdoms of Ghana, Mali, Songhai and the growth of these civilisations with the historian's eye for setting the record straight. Central to *Masks*, however, is the poet's encounter with this universe and his initiation into a world of rituals and mystery. 'The Forest' describes such a recognition of a hallowed state. The images of desolation in the previous section are replaced by a sense of awe and calm appropriate to an unfallen world, the poet's 'wom'd heaven':

> This
> was the pistil journey in-
> to moistened gloom. Dews
> dripped, lights twink-
> led, crickets chirped and still
> the dark was silence, still
> the dark was home.

This vision of 'wholeness' is not permanent. It is the preparation for the final stage of the poet's return. It is the attempt to restore such a moment of stillness and contemplation in his own broken landscape that represents the fundamental movement of the trilogy.

The analogy with Césaire's *Cahier* is useful in discussion of the final phase, *Islands*. In the Martinican poet's work we find that the process of return and fashioning a new poetic vision draws on Rimbaud and Surrealist technique as literary antecedents. The *Cahier* even more than an ideological 'prise de position' is an attempt to dislocate the traditional meanings of words so as to set the poetic imagination free. It was through such directed anarchy that language could be cleansed and become the poet's miraculous weapon for reconstructing the world after the flood. This is precisely what the poet is referring to when he speaks of 'the madness that sees'. Brathwaite's 'the eye must be free/seeing' also suggests this feature of modern poetry as he wishes to reach beyond the static and sterile to retrieve his world through his poetic vision. In this, an important literary ancestor is T. S. Eliot.

Eliot is as important to Brathwaite's creative imagination as the overwhelming moment of revelation in the African experience. To this extent Eliot's poetry almost becomes the literary pre-text for the Caribbean poet's trilogy. This is not to say that Brathwaite supports Eliot's religious and ideological dogma; what he does endorse is the latter's plea for the restoration of the numinous and his indictment of man's enslavement to materialism. In the same way that Eliot criticises modern man's attempt to fix time—indeed, his servitude to linear time, 'the enchainment of past and future', and the accompanying notions of material progress—so Brathwaite attempts to defy such a view of the New World which would make it an uncreative adjunct to Imperial expansion.

At this point Brathwaite the poet upstages Brathwaite the historian, in that he feels the need to go beyond the formal recorded history to a more open and speculative view of the New World experience. This is one way to avoid the knowledge that falsifies, to rediscover in myth a new, liberating sense of self and of possibilities in the Caribbean. When this intense moment of revelation is attained, the poet begins to see his community and landscape for the first time. It is his poetic vision that has the redemptive force of defying the tragic, mutilated, historical stereotype. Brathwaite is alluding to this moment of quasi-mystical illumination when he explains:

Like a worshipper possessed at shango or vodun, as with a jazz musician, time past and time future speak to the community in the trapped and hunting [sic] moment of awareness.[12]

The artist/shaman in this creative trance becomes a medium, the community's link with a world of mystery which involves a new potency for change.

Islands casts the poet in such a role and can be seen as the *raison d'être* of the trilogy. It begins by restating the sterile, materialistic world of *Rites of Passage*. In 'Homecoming' this initial state is made explicit:

> To this new doubt
> and desert I return,
> expecting nothing.

The universe to which the poet returns represents a harsh encounter with a lifeless, secular reality: God 'is glass with his type-/ writer teeth'; the land 'has lost the memory of the most secret places' and the people 'float round and round . . . without hope of the hook/of the fisherman's tugging-in root'. This state is poignantly evoked in the epigrammatic poem 'Pebbles' which in a sustained image presents a world which is barren and unheeding:

> But my island is a pebble.
> . . .
> It will slay
> giants
>
> but never bear children.

The humpbacked turtle of 'Francina' is a symbol of the past, of the sacred (like Eliot's river in 'The Dry Salvages') which is ignored and unpropitiated by an insensitive, complacent world. Francina's quiet, daring act of retrieval is mocked by a world that cannot comprehend such an act.

For the poet to accomplish his mission he must find the poetic equivalent to Francina's act. He must reinstate a sense of the sacred in this empty, destructively secular world. Ideology and political solutions are not adequate for this level of restoration. Yet this spiritually impoverished world resists the poet. The poetic word in its full literary and religious significance is the only means of redemption but the poet is daunted by the task. The 'word has been destroyed/ and cannot live among us', and the poet has difficulty restoring the word to its real importance. The way in which this strange, desecrated waste-land defies the poet is referred to in such lines as 'the stars/ remain my master's/property' and 'they'd rob the world I ruled.' The world is at least temporarily possessed by the Other. It can only be retrieved by an imagination and a language that have been set free.

Some of the poems in *Islands* can be seen as an allegory of the poetic act, namely the act of retrieving and renaming the landscape. A poem such as 'Veve' suggests this process of 'hallowing' as the fisherman's net or poetic vision falls gently over reality and retrieves it. The lyricism of the poem revolves around the invoking of this state of 'wholeness' and images of rebirth: 'The black eye travels to the brink of vision:/ look, the fields are wet,/ the sea sits gentle on the dawn.' Significantly placed towards the end of *Islands*, this poem represents the end of the quest, the attainment of this transcendental vision. The final poem, 'Jou'vert', is more than an attempt to re-use a local ritual—the carnival. It also represents the dawn of the risen god/word and the poetic vision retrieved with all its positive and healing resonances.

Brathwaite has included himself in the 'second phase' of West Indian writing because his work is so deeply involved in an aesthetic renascence. It is interesting to see how this vision of salvation for the Caribbean has certain implications for the poet's role. The relationship of the poet to his community becomes more complex than that of a poet–politician. It is no longer a question of a readily accessible ideal of commitment which would inspire some collective action. Central to Brathwaite's conception of the poet is the element of possession. Even though he identifies closely with his community, his superior vision inevitably isolates him. Each metaphor of the artist as he appears in Brathwaite's work is presented in terms of a sensitive but essentially lonely figure. For instance, 'Ananse' suggests such characteristics, 'creator/dry stony world-maker, word breaker' who survives with his memories in the 'dark attic'. The same is true of 'Littoral' with the frequently used image of the solitary fisherman/artist; 'his head/ sleeps in the surf's/ drone, his crossed/ legs at home/ on the rough sand.' He shares the same spiritual resources of Ananse—a voice in the dark—'his fingers knit as the dark rejoices/ but he has many voices.' The distance between this creative consciousness and the materialistic world around it is made clear in 'Ogun'. Ordinarily he appeared to be nothing but a carpenter making 'what the world preferred' but secretly he is a divine craftsman shaping the block of wood 'that would have baffled them . . . breathing air . . . still tuned to roots and water'. This sombre communion with the spiritual has little to do with the rhetorical gesture and iconoclasm of protest poetry. The contemplative state which frees the creative imagination creates an overwhelming kind of self-awareness in the poet. As the trilogy progresses, Brathwaite focuses more intensely on the relocation of his vision of the Caribbean in an artistic consciousness and not in the external history of the region.

So far we have treated literary preoccupations in Brathwaite's work and the emergence of a poetic self-consciousness. Such a resumé of his poetry would seem adequate if he simply saw himself as a cerebral poet, but even the most casual reading of Brathwaite's verse would reveal different or even conflicting voices in his work. The voice we have examined so far is easily recognised as the product of various literary concerns of his initiation into poetry. The other voice that is apparent is more direct and closely linked to the speech patterns and rituals of the folk.

Along with the use of sustained visual imagery and the dislocation of words, Brathwaite favours the use of speech patterns for purposes of irony or to bring immediacy to what he is saying. These intonations that often relieve the apparent plainness of his verse are frequently drawn from local dialects. This has both ideological and literary implications. Brathwaite accepts the need for a writer to be part of a tradition, indeed to be its growing edge. He has sought such a tradition in the creolised cultures of the Caribbean. The use of dialect (like the use of various deities and rituals) is his articulation of the consciousness of those who survived in the New World. The literary significance of what the poet is doing presents a more complicated problem.

The use of dialect in poetry is never considered just another literary device which a poet can exploit to dramatise certain features in his work. It has traditionally been seen as part of an anti-intellectual rejection of formalism in poetry. The spontaneity and simplicity of folk poetry did not seek academic acclaim—in the case of Langston Hughes it meant a defiance of the literary establishment—and so was apparently exempt from critical evaluation. However, it would be a simplification to see Brathwaite's use of dialect as a gratuitous rejection of formal poetic devices, especially with his own closeness to the conventions of modern poetry. The seriousness with which he considers this issue is revealed in a series of articles written in 1967 entitled 'Jazz and the West Indian Novel'.[13] The analogy between the novel form and jazz may be overdone but the point is that Brathwaite sees Caribbean writing in terms of literary improvisation, which explains the comparison with music. This improvisation is also part of a general shift away from traditional literary models towards the articulation of indigenous cultural forms. Repeatedly stressed is the need to bring the literary work closer to speech and the community experience. What is never really discussed is the inevitable differences between speech and the language of poetry.

Essentially any language in poetry is subjected to the conventions of the genre in that the language of everyday speech undergoes a process of transformation. The language of poetry moves beyond the familiar to a new mode that brings new ambiguities, new clusters of resonances and a certain atemporality to what is expressed. Brathwaite in his more successful poems subjects the English language to this process. The same should apply to his use of dialect. Brathwaite's better dialect verse is subjected to enough of a formal re-ordering and control that it rises above the commonplace to become the language of poetry. The poem 'Dust', which recounts the explosion of Mont Pelée in Martinique in 1902, effectively captures a feeling of deep-seated terror as well as the notion of a world that has become contingent, where bewildering things occur 'widdout rhyme/ widdout reason'. The metaphor of the

dust from the volcanic eruption is used with its full biblical
resonance to suggest a world where the people 'can't pray to no
priest or no leader/ an' God gone and darken the day'.
Similarly the cricket match of 'Rites' is more than a celebration
of a certain community ritual. It becomes an insight into a
debilitating passivity which afflicts the crowd. When a poet
uses a language in his work he makes it his own. Dialect is a
tool for exploring the Caribbean landscape and is moulded by
the poet's creative authority. It is in this way also part of the
conscious process of repossession.

Any attempt to extract either cultural or political prescrip-
tions from Brathwaite's work takes us onto treacherous
ground. The poetic concept of 'wholeness' and the importance
of myth and ritual can become distorted when converted into
ideological formulae. Brathwaite does not opt for the simplification of cultural decolonisation and does not see the colonial
past as a complete void. He has attempted to discover tangible
evidence for his essentially poetic perception of reality in the
investigation of the continuing process of creolisation in
Caribbean society. His historical work, *The Development of
Creole Society in Jamaica (1770–1820)*, is original in its attempts
to substantiate the integrating creole features which he sees at
work in Jamaican society. He has more recently returned to
this refutation of cultural plurality in his monograph, *Contradictory Omens: Cultural diversity and integration in the
Caribbean*.[14] This work, which sets out to be an objective
account of the creolising forces in the Caribbean, becomes
somewhat impenetrable as the language moves further away
from historical documentation towards the poetic imagination. Brathwaite's main thesis is that

> In spite of efforts to socialize individuals into separate racial
> groupings as demanded by the ethos of slavery, the ramifica-
> tions of personal relationships . . . brought new, unexpected
> exchanges into each group's repertoire of behaviour. This
> slow uncertain but organic process (from initiation/
> imitation to invention) . . . is what we mean by creolisation.

Art sometimes offers a way of seeing reality which may be left out of account in other kinds of investigation. *Contradictory Omens* is an attempt to combine poetry and history. The difficulties of such an endeavour are apparent in the obscure and paradoxical nature of this text.

In contrast to this monograph, Brathwaite's most interesting recent work, *Mother Poem*,[15] is a more appropriate medium for articulating his intuition of an authentic creole presence in the Caribbean. The monograph ends 'Unity is submarine' and the main theme and dominant imagery of *Mother Poem* are drawn from this idea. This is the continuation of the process begun in *Islands* as the poet returns to Barbados to discover the 'ancient watercourses' secreted in its limestone landscape. The collection presents a specific focus on Brathwaite's own beginnings and the landscape of Barbados. To this extent it is different from the more panoramic trilogy. We have a narrowing down of the same act of retrieval, the same desire to transcend a dehumanised, materialistic world and restore a sense of the past and a sense of 'wholeness'. The mother, however, is neither Europe nor Africa; the Caribbean poet is no longer a provincial. The image of 'black Sycorax', like the old Amerindian women of Wilson Harris's stories, is that of an ancestral, hidden symbol of survival from which the poet derives his vision.

To conceive of Brathwaite as either a folk poet or a political poet is to limit and even distort what has emerged from his creative imagination. Perhaps the most important single idea behind Brathwaite's work is the rejection of man as a product of ideology. His ability to shift back and forth between a palpably desolate world and the realm of the imaginative, and his consistently anti-materialistic position suggest that for him art has provided a way of liberating the individual from the confining grip of privation and brutality that cloud the documented, external history of the New World. It is this subversion of the traditional myths of an uncreative past and fragmented present that provides the crucial transition to the 'second phase' and enables the artist to conceive of the possibilities of growth and an authentic creole culture in the Caribbean experience.

Notes

1 Introduction

1. The first books of criticism on West Indian writing were Louis James (ed.), *The Islands In Between* (Oxford University Press, 1968), and Ivan Van Sertima, *Caribbean Writers* (London: New Beacon, 1968).
2. Early novels and *The Beacon* are discussed in Kenneth Ramchand, *The West Indian Novel and Its Background* (London: Faber & Faber, 1970).
3. V. S. Naipaul's Foreword to Seepersad Naipaul, *The Adventures of Gurudeva and Other Stories* (London: André Deutsch, 1976), pp. 9–10.
4. Louis James's Introduction to *Corentyne Thunder* (London: Heinemann, 1970), p. 1.
5. C. L. R. James's Introduction to Wilson Harris, *Tradition, the Writer and Society* (London and Port of Spain: New Beacon, 1967), p. 75.
6. Ramchand's *The West Indian Novel* discusses in detail the literary use of West Indian forms of speech.
7. Characteristic themes of West Indian literature are discussed in William H. New, *Among Worlds* (Erin, Ontario: Press Porcepic, 1975).
8. See, for example, J. E. Clare McFarlane, *A Literature in the Making* (Kingston: The Pioneer Press, 1956); and the anthology edited by Norman E. Cameron, *Guianese Poetry: 1831–1931* (British Guiana: Argosy, 1931; reprinted Nendeln: Kraus, 1970).

2 The Background

1. Ned Thomas, 'Meeting Jean Rhys', *Planet 33* (August 1976) 31.
2. Kenneth Ramchand, 'The Alfred Mendes Story', *Tapia* 7, 22 (29 May 1977) 6.

3. Edward Baugh, 'Small Town Story', in Mervyn Morris (ed.), *Seven Jamaican Poets* (Jamaica: Bolivar Press, 1971), pp. 26–7.
4. Derek Walcott, 'What the Twilight Says, an Overture', *Dream On Monkey Mountain and Other Plays* (New York: Farrar, Straus & Giroux, 1970), p. 22.
5. George Campbell, 'On This Night', *First Poems* (Kingston: City Printery, 1945), p. 67 (written on the occasion of the launching of the People's National Party on 18 September 1938 by N. W. Manley and Sir Stafford Cripps).
6. *Henri Christophe* reviewed by 'A Special Correspondent' in *West India Committee Circular* (February 1952) 38.
7. V. S. Naipaul, 'The Regional Barrier', *Times Literary Supplement* (15 August 1958) 38.
8. Some of this new work has been published in the anthology released after the Caribbean Festival of Arts in Guyana in 1972; see A. J. Seymour (ed.), *New Writing in the Caribbean* (Georgetown: National History and Arts Council, 1972).

3　　The Beginnings to 1929

1. See *Journal of Commonwealth Literature*, 9 (July 1970), 67.
2. *Savacou*, I, i (June 1970), 46–73.
3. Drayton in *Journal of Commonwealth Literature*, 9 (July 1970), 70.
4. For a discussion of the literary merits of this Latin ode, see Locksley Lindo, 'Francis Williams—a "Free" Negro in a Slave World', *Savacou*, I, i (June 1970), 75–80.
5. Joseph and Johanna Jones, *Authors and Areas of the West Indies* (Austin, Texas: Steck-Vaughn, 1970), p. 22.
6. *Ibid*.
7. *Thoughts on Life and Literature* (Georgetown: 1950), p. 59.
8. Georgetown: *Daily Chronicle*, 1949.
9. Kingston, Jamaica: Pioneer Press, 1952, p. 102.
10. Brathwaite, *Savacou*, I, i (June 1970), 72.
11. Kingston, Jamaica: The Jamaica Times, p. 48.
12. *Triumphant Squalitone* (Kingston, Jamaica: The Gleaner Co., 1916).
13. Publisher's foreword to *Becka's Buckra Baby*, 'The All Jamaica Library', I (Kingston: Times Printery, 1904).
14. For a discussion of his work, see Kenneth Ramchand, 'The Writer Who Ran Away', *Savacou*, I, ii (September 1970), 67–75.
15. *An Introduction to the Study of West Indian Literature* (Kingston, Jamaica: Nelson Caribbean, 1976), p. 5.

4   The Thirties and Forties

1. The observations of Arthur Calder-Marshall in *Glory Dead* (London: Michael Joseph, 1939) are a significant exception to the rule. Another Englishman, Robert Herring, devoted several issues of *Life and Letters* to West Indian literature in the late 1940s.

2. 'Talking about the Thirties', Alfred H. Mendes interviewed by Clifford Sealy in *Voices*, 1, 5 (December 1965) 5. Other comments by Mendes are drawn from 'The Turbulent Thirties in Trinidad', Mendes interviewed by R. W. Sander in 1972, *World Literature Written in English*, 12, 1 (April 1973).

3. *The Beacon*, *Bim* and *Focus* are now available in reprint editions by Kraus Reprint of New York and Liechtenstein.

4. Cameron's plays are discussed in Joycelynne Loncke, 'The Plays of Norman Cameron: The Price of Victory', *Bim*, 16, 61 (June 1977).

5. Albert M. Gomes, *Through a Maze of Colour* (Port of Spain, Trinidad: Key Caribbean, 1974), p. 19.

6. A selection of short fiction, poetry and essays from *Trinidad* and *The Beacon* has appeared as *From Trinidad: An Anthology of Early West Indian Writing*, ed. R. W. Sander (London: Hodder & Stoughton, 1978).

7. C. L. R. James, *Minty Alley* (London: Secker & Warburg, 1936. Republished by New Beacon Books: London, 1971). Alfred H. Mendes, *Pitch Lake* (London: Duckworth, 1934) and *Black Fauns* (London: Duckworth, 1935). (Both reprinted by Kraus Reprint in 1970.) Ralph de Boissiere, *Crown Jewel* (Melbourne: Australasian Book Society, 1952), *Rum and Coca-Cola* (ABS, 1956) and *No Saddles for Kangaroos* (ABS, 1964). *Crown Jewel* was completed before de Boissiere left for Australia in 1948.

8. A recent novel which also deals with the Portuguese community in Trinidad is Albert M. Gomes, *All Papa's Children* (Surrey: Cairi Publishing House, 1978).

9. W. Adolphe Roberts, *Royal Street* (Indianapolis: Bobbs-Merrill, 1944), *Brave Mardi Gras* (Bobbs-Merrill, 1946), *Creole Dusk* (Bobbs-Merrill, 1948) and *The Single Star* (Bobbs-Merrill, 1949); Claude McKay, *Home to Harlem* (New York: Harper & Brothers, 1928), *Banjo* (Harper, 1929), *Gingertown* (Harper, 1932) and *Banana Bottom* (Harper, 1933).

10. V. S. Reid, *New Day* (New York: Knopf, 1949. Republished in Heinemann's Caribbean Writers Series, 1973).

5   The Fifties

1. K. Ramchand, *The West Indian Novel and its Background* (London: Faber & Faber, 1970), p. 3.
2. Errol Hill, 'West Indian Drama', *The Artist in West Indian Society* (Department of Extra-Mural Studies, University of the West Indies).
3. *Black Jacobins* was written in 1938.
4. *The Negro in the Caribbean* (1942); *Capitalism and Slavery* (1944).
5. L. Edward Brathwaite, 'Sir Galahad and the Islands', *Bim* 25 (1957) 8.
6. L. Edward Brathwaite, 'The New West Indian Novelists', *Bim* 32 (1961) 278.
7. George Lamming, *The Pleasures of Exile* (London: Michael Joseph, 1960), p. 38.
8. *Ibid*, p. 36.
9. Mervyn Morris, Introduction to V. S. Reid's *New Day* (London: Heinemann, 1973).
10. See Edward Baugh, 'The West Indian Writer and His Quarrel with History', *Tapia* 7, Nos. 8 and 9 (1977).
11. John Hearne, Colloquium on *Voices Under the Window*, at the University of the West Indies, Mona, November 1976.
12. *Ibid*.
13. *Ibid*.
14. Brathwaite, 'The New West Indian Novelists', 277.

6   Since 1960: Some Highlights

1. In *The Yale School of Drama Presents*, ed. Gassner (New York: Dutton, 1964).
2. In *Penguin Plays*, Vol. 68, 1966, but not about the West Indies.
3. In *A Time and a Season; 8 Caribbean Plays*, ed. Hill (Trinidad: University of the West Indies, Extra-Mural Studies Unit, 1976).
4. *The Meeting Point* (London: Heinemann, 1967), p. 23.
5. *The Bigger Light* (Boston & Toronto: Little, Brown, 1975), pp. 133–4.
6. *J—, Black Bam and the Masqueraders* (London: Faber, 1972), pp. 7–8.
7. *A Room on the Hill* (London: Faber, 1968), p. 37.
8. *Uncle Time* (University of Pittsburgh Press, 1973), p. 8.
9. *The Pond* (London and Port of Spain: New Beacon Books, 1973), p. 14.
10. *Shadowboxing* (London and Port of Spain: New Beacon Books, 1979).

11. *The Pond*, pp. 42–3.
12. *Reel from 'The Life-Movie'* (Kingston: Savacou, corrected edition 1975; first published 1972).

7 Edgar Mittelholzer

1. From the unpublished second part of Mittelholzer's autobiography, 'A Pleasant Career' (in the possession of Mrs Jacqueline Ives).
2. He allowed *The Mad McMullochs* (1959) to appear under a pseudonym, 'H. Austin Woodsley'. By then, however, he was an established author, and there is some evidence to suggest that the novel was written *pour épater la bourgeoisie*.
3. Republished in hard covers in 1976 by Secker & Warburg as a 'quartet'. The original first volume, *The Children of Kaywana*, is split in two; the 'second' volume becoming 'Kaywana Heritage'.
4. 'The New West Indian Novelists,' part II, *Bim*, 8, 32 (1961) 274.
5. *The Edgar Mittelholzer Memorial Lectures*, Georgetown, Guyana (1969), p. 10.
6. In V. S. Naipaul's *The Mystic Masseur* (André Deutsch, 1957), Ganesh and his wife Leela, East Indian peasants newly arrived at middle-class respectability, display the same vulgar benevolence to social inferiors. Even the status symbols are similar: 'The deputation sat down carefully on the Morris chairs in the verandah and Ganesh shouted for Leela to bring out some Coca-Cola' (p. 162).
7. *With a Carib Eye* (London: Secker & Warburg, 1958), pp. 134–5.
8. *The Jilkington Drama* (London: Corgi, 1966), p. 124.
9. The novel, or a version of it, had already been completed by 1948. Mittelholzer's diary entry of 19 July of that year reads: 'Rec'd letter from Macmillan's (rejected *Sylvia*). Wrote Hart and Bucklin Moon of Doubledays.'
10. Manuscript in the possession of Mrs Jacqueline Ives. The title page bears Mittelholzer's 1948 Trinidad address, and the note: 'Previously Published: *Corentyne Thunder*, a novel (Eyre & Spottiswoode, London).'
11. In 'A Pleasant Career', the unpublished second part of his autobiography, Mittelholzer wrote: 'In February 1948, I sailed for England, taking with me the completed script of a novel that treated of the social scene in Trinidad. It was entitled *A Morning at the Office*.'
12. There are interesting similarities between Mittelholzer and Hawthorne. Both New World writers regarded the heritage of

the colonial past as occasion for family pride as well as for a feeling of hereditary guilt. Both seem obsessed by an apparently hopeless dualism of 'higher' and 'lower' motives; and their work harbours a curious moral ambiguity. The story 'Main Street', in Hawthorne's *Twice-Told Tales*, is (like the *Kaywana* novels) a nostalgic, clearly ironic reconstruction of a historical legacy, beginning in the pre-colonial past. Hawthorne's New England is seen to be founded as much on exploitation as on heroic 'vision'.

13. The last section of the book is headed 'Perdendosi': a musical term which means 'gradually fading away'.

14. *The Aloneness of Mrs Chatham*, p. 144.

15. *A Swarthy Boy* (London: Putnam, 1963), p. 126.

16. Six typed scripts in thin cardboard file-covers. No handwritten scripts are extant. Mittelholzer composed on the typewriter, generally producing a 'fair copy' right away. Lodged in the Guyana National Library, Georgetown, Guyana.

17. Derek Walcott, 'What the Twilight Says: An Overture', Preface to *Dream on Monkey Mountain and Other Plays* (London: Jonathan Cape, 1972), p. 9.

18. *Ibid*.

8   Samuel Selvon

1. Books by Samuel Selvon: *A Brighter Sun* (London: Wingate, 1952; Longman, 1971); *An Island Is A World* (Wingate, 1955); *The Lonely Londoners* (Wingate, 1956; Longman, 1972); *Ways of Sunlight* (London: MacGibbon & Kee, 1958); *Turn Again Tiger* (MacGibbon & Kee, 1958; Longman, 1978); *I Hear Thunder* (MacGibbon & Kee, 1963); *The Housing Lark* (MacGibbon & Kee, 1965); *A Drink of Water* (London: Nelson, 1968, an adaptation for children of the novella in *Ways of Sunlight*); *The Plains of Caroni* (MacGibbon & Kee, 1970); *Those Who Eat the Cascadura* (London: Davis–Poynter, 1972); *Moses Ascending* (Davis–Poynter, 1975). Quotations in my text refer to the original editions, except in the case of *The Lonely Londoners*.

2. Interview with Samuel Selvon by the author (London, 11 November 1977).

3. *Ibid*.

4. I am indebted to Sandra Pouchet Paquet for sending me her introduction to a new edition of *Turn Again Tiger* in the Heinemann Caribbean Writers Series. This thorough analysis of the novel also emphasises Selvon's habit of reversing stereotypes and his metaphorical use of interracial sexual relationships.

9 George Lamming

1. 'West Indian Dutch Party', B.B.C., *Caribbean Voices*, Script No. 271, 22 August 1948.
2. 'Birds of a Feather', *Bim*, 9 (December 1948), 34.
3. 'February 1949', *Bim*, 10 (June 1949), 111.
4. 'Birthday Poem (For Clifford Sealy)', B.B.C., *Caribbean Voices*, 24 September 1950.
5. 'A Dedication from Afar: Song for Marian', B.B.C., *Caribbean Voices*, 1 April 1951.
6. 'The Illumined Graves', *Bim*, 15 (December 1951), 165–6.
7. *In the Castle of My Skin* (New York: McGraw-Hill, 1953), p. 4.
8. *The Emigrants* (New York: McGraw-Hill, 1954), p. 8.
9. *The Pleasures of Exile* (London: Michael Joseph, 1960), p. 27.
10. 'The Negro Writer and His World', *Présence Africaine*, 8–9–10 (June–November 1956), 322.
11. 'Caribbean Literature: The Black Rock of Africa', *African Forum*, 1 (Spring 1966), 48.
12. *The Pleasures of Exile*, p. 36.
13. *Season of Adventure* (London: Michael Joseph, 1960), p. 50.
14. 'The West Indian People', *New World Quarterly*, 2 (Croptime 1966), 71.
15. George E. Kent, 'A Conversation with George Lamming', *Black World*, 22 (March 1973), 96.
16. *Ibid.*
17. *Natives of My Person* (New York: Holt, Rinehart & Winston, 1972), p. 120.
18. *The Pleasures of Exile*, p. 13.
19. Kent, p. 6.
20. 'But Alas Edgar', *New World: Guyana Independence Issue* (1966), p. 19.
21. Interview with George Lamming, London, 2 October 1975.
22. *Water With Berries* (London: Longman Caribbean, 1971), p. 145.
23. 'West Indian People', p. 65.

10 Derek Walcott

1. 'What the Twilight Says: An Overture', *Dream on Monkey Mountain and Other Plays* (New York: Farrar, Straus & Giroux, 1970; London: Jonathan Cape, 1972), pp. 3–40, p. 10.
2. 'The Muse of History', *Is Massa Day Dead?*, ed. Orde Coombs (New York: Anchor Press/Doubleday, 1974), pp. 1–27, p. 1.

3. 'Leaving School', *The London Magazine*, 5, 6 (September 1965), 4–14, p. 6.
4. 'Meanings', *Savacou* 2 (September 1970), 45–51. *Another Life* (New York: Farrar, Straus & Giroux, 1973; London: Jonathan Cape, 1973).
5. 'What the Twilight Says', p. 4.
6. 'Some West Indian Poets', *The London Magazine*, 5, 6 (September 1965), p. 15.
7. 'Meanings', pp. 47–8.
8. Selden Rodman, *Tongues of Fallen Angels* (New York, 1972), p. 252.
9. 'The Muse of History', pp. 2, 5.
10. *25 Poems* (Bridgetown: Advocate Co., 1949); *Epitaph for the Young* (Bridgetown: Advocate Co., 1949); *Poems* (Kingston: Jamaica Printery, 1952); *In a Green Night* (London: Jonathan Cape, 1962); *Selected Poems* (New York: Farrar, Straus & Co., 1964); *The Castaway and Other Poems* (London: Jonathan Cape, 1965); *The Gulf and Other Poems* (London: Jonathan Cape, 1969); *The Gulf* (New York: Farrar, Straus & Giroux, 1970); *Sea Grapes* (London: Jonathan Cape, 1976; New York: Farrar, Straus & Giroux, 1976).
11. *Another Life*, p. 106.
12. 'The Muse of History', p. 25.
13. *Another Life*, p. 106.
14. *Trinidad and Tobago Review*, May 1978 (special insert).
15. The notebooks and succeeding drafts have been deposited in the library of the University of the West Indies, Mona, Jamaica. See Edward Baugh, *Another Life: Memory as Vision* (Longman Caribbean, 1979).
16. *The Joker of Seville* (first performed 1974) and *O Babylon* (first performed 1976) have recently been published in a single volume (New York: Farrar, Straus & Giroux, 1978).
17. See: Eric Roach, 'The Musical Fuses Both Traditions of Folk Legend', *Sunday Guardian* (Trinidad), 28 June 1970; Syl Lowhar, 'A Struggle for Freedom': Derek Walcott's *Ti-Jean*', *Tapia*, 9 August 1970; Anon. [Gordon Rohlehr], 'The Three Stages of Black Revolution: A Brief Look at Derek Walcott's *Ti-Jean and His Brothers*', *Liberation* (Trinidad), September 1970; Theodore Colson, 'Derek Walcott's Plays: Outrage and Compassion', *World Literature Written in English*, Vol. 12, No. 1 (April 1973); Albert Olu Ashaolu, 'Allegory in *Ti-Jean and His Brothers*', *World Literature Written in English*, 16, 1 (April 1977); Robert D. Hamner, 'Mythological Aspects of Derek Walcott's Drama', *Ariel*, 8, 3 (June 1977).
18. Derek Walcott, 'Derek's "most West Indian play"', *Sunday*

Guardian magazine (Trinidad), 21 June 1970, p. 7.

19. *Ibid.*
20. 'Meanings', p. 48.
21. *Another Life*, p. 75.
22. Robert Graves, *The White Goddess* (London: Faber & Faber, 1961), p. 24.
23. Selden Rodman, *Tongues of Fallen Angels*, p. 249.
24. *Ibid.*
25. Derek Walcott, in 'Man of the Theatre', report of an interview with Derek Walcott, *The New Yorker*, 26 June 1971, p. 30.

11   V. S. Naipaul

1. Landeg White's excellent study, to which I am indebted, *V. S. Naipaul: A Critical Introduction* (London: Macmillan, 1975), shows how Mr Biswas is based upon details in the life of Seepersad Naipaul, V. S. Naipaul's father. Seepersad's stories have been reprinted, with an introduction by V. S. Naipaul, in *The Adventures of Gurudeva and Other Stories* (London: André Deutsch, 1976). His work is discussed in *New Voices* (Trinidad), vol. 4, nos. 7 and 8 (1976).
2. Dates in my text refer to the first London publication of Naipaul's books by André Deutsch.
3. The accuracy with which Naipaul follows the history of the East Indians in Trinidad can be seen by reading *Calcutta to Caroni*, edited by John La Guerre (London: Longman, 1974).

12   Wilson Harris

1. The *Guiana Quartet* includes *Palace of the Peacock* (1960), *The Far Journey of Oudin* (1961), *The Whole Armour* (1962) and *The Secret Ladder* (1963). These and all other novels by Harris are published by Faber.
2. Wilson Harris, 'The Making of Tradition', in Alastair Niven, *The Commonwealth Writer Overseas* (Brussels: Didier, 1976), p. 35.
3. Wilson Harris, *Tradition, the Writer and Society* (London: New Beacon Publications, 1967), p. 48.
4. *The Eye of the Scarecrow*, p. 14.
5. *Ascent to Omai*, p. 96.
6. The 'black hole', a recent scientific discovery, has been described as 'formed by the collapse of a heavy star to such a condensed state that nothing, not even light, can escape'. John Taylor, *Black Holes, The End of a Universe?* (Glasgow: Fontana/Collins, 1976), p. 9.

7. In *The Sleepers of Roraima* (1970) and *The Age of the Rainmakers* (1971), two collections of novellas, Harris reinterprets Amerindian myths, modifying their content and showing that they can elicit a wholly new conception of life. In this entirely native context Harris pursues the same concerns as in his novels. They thus represent a true developmental stage between phase two and phase three.

8. *Ascent to Omai*, p. 85.

9. *Da Silva da Silva's Cultivated Wilderness* (published in a single volume with *Genesis of the Clowns*) and *The Tree of the Sun* (1978).

13   Jean Rhys

1. *The Left Bank* (1927); *Postures* (1928), later republished as *Quartet*; *After Leaving Mr Mackenzie* (1930); *Voyage in the Dark* (1934); *Good Morning Midnight* (1939).

2. *Quartet* (London: André Deutsch, 1969), p. 13. Quotations are taken from the later editions.

3. *After Leaving Mr Mackenzie* (London: André Deutsch, 1969), p. 9.

4. *Voyage in the Dark* (Penguin, 1969), p. 120.

5. *After Leaving Mr Mackenzie*, pp. 69–70.

6. *Sleep it off Lady* (London: André Deutsch, 1976).

7. *After Leaving Mr Mackenzie*, p. 11.

8. *After Leaving Mr Mackenzie*, p. 53.

9. *Good Morning Midnight* (Penguin, 1969), p. 159.

10. *Wide Sargasso Sea* (Penguin, 1968), pp. 16–17.

14   Edward Brathwaite

1. *Savacou 2* (September 1970) 36.

2. See 'West Indian Prose Fiction in the sixties', *Critical Survey* (Winter 1967), 169–74.

3. *Bim*, 3, 12 (1950), 325.

4. *Bim*, 7, 28 (1959), 191.

5. *Bim*, 9, 33 (1961), 18.

6. *Bim*, 10, 40 (1965), 250.

7. *Other Exiles* (London: Oxford University Press, 1975).

8. *The Arrivants* (A New World Trilogy). (London: Oxford University Press, 1973).

9. *Bim*, 8, 30 (1960).

10. *The Middle Passage* (Harmondsworth: Penguin, 1969), p. 29.

11. *The Overcrowded Baracoon* (Harmondsworth: Penguin, 1972), p. 26.

12. *Savacou 2*, p. 43.

13. *Bim*, 44/45/46 (1967–68).
14. *Savacou*, monograph no. 1 (1974).
15. *Mother Poem* (London: Oxford University Press, 1977). *Black and Blues* (Havana: Casa de les Américas, 1976) won the Casa de las Américas poetry award for 1976. It is a compilation of material old and new which tends to restate themes raised in the trilogy.

INDEX

Aaron, R. L. C. 57
Abeng 28
Abrahams, Peter 47
Adams, Grantley 19
Adventures of Jonathan Corncob 35
Advocate 58
Allfrey, Phyliss 12, 209
'All Jamaica Library' 2, 12, 39, 230
Anderson, Izett 36
Anderson, Marian 127
Anthony, Michael 43, 78, 80–1,
    209
Archibald, Kathleen 51
Argosy 34
Arthur, William S. 58
Auden, W. H. 146

Balgobin, Basil 47
Barbados Herald 15
Barrat, Jim 56
Barraud, C. W. 35
Barrett, Lindsay 13, 78
Barrow, Raymond 60
Baugh, Edward 18, 230, 232, 236
Beacon, The 2, 15, 46, 49–51, 58,
    229, 231
Beckwith, Martha 36
Behn, Aphra 30
Bell, Vera 47
Bennett, Louise 25, 47, 58, 60
Bim 2, 20, 46, 50, 63, 76, 147, 211,
    212, 216, 231, 232, 233, 235,
    238, 239

Bogle, Paul 12
Bongo Man 28
Bourne, J. A. V. 48, 57
Brathwaite, Edward 1, 6, 26, 27,
    31, 33, 35, 36, 44, 63, 65, 69, 73,
    79, 83, 87, 90, 96, 210–27, 230,
    232, 238, 239
    The Arrivants 6, 44, 215–26, 238
    Contradictory Omens 226–7
    Islands 212, 215, 216, 220–4, 227
    Masks 215, 219–20
    Mother Poem 83, 227, 239
    Odale's Choice 215
    Other Exiles 213–14, 238
    Rites of Passage 6, 212, 215,
        217–19, 222, 226
    'Timehri' 210
Bridgetown Players 47
Brown, Charles Brockden 110
Brown, R. C. 57
Brown, Wayne 79, 87
Burnham, Forbes 24
Bustamante, Alexander 16, 139
Butler, Uriah 15, 56

Calder-Marshall, Arthur 231
Callaloo 15, 46
Calypso 15, 28, 29, 64, 113, 119,
    218
Cameron, N. E. 10, 31, 34, 35, 47,
    49, 58, 229, 231
Campbell, George 19, 47, 58, 59,
    230

Campbell, W. A. 39
Carberry, H. D. 47
Carew, Jan 66, 73–4, 77
Caribbean Artists Movement 27, 28
Caribbean Festival of Arts 28, 230
Caribbean Quarterly 46
Caribbean Voices (B.B.C.) 2, 3, 8, 21, 46, 63, 161, 235
Carmichael, Stokely 27
Carpentier, Alejo 151
Carr, Ernest A. 50–1, 57
Carter, Martin 3, 24, 28, 48, 59, 63, 66, 74–6, 77
Casimir, J. R. 58
Castro, Fidel 64, 72
Césaire, Aimé 146, 215, 216, 218, 219, 220
Chapman, Esther 42
Chapman, M. J. 33
Charles, Frederick, *see under* Tomlinson, Frederick
Chase, Sam 47
Chronicle 58
Cipriani, Arthur 15, 56, 139
Clarke, A. M. 57, 58
Clarke, Austin 29, 78, 81–5, 232; *The Bigger Light* 82, 83–5, 232
Coard, Robert M. 46
Collymore, Frank 46, 47, 48, 50, 58, 60, 63
Congress de Habana 28
Conrad, Joseph 70, 98
Cripps, Stafford 230
Cruickshank, Graham 36
Cundall, Frank 36

Dalton, Henry G. 34
Dalzell, Frank E. 48
Dathorne, O. R. 31, 32
Dawes, Neville 17
de Boissiere, Jean 46
de Boissiere, Ralph 15, 53, 54, 55–6, 231
Deeble, Michael J. 50
de Lisser, H. G. 2, 6, 10, 11, 13, 14, 37–8, 40, 42–4, 46, 230; *Jane's Career* 2, 13, 43; *Revenge* 43; *Susan Proudleigh* 14, 43–4;

Triumphant Squalitone 37, 42, 43, 230; *Twentieth Century Jamaica* 37–8; *The White Witch of Rosehall* 11, 43, 44
Dizzy, Ras 28
Dodd, E. A. (Snod, E.) 39
Don, Thomas 34
Donne, John 173
Dos Passos, John 114
Drayton, Arthur 30, 31, 230
Drayton, Geoffrey 12, 209
Drummond, Don 94

Elcock, Howick 58
Election, The 32
Eliot, T. S. 5, 146, 173, 211, 221, 222
Ellison, Ralph 124
Emtage, J. B. 26, 209
Equiano, Olaudah 30
Escoffery, Gloria 46

Faulkner, William 70
Figueroa, John 47
Focus 2, 20, 46, 47, 50, 59, 63, 231
Forum Magazine 46
Forum Quarterly 46
Froude, James Anthony 31
Fuller, Roy 3

Gandhi, Mahatma 50, 169
Garvey, Marcus 25, 26
Georgetown Dramatic Club 47
Gilkes, Michael 79
Gleaner 42, 58, 230
Goldson, Philip S. W. 46
Gomes, Albert 46, 49, 50, 57, 231
Gordon, George William 12
Goveia, Elsa 64
Grainger, James 32–3
Graves, Robert 159, 237
Guardian (Trinidad) 3, 58, 161, 236, 237
Guianese Poetry 31, 58, 229
Guiseppi, Neville 57, 58

Haile Selassie 16, 25
Hakluyt 138
Haldane, George 32

Hallinan, Judge 57
Hamel, The Obeah Man 35, 36
Harris, Wilson 5, 6, 7, 9, 24, 28, 48, 51, 63, 69, 73, 78, 110, 179–195, 211, 227, 229, 237
  Ascent to Omai 179, 188, 189, 192, 194, 237, 238
  Black Marsden 192–3, 194
  Companions of the Day and Night 185, 193–4
  Da Silva da Silva's Cultivated Wilderness 194, 195, 238
  Eternity to Season 180
  The Eye 188, 189, 190, 194, 237
  The Far Journey of Oudin 24, 186, 237
  Guiana Quartet 5, 9, 183–7, 237
  Heartland 187
  Palace of the Peacock 5, 78, 179, 183–6, 189, 194, 237
  The Secret Ladder 186, 187, 237
  Tumatumari 180, 185, 188, 189, 190, 191, 192
  The Waiting Room 188, 189, 190, 191
  The Whole Armour 186, 237
Hawthorne, Nathaniel 106, 110, 233, 234
Hearne, John 3, 17, 26, 47, 66, 69–72, 73, 77, 232; *The Autumn Equinox* 70, 72; *The Faces of Love* 70, 71, 72; *Strangers at the Gate* 70, 71, 72; *Voices Under the Window* 3, 17, 69, 70–1, 232
Hemingway, Ernest 70
Hendriks, A. L. 46, 47, 79
Herbert, Cecil 46
Hill, Errol 21, 57, 63, 232
Hobbes, Thomas 173
Hollar, Constance 41, 58
Hosack, William 33
Howland, Cicely 47
Hughes, Langston 225
Hutchinson, Lionel 11
Hutton, Albinia 41, 58

Ingram, K. E. 47

Jagan, Cheddi 24
Jamaica: a poem in Three Parts 33
Jamaican Daily Express 42
Jamaica School of Arts and Crafts 64
Jamaica Times 38, 230
James, C. L. R. 2, 10, 13, 28, 46, 49, 50, 51, 52, 53, 54, 55, 64, 96, 229, 231, 232; *The Black Jacobins* 50, 323; *Minty Alley* 2, 53, 54, 55, 56, 231
James, Louis 229
Jekyll, Walter 36, 37
Jerry, Bongo 28
John, Errol 21
Johnson, Linton Kwesi 29, 79
Jones, Johanna 33, 230
Jones, Joseph 33, 230
Joyce, James 5, 140

Kent, Lena 41, 58
Kingsley, Charles 31
Kyk-over-al 2, 19, 20, 46, 47–9, 58, 63, 179

Lamming, George 4, 9, 17, 18, 20, 21, 22, 23, 24, 27, 46, 51, 63, 65, 66, 67, 68, 69, 76, 78, 81, 100, 110, 115, 124, 126–43, 217, 232, 235
  Of Age and Innocence 23, 132–5, 140
  In the Castle of My Skin 4, 17, 18, 21, 67–8, 80–81, 126, 127, 128–30, 131, 137, 140, 217, 235
  The Emigrants 69, 115, 130–2, 137, 141, 235
  Natives of My Person 9, 24, 126, 137–41, 143, 235
  The Pleasures of Exile 20, 100, 130, 134, 138, 142, 232, 235
  Season of Adventure 126, 135–7, 140, 235
  Water with Berries 23, 78, 126, 140, 141–3, 235
La Guerre, John 237
La Rose, John 27, 28

Lawrence, Walter MacArthur 10, 42, 49

Left Book Club 16

Leo, *see under* Martin, Egbert

Lewin, Olive 64

Lewis, Monk 30

Liberation 236

Life and Letters 231

Lindo, Archie 47, 57

Little Carib Dance Company 47, 64

Little Theatre Movement 47

Long, Edward 32

McBurnie, Beryl 47, 64

MacDermot, Thomas ('Tom Redcam') 2, 10, 12, 35, 36, 38–41, 230

McDonald, Ian 12, 81

MacFarlane, Basil 47, 59

McFarlane, J. E. Clare 41, 58–9, 229

McKay, Claude 2, 6, 10, 14, 22, 24, 27, 36, 37, 38, 41, 44, 60–1, 73, 96, 115, 211, 231; *Banana Bottom* 2, 14, 24, 36, 37, 41, 61, 73, 211, 231; *Banjo* 27, 41, 61, 115, 231; *Gingertown* 61, 231; *Home to Harlem* 27, 41, 231

McNeill, Anthony 26, 79, 87, 88, 93–4, 232

McTurk, Michael ('Quow') 34

Mais, Roger 3, 16, 26, 47, 57, 66, 67–9, 70, 73, 77, 96; *Black Lightning* 69; *Brother Man* 68–9, 73; *The Hills Were Joyful Together* 3, 67–8

Manjak 28

Manley, Edna 46, 47, 49, 50

Manley, Norman 19, 139, 230

Marley, Bob 29

Marley 35

Marshall, Paule 78

Marson, Una 41, 59

Martin, Egbert ('Leo') 34, 49

Martin, Sidney 35

Maxwell, Marina 28

Maynard, Percival C. 51, 52

Mendes, Alfred 2, 10, 11, 14, 45, 46, 49, 51–5, 96, 229, 231; *Black Fauns* 2, 53–4, 56, 231; 'Her Chinaman's Way' 52, 53; *Pitch Lake* 2, 11, 53, 55, 231

Mentor, H. C. 14

Mentor, Ralph 50

Miles, Jean 154

Miniature Poets 21

Mitchell, Horace L. 48

Mittelholzer, Edgar 1, 3, 4, 9, 10, 18, 22, 24, 46, 48, 57, 95–110, 140, 233, 234, pseudonym H. Austin Woodsley, 233

The Aloneness of Mrs Chatham 100, 103, 108, 109, 234

Corentyne Thunder 4, 18, 24, 58, 95, 97–101, 102, 229, 233

The Harrowing of Hubertus 100, 105

Kaywana trilogy 4, 9, 95, 101, 103, 105–7, 233, 234

The Life and Death of Sylvia 102–3, 233

A Morning at the Office 3, 4, 104–5, 233

My Bones and My Flute 4, 101, 103

Shadows Move Among Them 100, 101

A Swarthy Boy 96, 234

Moko 28

Montagu, Duke of 32

Montgomery 35, 36

Morant Bay rebellion 11, 12, 43, 62, 66, 203

Morris, Mervyn 26, 79, 87, 88, 90–3, 230, 232

Naipaul, Seepersad 2, 57, 161, 229, 237

Naipaul, Shiva 161

Naipaul, V. S. 2, 3, 5, 18, 22, 23, 24, 44, 57, 73, 110, 111, 161–78, 211, 216, 217, 229, 230, 233, 237, 238

An Area of Darkness 169

A Flag on the Island 173

In a Free State 172, 174–5
Guerrillas 23, 172, 176–8
A House for Mr Biswas 5, 18, 24,
    57, 161, 165–8
The Loss of El Dorado 170
The Middle Passage 24, 44, 168,
    216, 238
Miguel Street 73, 163
The Mimic Men 171–3
*Mr Stone and the Knight's
    Companion* 170
The Mystic Masseur 5, 73, 111,
    163–4, 172, 233
The Overcrowded Barracoon 176,
    217, 238
The Suffrage of Elvira 5, 73,
    164–5
National Dance Company
    (Jamaica) 64
Neruda, Pablo 146
Nettleford, Rex 64
New, William 229
New World Quarterly 235
Ngugi wa Thiong'o 67
Nicholas, Arthur 41
Nicole, Christopher 10
Nolte, Austin M. 46
Nugent, Lady 30

Oliver, Simon Christian 34
Orderson, J. W. 35, 36
Outlook, The 46

Papa Bois 57
Paquet, Sandra 119, 234
Patterson, H. Orlando 26, 78
Payne, Clement 16
Perse, Saint-John 146
Picong 15, 46
Pioneer Press 63, 229
Planters' Punch 43, 46
Pocomania 10, 59, 60, 72, 73, 147
Poetry League of Jamaica 58
Politics and Patriots of Jamaica 32
Pound, Ezra 146

Quarterly Magazine, The 46
Quow, *see under* McTurk, Michael

Radcliffe, John 36
Ramchand, Kenneth 30, 43, 63,
    229, 230, 232
Ramcharita, C. E. J. 58
Ramon-Fortuné, B. J. 46, 57
Rashomon 158
Rastafarians 16, 25, 26, 28, 68, 69,
    88, 94
Ratoon 28
Reckord, Barry 79–80, 83
Redcam, Tom, *see under* MacDer-
    mot, Thomas
Reid, V. S. 3, 11, 20, 43, 47, 61, 62,
    65, 66–7, 77, 231, 232; *The
    Leopard* 66–7; *New Day* 3,
    11, 20, 44, 61–2, 66, 67, 231, 232
Rhone, Trevor 79–80
Rhys, Jean 6, 11, 12, 42, 44,
    196–209, 229, 238
    After Leaving Mr Mackenzie 197,
        199–200, 238
    Good Morning Midnight 6, 197,
        200–1, 238
    The Left Bank 42, 238
    Quartet 197, 199, 208, 238
    Sleep it off Lady 196, 198, 201,
        207, 238
    Voyage in the Dark 197, 201, 206,
        238
    Wide Sargasso Sea 6, 11, 42, 196,
        197, 198, 200, 201–9, 238
Rienzi, Adrian 50
Rimbaud, Arthur 220
Roach, Eric M. 63, 66, 76–7, 236
Roberts, W. Adolphe 7, 35, 38, 41,
    43, 60–1, 231
Rodney, Walter 27
Rogers, De Wilton 57
Rohlehr, Gordon 236
Royalian, The 14
Russell, Thomas 36

St George's Literary League
    Magazine 46
St Omer, Dunstan 151, 152, 154
St Omer, Garth 78, 85–7, 110, 232
Salkey, Andrew 23, 27, 28,
    66, 72–3, 77, 78, 124;

Salkey, Andrew—*cont.*
  *Come   Home,   Malcolm
    Heartland* 23, 78; *Georgetown
    Journal* 28; *Havana Journal* 27;
    Joey Tyson 27; *Quality of
    Violence* 72–3, 78
Savacou 28, 230, 233, 236, 238,
  239
Schopenhauer, Arthur 96
Scott, Dennis 79, 87–90, 92, 94,
  232
Scott, Michael 30, 31
Sealy, Clifford 231, 235
Selvon, Samuel 4, 18, 22, 23, 24,
  25, 29, 46, 65, 66, 67, 82, 83,
  111–25, 234
  A Brighter Sun 4, 18, 24, 65, 67,
    111–4, 115, 116, 117, 124, 234
  An Island Is A World 114–5, 234
  The Lonely Londoners 4, 29, 66,
    82, 115–7, 121, 122, 124, 234
  Moses Ascending 23, 83, 122–4,
    234
  *Those   Who   Eat   the
    Cascadura* 120–1, 234
  Turn Again Tiger 4, 18, 65, 116,
    117–20, 121, 234
Senghor, L. S. 219, 285
Seymour, A. J. 46, 47, 48–9, 53,
  58, 60, 230
Shakespeare, William 35, 138, 142,
  145
Sherlock, Philip 47, 48, 59–60
Simmons, Harold 46, 151, 152
Smith, M. G. 47, 59
Snod, E., *see under* Dodd, E. A.
Strindberg, August 159
Surrealism 220
Swanzy, Henry 3, 46
Swift, Jonathan 173
Synge, J. M. 155

Tanker, André 158
Tapia 28, 229, 232, 236
Telemaque, Harold 46, 58, 60
Tennyson, Alfred, Lord 35
Thomas, Dylan 146
Thomas, J. J. 31, 36

Thomasos, C. A. 50, 51, 52, 53, 57,
  58
Thompson, Claude 47, 57
Tomlinson, Frederick Charles
  ('Frederick Charles') 42
Trinidad 46, 49, 50, 52, 231
Trinidad and Tobago Review 236
Trinidad Theatre Workshop 145
*Trinidad Workingmen's
  Association* 15
Trollope, Anthony 30
'Tropica' (M. A. Wolcott) 41
Trowbridge, W. R. H. 51

University of the West Indies 1, 20,
  26, 46, 152, 232

Van Sertima, Ivan 229
Vaughan, H. A. 15, 58
Virtue, Vivian L. 2, 47, 58, 59
Voices 231
Voices from Summerland 41

Wagner, Richard 96
Waite-Smith, Cecily 57
Walcott, Derek 3, 5, 7, 18, 19, 21,
  26, 46, 58, 60, 63, 69, 79, 83, 87,
  144–60, 230, 234, 235, 236
  Another Life 5, 144, 145, 146,
    148, 150–3, 154, 236, 237
  The Castaway 146, 147, 148–50,
    236
  Dream on Monkey Mountain 5,
    79, 155, 159–60, 230, 234, 235
  Epitaph for the Young 58, 63, 146,
    236
  In a Green Night 5, 79, 146, 147,
    236
  The Gulf 146, 148–50, 236
  Henri Christophe 21, 230
  The Joker of Seville 83, 155, 236
  Malcochon 158
  The Sea at Dauphin 155–6
  Sea-Grapes 146, 147, 153–5
  Ti-Jean and His Brothers 156–8,
    236
  Twenty-Five Poems 3, 58, 63, 146,
    236

Walcott, Roderick   18, 79, 144, 147
Walke, Olive   64
Walrond, Eric   6, 13, 42, 44, 230
Webber, A. R. F.   42
West Indian Committee Circular   21, 230
West Indian Federation   3, 8, 17, 20, 21, 23, 25, 48, 49, 64, 133, 154
West Indian Review   42
Whitehall Players   47
White, Landeg   237
Wickham, Clennell   15
Wills, S. E.   34

Williams, Denis   28, 78, 96, 110
Williams, Eric   17, 27, 50, 64
Williams, Francis   32, 230
Williams, N. D.   26, 27, 78
Wong, Orlando   79
Woodsley, H. Austin (pseudonym E. Mittelholzer)   233
Woolford, E. N.   36
Wordsworth, William   35
Wynter, Sylvia   26

Yaatoff, Olga   51
Youth   46